W9-BIE-029

LOOPHOLES
OF
REAL ESTATE

SECRETS OF SUCCESSFUL REAL ESTATE INVESTING

GARRETT SUTTON, ESQ.

FOREWORD BY ROBERT KIYOSAKI

RDA
PRESS

This publication is designed to provide competent and reliable information regarding the subject matter covered. However, it is sold with the understanding that the author and publisher are not engaged in rendering legal, financial, or other professional advice. Laws and practices often vary from state to state and country to country and if legal or other expert assistance is required, the services of a professional should be sought. The author and publisher specifically disclaim any liability that is incurred from the use or application of the contents of this book.

Published by RDA Press

Rich Dad Advisors, B-I Triangle, CASHFLOW Quadrant and other
Rich Dad marks are registered trademarks of CASHFLOW Technologies, Inc.

RDA Press LLC
15170 N. Hayden Road
Scottsdale, AZ 85260
480-998-5400
Visit our Web sites: RDAPress.com and RichDadAdvisors.com

Printed in the United States of America
Cover design by Chris Collins | American Design Co.

First Edition: May 2013
Second Edition: January 2015
Third Edition: November 2018
ISBN: 978-1-937832-22-3

072020

Preface and Acknowledgements

The genesis of this book begins with *Real Estate Loopholes*, which was first released in January 2003 (and was on the bestseller lists that summer). Then, with additional information on landlord liability, insurance, and other legal and tax issues included, it was published as *Real Estate Advantages* in 2006. Of note, in his Foreword to that edition Robert Kiyosaki called the real estate bubble.

After the bubble burst there were many new issues for real estate investors to consider, including the importance of clear title in the wake of record foreclosures. So we have brought in new and updated material, including a chapter that questions the utility of land trusts as well as new changes in the laws of asset protection.

Fair warning: Some of the chapters contain the same information as the previous editions. This is because, with all due modesty, there is no reason to redo what was brilliantly brought forth the first time. But there are many new sections as well. We have incorporated up-to-date sections written by CPA and Rich Dad Advisor Tom Wheelwright on cost segregations, using IRAs for investing, and becoming a real estate professional. We have updated Gary Gorman's chapter on 1031 Exchanges from several years ago. And in this edition, and the reason we now call it *Loopholes of Real Estate,* we explore the medieval history of loopholes. I find it fascinating—and it only took me a decade to tie it together.

For this new edition I would like to thank Robert Kiyosaki, Tom Wheelwright, Gary Gorman, Brandi MacLeod, Mona Gambetta, Jessica Santina, Ken McElroy and Kathy Spitzer for all your valuable contributions. They are greatly appreciated.

Best-Selling Books in the Rich Dad Advisors Series

BY BLAIR SINGER

Sales Dogs
You Don't Have to Be an Attack Dog to Explode Your Income

Team Code of Honor
The Secrets of Champions in Business and in Life

Summit Leadership
Taking Your Team to the Top

BY GARRETT SUTTON, ESQ.

Start Your Own Corporation
Why the Rich Own their Own Companies and Everyone Else Works for Them

Writing Winning Business Plans
How to Prepare a Business Plan that Investors will Want to Read and Invest In

Buying and Selling a Business
How You Can Win in the Business Quadrant

The ABCs of Getting Out of Debt
Turn Bad Debt into Good Debt and Bad Credit into Good Credit

Run Your Own Corporation
How to Legally Operate and Properly Maintain Your Company into the Future

The Loopholes of Real Estate
Secrets of Successful Real Estate Investing

Scam-Proof Your Assets
Guarding Against Widespread Deception

Piercing the Corporate Veil
When LLCs and Corporations Fail

BY KEN MCELROY

The ABCs of Real Estate Investing
The Secrets of Finding Hidden Profits Most Investors Miss

The ABCs of Property Management
What You Need to Know to Maximize Your Money Now

The Advanced Guide to Real Estate Investing
How to Identify the Hottest Markets and Secure the Best Deals

ABCs of Buying Rental Property
How You Can Achieve Financial Freedom in Five Years

Contents

Foreword
by Robert Kiyosaki

Before I began my business career, my rich dad insisted that I learn to be a real estate investor. At first, I thought he wanted me to invest in real estate simply for the real estate itself. As the years went on and my base of education grew, I came to better understand the bigger picture of the world of investing. Rich dad said, "If you want to be a sophisticated investor, you must train your mind to see what your eyes cannot see." What my eyes could not see were the legal and tax advantages that real estate investing offers the more informed investor. In other words, there is far more to real estate than dirt, sticks, and bricks. This book, written by Garrett Sutton, one of our Rich Dad Advisors, goes into the real reasons why the rich invest in real estate. *Loopholes of Real Estate* will take you into the world of real estate investing that the average investor rarely sees.

Today I make my money from all three asset classes: businesses, real estate, and paper assets. But I hold the bulk of my wealth in real estate. I am able to magnify my wealth using the advantages that real estate offers the sophisticated investor.

There have been challenges for real estate investors in the recent past. But if you learn the ins and outs of real estate investing, you can make money in real estate whether the market is going up, down, or sideways. That is why my rich dad preferred investing for cash flow instead of capital gains. As long as your property is cash-flow positive, you can ride out a downturn in the real estate market. The flippers and capital-gains buyers who are left holding properties for resale in a plummeting market are the ones who will be hurt the most.

You also need to surround yourself with good advisors. As a real estate investor you must seek tax and legal advice from professionals, which is why Garrett wrote this book. I do not know all of the details of the tax and legal advantages he describes—but I am glad that he, as my advisor, does.

If you are ready to become a sophisticated investor, find out how to use tax, legal, and other little-known advantages that investing in real estate offers, and how to find your own team of advisors, this book is for you.

Robert Kiyosaki

Part One:
Real Estate Advantages

Do you want to know a secret? Do you want to know the loopholes that allow successful real estate investors to do it so well?

You don't have to be a genius to understand and apply these loopholes. You just have to be willing to follow a proven path toward success. Basically, you need to be smart about following what others have used to their advantage before you.

The truth is that there are two types of real estate loopholes.

From a tax standpoint, there are real estate loopholes to be opened. The Tax Code, as put forth by Congress and the IRS, encourages certain real estate activities. Smart investors know how to open these loopholes to their maximum advantage.

From the legal side, there are real estate loopholes to be closed. There is liability and risk associated with owning real estate, leading to loopholes of increased personal liability and responsibility for the claims of others. These legal loopholes must be closed in order to gain asset protection and best protect yourself and your family.

How can I learn these secrets, you ask? And how can I apply them?

The secrets of real estate loopholes are not handwritten on aged parchment, locked in a dark and inaccessible vault in the depths of a well-fortified castle, and guarded by huge rabid dogs, fed by the rich and powerful as a way to exclude all newcomers. On the contrary, although not set out everywhere, the important loophole strategies—the ones you must know—are found in the pages of this book.

In using these loopholes, you have to be willing to combine the experience of others with the specifics of your own situation. This is not hard to do. In all aspects of our lives we synthesize and apply information. But unlike most other activities, by learning when to open loopholes and when to close them, you are going to significantly improve your results as a real estate investor.

And in applying these loopholes, you will become smart about selecting real estate, as we will review in the final section of this book.

Let's begin by answering several interesting questions...

Introduction

What are the Advantages of Real Estate?

Does the government care if you own real estate?

Not really.

Does the government offer significant advantages if you do own real estate?

Absolutely.

But aren't there risks that limit the benefits of owning real estate?

Perhaps.

Have the rich figured out ways to minimize that risk to their advantage?

Of course.

And so can you.

Real estate offers huge financial advantages to those who will learn the system. And, as this book will illustrate, any risks can efficiently be managed through insurance, legal structures, and other common strategies that are neither difficult nor expensive. There are great advantages to investing in real estate, both as a cash flow business and as a wealth builder. And the financial benefits flow from several sources, including the appreciation of your land and property values and the monthly cash flow you can earn by renting out residential, office, or commercial space in a structure on your land. In addition, you stand to benefit greatly through tax reduction from depreciation on those structures and through options to roll over profits, as allowed in the tax code. You can even benefit from writing off business expenses associated with your investment. And because of these advantages, it is easier to raise capital for real estate ventures.

Real estate investors can accelerate their wealth building much faster than with other assets, such as stocks, bonds, and tax-deferred retirement funds. Our financial, tax, and legal systems are set up to reward property owners who are educated enough to seize the available advantages. And best of all for starting investors, they don't need enormous cash reserves to buy real estate. They can start small.

Like first-time home buyers, real estate investors can secure bank loans and make monthly payments as owners of rental property. And as they watch their equity grow, they can parlay their initial investment property's increased value into garnering a new loan to purchase a second property. Pulling this cash out has a second benefit, in that they do not have to pay taxes on the money they receive because it is from their equity. And so on. They can learn as they go, perhaps making some mistakes and increasing their knowledge through experience, as their holdings expand.

The financial, tax, and legal advantages—as spelled out in this book— of owning real estate are enormous. And the question you, the reader, may ask is, "Why don't more investors follow this route to success?"

The answer is twofold and simple: Lack of knowledge and fear.

Begin Your Education Now

Many investors who avoid real estate are afraid of the anticipated difficulties of being landlords. They hear horror stories. They think to themselves, "I don't want to fix toilets," and "I don't want to get calls from tenants in the middle of the night." But know that there are strategies for intelligently managing a property that any capable person can implement. As well, many people fear the threat of a lawsuit. And rightly so. We are a litigious society. Attorneys are rewarded for bringing claims against wealthy individuals. But know that there are asset protection strategies we'll discuss that can reduce your exposure and limit your liability. In all, the rewards of owning real estate far outweigh the drawbacks for most prudent investors.

In recent years, many have come to fear the entire market. With the meltdown in 2008, thousands of real estate investors were caught with properties worth less than the mortgage on the parcel. These underwater properties have caused a great deal of turmoil for many investors. Some will never re-enter the real estate market. But others, who do not fear but rather appreciate the market, will do well. For in any environment there is room to make money in real estate.

Similarly, when it comes to lack of knowledge, most people are unaware of the advantages to be gained from investing in real estate. This is understandable. Most of us in our society aren't raised to consider investing in real estate. It's certainly not taught in schools. The standard pattern is to go to school, get a job, climb up the corporate ladder of a career, put earnings in a bank, maybe buy stocks, mutual funds, and bonds, and save for a rainy day, including retirement. Most of us don't realize that real estate investments allow our money to accelerate at a greater pace than typical paper investments. In fact, real estate has historically over the long term trended up in value and yielded higher returns than the securities markets.

There are really three types of income:

Earned Income: This is what you bring home from work in the form of a paycheck. You go to the office from eight to five. If you stopped going to work, your earned income would end.

Passive Income: This is what comes to you from an investment such as real estate. If you get sick and can't earn a paycheck from your job, your real estate is still working for you. (Even better, most of this income may not be subject to Social Security and Medicare withholdings, and in some cases incurs no tax at all because of your ability to depreciate a property's value, or to defer claimed gains by rolling over a sale to another property.)

Portfolio Income: This is what comes from the dividends and increases in value of paper assets such as stocks, bonds, and mutual funds. It's the most popular form of investment income for the masses, because it's easier to manage than real estate and other investments.

The point of this book isn't to encourage you to invest only in real estate. The Rich Dad philosophy is to diversify (although in a different sense of the word as used by financial planners), and to put your savings and earnings into three different areas: businesses, real estate, and paper assets. This is because each sector is subject to market fluctuations and corrections, and your investment risk must be spread out. The point of this book is to explain the financial, tax and legal advantages of investing in real estate as a passive-income earner and to educate you on how to utilize these investment advantages.

If this is the first Rich Dad book you're reading, please know that Rich Dad's philosophy is that your primary residence should not be considered an asset, because it is not generating regular income for you. (Rich Dad has a simple definition for "asset": something that puts money in your pocket. A "liability," conversely, is something that takes money *from* your pocket.) With your primary residence, you're paying the mortgage, and therefore the cash flow is going *from* you (to the bank), not *toward* you. Your home mortgage is an example of "bad debt." Still, the tax code offers some advantages for homeowners, which we'll discuss in later chapters.

Real estate becomes an asset when it brings you cash flow. By following the advice in this book, as a real estate investor, you will be putting other people's money—the lender bank's and your tenants'—to work for you. If your monthly mortgage on a rental property is $5,000, but your tenants are paying you $6,000, then you're earning $1,000 in cash. Your bank loan is "good debt."

Loophole #1

Good debt is debt that is used to purchase an asset that puts money *in* your pocket. Bad debt is debt that is used to purchase something that takes money *out* of your pocket. A real estate investment (which does not include your house) makes use of good debt.

How This Book Will Help You

This book is divided into five parts:

"Real Estate Advantages" explains the theories and facts behind the benefits of real estate investing.

"Get in the Game" instructs how to create an investment plan, assemble a team of advisors, and choose investments.

"Tax Strategies" teaches how to crunch the numbers of potential investments, make full use of tax advantages, and manage your investments.

"Legal Strategies" covers methods for protecting your investments and yourself.

"Selection Strategies" reveals the legal and other issues for choosing profitable properties.

This book is not intended to make you a tax expert or legal expert on real estate. Nor is this book offering a get-rich-quick scheme. (There are enough of those pipe dreams being sold all the time in books and brochures, seminars and infomercials.) *Loopholes of Real Estate* is for readers who are serious about educating themselves about investing in real estate. It's for readers who want to learn about these advantages that the rich already know about. And because the law applies to everyone–rich or poor–these advantages are available to all of us.

This book will help you know what questions to ask the advisors who will constitute your investment team. In *Rich Dad Poor Dad,* Robert Kiyosaki has famously cited the advice his "rich dad" gave him: "Business and investing are team sports." While most successful real estate investors learn by doing, as you forge ahead in real estate, you won't be on your own. You will assemble a team of advisors—as discussed in Chapter 6. You'll know whom you need and when.

Also know that you need not absorb the contents of this book like a sponge. As you progress in your real estate investing career, you can return time and again to the book. And since your education will be ongoing, we strongly urge you to explore the other titles listed in our resource section found in Appendix A.

Your Opportunity Awaits

Becoming a successful real estate investor is within most investors' reach. I am a living example of this. I am building my personal wealth through real estate. I am an attorney, Rich Dad Advisor, and author. I never enjoyed a previous career as a real estate professional. But I've practiced the principles in this book and reaped the rewards. So can you.

As with other investment options, the world of real estate is vast, and no one can become an expert in every area. Nor should anyone try. You are wise to specialize in one type of market—such as small single-family homes, or apartment complexes with a certain number of units, and in a geographic area familiar to you.

If you're a small investor, successfully investing in real estate will allow you to move out of the great mass of fellow investors who put their paycheck savings into modest paper investments. Real estate investing will power up your earning potential and put you into a different class of investor entirely.

Chapter One

Understanding the "Why" of Real Estate

If you're familiar with the *Rich Dad* series, you're probably familiar with this:

    The CASHFLOW Quadrant above appeared in the second book in the series, *Rich Dad's CASHFLOW Quadrant: Rich Dad's Guide to Financial Freedom.*

    This quadrant represents the four types of income earners:

E is for employee, which is the most common type. E people earn their money by working for other people and taking home paychecks.

S is for self-employed. S people work for themselves, often as sole-proprietors or independent contractors, and are entirely reliant on their own productivity to produce a paycheck.

B is for business owners. B people have other people working for them to generate income.

I is for investors. I people invest their money in assets, so that their money is working for them.

The people on the left side of the CASHFLOW Quadrant manage their finances in the traditional way that most of us have learned from our parents or society at large: They establish careers in income-generating occupations, earn paychecks, and sock away savings in order to 1) pay off debts, 2) buy homes, or 3) invest in stocks, bonds, or retirement funds. This is the status quo. Few of us learn anything about money in school, but what most of us are brought up to understand is that our primary goal as adults should be to go to school, use our educations to get good jobs that pay well, put a little bit of money into savings each month for a "rainy day," and save for our retirement.

We're taught to "park" our money. So it sits there, doing very little but waiting for us to use it.

Most people are on the left side of the Quadrant, working for their money instead of having their money working for them. In that scenario, the bulk of their money pays off bills—liabilities—while only the "leftovers" go into savings or investments. So, most of their money is flowing *away* from them.

But for the people on the right, the B-I people, their money is working for them. It's flowing *toward* them. Their income is passive; their own money, as well as other people's money, time, and energy, all generate wealth for them.

This chart illustrates the inherently different mentalities of the two kinds of investors—those who rely on their earned income to slowly grow investments, and those who rely on their assets to grow and accelerate wealth. Put simply, if you want to grow wealth, it's desirable to move to the right side of the Quadrant.

Doing this means establishing a business, or a portfolio comprised of passive income-generation, diversified among real estate, businesses, stocks and bonds.

Does this mean you have to give up your current career or employment? Absolutely not. It simply means that your goal should be to increase your assets—right-sided, dynamic income generators—in order to get your income working for *you,* and not the other way around.

Real Estate is an Essential Building Block of Your Investment Portfolio

For those of you who don't know, in Robert Kiyosaki's first book, *Rich Dad Poor Dad,* he shares the financial lessons he learned from observing his "rich dad"—the wealthy father of Robert's best friend, who was very rich and became a mentor to Robert—and his "poor dad"—his own father, who earned a traditional salary, invested only in long-term, conservative paper assets, and died poor.

One of the things Robert learned from rich dad was how investing in the three asset classes—business, real estate, and paper assets— contributed to his wealth. Rich dad's formula for wealth was starting a business, taking the cash flow from that business (mostly after-tax monies) and investing in real estate, and keeping that wealth in real estate and paper assets, where it will keep growing.

This formula was illustrated in Robert's "Why the Rich Get Richer" chart, as shown below, which appeared in his book *Rich Dad's Who Took My Money?*

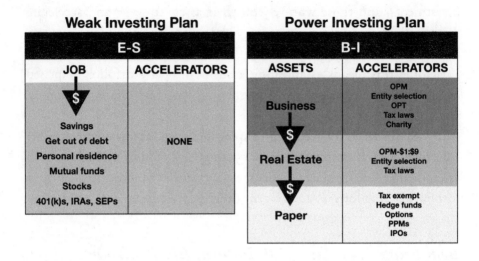

As you can see, E and S people on the left have one source of income generation: a job. But the B-I people on the right-hand side of the chart have three sources, or assets, as well as a multitude of accelerators to speed up the income that those assets provide.

Here's an explanation of the chart abbreviations.

OPM: Other People's Money (Money from lenders, like banks or investors)

OPT: Other People's Time (In a business, employees work for you, using their time to benefit the bottom line.)

OPM—$1:$9: This refers to a real estate investor's ability to borrow, from a bank or other lender, nine-tenths of the cost of an investment; the investor's own money covers the remaining one-tenth. This is an example of leveraging "good debt."

PPM: Private Placement Memorandum, which young companies use to attract investment capital

IPO: Initial Public Offering, which enables a company to begin issuing stock for purchase by investors outside the company, usually with an attractive opening price to entice investors

In this book, I'll be dealing specifically with those accelerators that pertain to real estate.

Additionally, you might be wondering, after having read *Rich Dad's Who Took My Money?*, whether you actually have to start a business in order to invest in real estate. The answer is no. In fact, even as an E or S, you can funnel after-tax earnings into real estate. But many people eventually make real estate investing itself their business (which we will further discuss in Chapter 9).

Real estate investment offers several benefits. There are, of course, certain tax benefits involved in owning real estate. As you'll notice in the chart, the real estate asset class shows the tax laws pertaining to Depreciation and Passive Loss as income accelerators. We'll be covering these topics in detail in Chapters 3 and 8, but for the purpose of understanding, when passive income is negative (or a passive loss), the government allows us to write off a deduction, or what accountants call "paper loss," each year, based on business expenses plus the calculated loss, or depreciation, of repairing a structural component or piece of personal property that was used in the building on your land, with the assumption that these items naturally will deteriorate over time.

What I'm saying here, basically, is that if you educate yourself, real estate can be the key to moving you from the left side of the Quadrant to the right, and to building your own estate.

The easiest way to invest (although not always the most successful) in order to build an estate through portfolio income is by putting your earnings into stocks, bonds and mutual funds. Some people do this themselves, some use a tax-deferred retirement plan, and some rely on the assistance of a financial planner. Most people on the left side of the Quadrant take this route.

Meanwhile, what is arguably the most difficult method of investment is running a business with employees. Whether your business is entirely your own or a franchise, your success is dependent on your education, time commitment, finding the right members to make up your team and significant risk. Though it could potentially offer the greatest rate of return of any investment type—even real estate investment—the deck is stacked against most business owners. Nine out of ten businesses fail in their first five years.

Between those two ends of the spectrum is real estate investing, which requires a little more education than investing for portfolio income but is a lot less daunting than running a business. Plus, real estate offers a far greater rate of return, as well as tax savings, than does portfolio income.

With real estate investing, you're likely to make mistakes, especially as you're getting started. But if you educate yourself, and build a solid team of knowledgeable experts who you can trust, you will mitigate those mistakes and begin to see the benefits of leveraging to grow wealth.

Before we proceed, it is important to fully appreciate the meaning of loopholes...

Chapter Two

More about Loopholes

Today's meaning for 'Loophole' is that of a technicality that allows one to get out of a contract or a tax provision allowing for lower taxes. For some the term has a slightly negative connotation, which, when you know its history, is understandable.

The origins of the word loophole, like so much else in the lexicon of real estate, dates back to the Middle Ages. In the 1300's, *loupe* in the Middle English dialect meant window. Similarly, in Middle Dutch, *lupen* meant to peer.

Now think back to every great defensive medieval castle you've ever seen. Not the likes of the fancy, fairy book Neuschwanstein Castle in Bavaria, which has regular size windows and was only built between 1869 and 1892, long after castle sieges ended. Instead, think of Blarney Castle (home of the famous Blarney Stone), a gritty monolith built in County Cork, Ireland, in 1446. You can Google photos of the castle. While the tower in front has regular window size apertures, the castle itself has narrow, vertical slit like openings. These are called loopholes.

A *loupehole*, in Middle English, is a window hole, or a hole to peer out of in Middle Dutch. These narrow windows were used to defend the castle. You could fire arrows and other projectiles through these slits onto the invaders below. In later times muskets were used to shoot through the window holes. And it was very difficult for the masses on the ground to get anything back in and through the very narrow openings. It is no wonder some people think negatively of loopholes. A loophole allowed a skilled archer to fire an arrow through your heart.

Of course, let's remember that archer was defending his castle. And the person on the ground in the archer's sights who doesn't like loopholes was trying to forcibly and violently take the castle. We will remember this scenario as we discuss the legal loopholes used to defend your own real estate in future chapters.

Over time, loopholes gained a second usage in castle fortifications. Well placed slits in an otherwise impenetrable wall allowed children and small adults to squeeze through for escape. If you were well informed, if you knew where the loopholes were hidden, you could get away from the destructive and deadly siege.

From there, in the 1600's, the word loophole had evolved to describe a means of escape, an "out" in an unpiercable contract or tax setting. Only the clever few who knew where the loopholes were could escape.

Today, loopholes carry the same meaning. But with one significant change. Loopholes are no longer hidden for the clever few. Instead, they are available for anyone to use. By educating yourself, by reading this book and others like it, you can take advantage of all the tax and legal loopholes the well-informed have used for years.

By opening up the tax loopholes and narrowing down the legal ones, you will greatly benefit you and your family through your real estate investments.

Loophole #2

When you think about loopholes, remember their historical context of defense and escape. While castle sieges have faded away, tax and legal sieges are on the rise.

Chapter Three

The Benefits of Leverage

In the "Why the Rich Get Richer" chart from Chapter 1, you will note the "OPM—$1:$9" accelerator for the real estate asset category. To reiterate, this accelerator exemplifies leveraging "good debt" — that which brings income flowing toward you that exceeds your payment on the debt. This accelerator refers to an investor's ability to borrow from a bank (or other lender) 90 percent of the cost of an investment, while using the investor's own money to cover the remaining 10 percent. It's a 9:1 leverage. (In today's market it may be 8:2 leverage where a 20% down payment is required to purchase investment real estate. Even so, the leverage is dramatic. For the purposes of illustration we will use 9:1 accelerator in this discussion.)

What this accelerator does is allow you to use a bank or other people's money to cover 90 percent of your investment, while enjoying 100 percent of the investment advantages in building up equity in your property. As well, you also enjoy 100 percent of the tax advantages that further increase the value of your investment. As such, the accelerator gives you the ability to use any equity you build up in each property to buy more properties at leveraged rates and increase your wealth exponentially.

We'll discuss the tax advantages of depreciation a little later. For now, let's consider an example of how the OPM—$1:$9 accelerator can increase the velocity of your money far more than two other common investment strategies. Suppose you have $20,000 to invest. Here are three choices:

- Choice 1: Invest $20,000 in a mutual fund that earns 5 percent a year. (This is what most E-S investors do: Put their savings into paper.)
  After seven years, your $20,000 should have grown to $28,142, assuming no market fluctuations.

- Choice 2: Invest $20,000 and borrow $180,000 from the bank for a $200,000 rental property, and let your equity compound. (This is using the OPM—$1:$9 accelerator, but only initially.) Assume rental income only breaks even with expenses and the property appreciates at a rate of 5 percent a year.
  After seven years, the property will be worth $281,000, and your equity (the $281,000 minus what you still owe the bank) is $101,420, assuming no market fluctuations.

- Choice 3: Invest $20,000 and borrow $180,000 from the bank for a $200,000 rental property. Rather than letting the equity compound, you borrow out the appreciation every two years and invest it in a new property at 10 percent down. (See, you're repeating your use of the OPM—$1:$9 accelerator.)
  After seven years, your four properties will be worth $2,022,218, and your net equity will be $273,198, assuming no market fluctuations.

To summarize the hypothetical $20,000 investment:

Net Equity After Seven Years	Average Annual Return
Choice 1: $28,142	5.8%
Choice 2: $101,420	58.2%
Choice 3: $273,198	180.9%

Choices 1 and 2 are examples of parking your money. Choice 3 is an example of increasing the velocity of your money. While borrowing out your appreciation may not be right for everyone it may be the correct choice for the investor who wishes to significantly increase wealth through real estate leveraging.

This is the formula for using Choice 3:

1. Invest money into an asset
2. Get the original investment money back
3. Keep control of the original asset
4. Move the money into a new asset
5. Get the investment money back
6. Repeat the process

What Choice 3 actually does is allow you, the personal investor, to invest much like a bank does. The strategy allows you to expand your money supply to increase your earning power. Like a bank or other financial institution, you can make your money move. The more times a dollar moves (being reinvested in a new moneymaking property), the greater the money supply you tap (since the dollar leverages other dollars), and the greater that dollar's earning power.

Now can you see the value of using other people's money to build your wealth? Of course, the ability to work this magic doesn't come at once. It requires an initial investment in financial education. That education can begin by reading this book. But it also will involve implementing the directions in this book, learning by doing and ongoing learning—which should continue throughout your life.

Which brings us to a cautionary note: You must always make intelligent investment decisions based soundly on your education and experience, for if you don't you may end up overleveraged. Of course, many learned this lesson the very hard way after the shocks beginning in 2008. If you own multiple investment properties and one of them proves to be a bad investment—not providing sufficient returns, or even losing money—it can cause your whole house of cards to collapse. You may find yourself robbing Peter to pay Paul. You must be prudent and ensure that if, say, one of your properties goes vacant, you can survive the downturn in your anticipated income. This can be accomplished by keeping a reserve, which is an account where you hold enough cash or liquid assets to help you pay your real estate expenses in case you have a vacancy. People usually keep from three months up to a year of expenses in their reserve account.

Again, that ability to plan your investments and continually assess their performance will come with education and knowledge gained from experience, and from building your team of advisors.

The Advantage of Depreciation with Leverage

Another key real estate advantage is the available tax savings. When you borrow 90 percent of a payment on a property, it doesn't mean you own only 10 percent of that property. You own 100 percent of it. Therefore, you are entitled to 100 percent of the tax deductions.

There are two categories of deductions for real estate: Depreciation and passive loss. We'll discuss these a bit further on in this chapter, and explain the applicable federal tax laws more fully in Chapter 8. For now, let's look at the following chart to see how using the OPM—$1:$9 accelerator can benefit you beyond the appreciation.

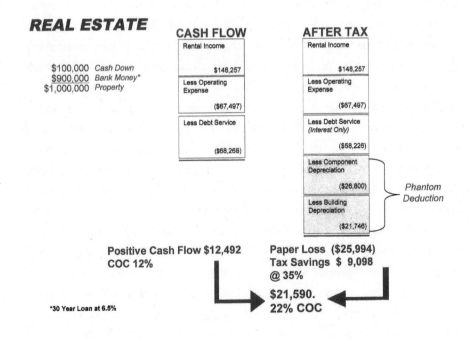

In this chart's example, you put $100,000 of your own cash down on a $1 million rental property, and borrow the remaining $900,000 from a bank at a 30-year loan rate of roughly 6.5 percent. Note the Cash Flow column on the chart. Your rental income for the first year is $148,257. Your operating expense is $67,497 and your debt service (the interest on the bank loan plus other payments you've made on the loan) is $68,268. Subtract these amounts from your income and you arrive at $12,492. That positive cash flow represents the cash-on-cash ("COC") return on your cash investment of $100,000. This return is better than 12 percent.

But that double-digit return isn't the only benefit accruing to you from your rental property. Look at the After Tax column on the chart. Your reportable income on your tax return will be your rental income minus your operating expense and only the interest you've paid on your debt service (not the principal payments)—plus two other deductions, what we term "phantom deductions." One phantom deduction is "component depreciation" (also known as "cost segregation depreciation" and discussed further in Chapter 8). The annual decline in the various components of a building, such as its shell and walls, roofing and flooring, carpets and furniture, electrical, heating and plumbing systems, are entitled to be depreciated. Each of these has a "useful life," or life expectancy, of more than one year, and will need replacement at some point. Their costs can be capitalized and prorated over the years you own the property. The other phantom deduction is "building depreciation," which means the annual decline in the useful life of a building's structure.

In all, your "paper loss" recognized by the Internal Revenue Service is $25,994. If you are in a tax-effective rate of 35 percent (which is higher than most income earners' rate), you can claim 35 percent of your paper loss ($9,098 in this example) to offset other income. Add that savings of $9,098 to your $12,492 in positive cash flow, and you have actually realized a $21,590 cash-on-cash return for the year on your $100,000 investment—roughly 22 percent. That is an excellent return.

The Government Respects Real Estate

We've mentioned the tax write-offs for the phantom deductions—component and building depreciations. There is another write-off to consider: Passive loss. After you've taken your rental income and deducted your operating expenses, interest on debt service, and phantom deductions, the resulting income or loss is considered your passive income or passive loss. The tax laws allow you to offset your earned income by up to $25,000 in passive losses from real estate, as long as your adjusted gross income is below $100,000. Above the $100,000 level to $149,999, there is a sliding scale for what you can deduct from real estate losses. Those with $150,000 or more of adjusted gross income can't claim this deduction. Unless, that is, you utilize the real estate professional strategy we'll discuss in Chapter 9.

Why are there such great tax advantages for owning and investing in real estate? Our nation's tax laws are written to support those people—business owners and investors—who create jobs and housing. The laws benefit the risk-takers, the doers, who spur the economy. Therefore, if you invest capital into your community by buying real estate, you are rewarded with tax breaks so that you can maintain and continue investing while, at the same time, you provide a much needed social service.

The government learned its lesson several generations ago that it does a very poor job of providing low-cost housing. The old joke that there is nothing more permanent than temporary government housing arose from these past and unsuccessful efforts. In some cities, such as San Francisco, the municipal government still owns large housing complexes. They are the most mismanaged rat traps around. All in all, the private sector just does a much better job of it, which most governmental agencies now keenly recognize. Accordingly, it is more efficient to encourage individual investors through tax advantages to perform this service than for the government to muddle its way through the important community need of housing.

The government also allows special tax and legal protections for property owners in the form of legal entities. As detailed in my book

Start Your Own Corporation, an entity is an organization which has a legal identity separate from its owners. It is derived from the Latin word '*ens,*' meaning an existing or real thing. When we refer to entities in this book, think of limited liability companies (LLCs), corporations and limited partnerships (LPs).

How you hold your property and use your entities becomes very important as your investments increase. You don't want a legal problem arising at one property — such as a tenant tripping on the stairs — to put your other holdings and personal assets at risk of a lawsuit settlement or judgment. These legal entity strategies will be discussed in depth in Part Four: Legal Strategies.

Loophole #3

The government grants tax and legal loopholes to real estate investors to encourage them to do a job that the government can't. Know that these loopholes lead to a societal benefit.

Summary of Leverage Advantages

Using the OPM—$1:$9 accelerator, your cash investment of 10 percent into a property is rewarded with income potential, full ownership, appreciation of equity, and tax deductions. The lender, which invests 90 percent of the purchase price, realizes only one benefit while being repaid its capital: Interest payments. As long as you pay the debt service to the bank, you enjoy the leverages of ownership, appreciation and depreciation. It's almost too good to be true and looks like this:

	YOU	YOUR LENDER
Money	10%	90%
Ownership	100%	0%
Appreciation	100%	0%
Deductions	100%	0%

The returns from leveraging equity and the tax advantages of ownership make real estate a very steady path to wealth for many people. And please know that even people who are struggling out of financial straits can invest in real estate. There are plenty of strategies for those with challenged credit to utilize to gain real estate success, including no money down deals and wrap around mortgages, which are discussed in numerous other real estate guides.

Better yet, when real estate is treated as a business your income potential increases even further.

Capital Gain and Cash Flow

As we saw in the CASHFLOW Quadrant in Chapter 1, the business owners and investors on the right-hand side of the Quadrant benefit from the work, time and money of other people. When it comes to investing in real estate, you want to increase your wealth not only from the property's appreciation—its "capital gain"—over time, but also from the cash flow the property can generate.

There are thus two goals for real estate investing. One is for the value of your property to appreciate over time so you'll be able to sell it for more than you bought it. Those are the two crucial points in time for your property: When you buy it, and when you sell it. This is *capital gains investing*.

The other goal is for your property to generate a positive income for you each and every month. You want the revenue from rental income to exceed the operating costs and mortgage payment. This is *cash-flow investing*. Having your money generate passive income for you—monies that come to you whether you are at work or on vacation—is a *Rich Dad* investment principle. An income-generating property is like an employee working for you. This passive income from a property would end if you sell that property. You may enjoy a capital gain from the sale, but you no longer have that money actively working for you to earn you even more money. To replace it, you may need to reinvest that money into another investment that yields positive cash flow.

A person who is solely a capital-gain investor looks at the optimal time to buy a property (i.e., when its market price is relatively low) and the optimal time to sell (when it appears the market value has peaked or risks plummeting). A cash-flow investor looks at the income history and potential of a property, and usually considers selling only when indicators (such as a decrease in an area's population) point to a drop in cash flow; or when money from capital gains can be parlayed into a more lucrative income-generating investment, such as a larger property; or when the property has fully depreciated over time and this tax advantage can no longer be enjoyed.

Rich Dad's philosophy is that once you have your dollar in your asset column, you want to keep it working for you, generating even more dollars that, in turn, will work for you, too. And so on. You may not want to do what most small investors do, which is park your money and hope that it will increase in value (appreciation) over time.

When it comes to real estate, you want to enjoy its appreciation *and* its generation of income. You want capital gain *and* cash flow.

In Real Estate, Time Is Your Ally

While the theory has been tested recently, from a long term perspective real estate values historically go up. Land is finite. As Will Rogers famously said, "They're not making any more of it." As the population increases, there is always a demand for real estate.

Furthermore, as our central banks continue to print more and more money, assets with a tangible worth such as gold and real estate hold and gain value while the fiat currencies (which are backed by absolutely nothing) continue to decline. Well purchased real estate is an excellent hedge against government recklessness.

There will always be market cycles lifting or lowering values, including market corrections, downward trends and artificially inflated price bubbles that burst. There will always be natural disasters such as hurricanes, flooding or drought and manmade disasters such as crime waves and pollution that can diminish property values. Financial markets and interest rates, and the changing fortunes of area industries that employ people and create wealth, will always have a bearing on real estate markets. But in general, over the long term, real estate goes up. If you buy property it stands to appreciate over time. But remember, there are no guarantees.

What's more, there's always a good deal to be found. If prices seem too high in a certain market, it may scare off competitors and leave an opening for the savvy buyer who looks a little harder. Or if it seems like a particular market or segment has tanked, it offers opportunity to the aggressive investor to buy at a reduced rate.

Here's an example. *Rich Dad Poor Dad* author Robert Kiyosaki moved to Phoenix in 1991 because of a plunge in real estate values in that city. Nationwide, the default of savings and loan lenders, along with overvaluation in real estate and overleveraged debt among investors, led to crashes in many markets. Robert purchased two apartment complexes in Phoenix for dimes on the dollar. By 1994, these investments had proved profitable enough to make him financially free. He had enough passive cash flow from those two properties alone to cover his monthly living expenses, hence financial freedom.

A key for capital gains investing is to hold onto a property for a minimum of one year. This is because you'll get a capital-gains tax rate (at this writing 20 percent at the federal level for the United States), which is lower than the rate on ordinary income, if you've held a property for at least one year.

Some investors pursue a strategy of "flipping" properties—buying low and selling high as soon as possible, often without holding onto a property for at least a year. These "fix-and-flippers" who sell before owning a property for a year get hit with the higher tax rate. That defeats the purpose of banking on a capital gain. In addition, if they do it too often, the IRS could categorize them as "dealers" and the capital gains income could be considered earned income and subject not only to the higher rates but also to employment taxes. But with their money accelerated, even at a higher capital gains rate, the strategy works for some people. Some people use the flipping strategy to help them build up cash more quickly in order to move into larger properties.

One more word of caution: When real estate is at its highest and the bubble is about to burst, the flippers may get caught holding properties with no cash flow, and with declining values due to the real estate bubble bursting. This is another reason why Rich Dad prefers cash flow investing over flipping.

Case #1
Tony and Terri

Tony and Terri were a couple who had once dated and found it was easier and less complicated to simply be friends. Their friendship was strengthened by their mutual interest in investing in real estate. But as they had found in their prior closer relationship, each had their own way of doing things.

Tony was impatient. He wanted to get in, do his work and move on. He liked turning his assets as quickly as possible. Terri was just the opposite. She wanted to get to know her property and liked the benefits of long term ownership, monthly cash flow and appreciation over time. It was clear that their investing strategies mirrored their romantic predilections, and never the twain would meet.

Tony's desire for accelerated action came with a greater financial burden. By flipping properties every few months, he was subject to short-term capital gains at his ordinary income rate. Of greater consequence, by doing these turns on a regular basis, it became his trade or business. As such, a salary was properly paid along with payroll taxes. Accordingly, Tony paid a 35% ordinary income tax, payroll taxes of 15.3% on the first $137,700 or so of income and state taxes on top of that. Over 50% of Tony's short term profits were eaten up in taxes.

Terri, on the other hand, did not jump from property to property. When she found one she liked she held onto it for over a year or longer. As such, she enjoyed the benefit of a 20% capital gains tax when she sold a property. So, for example, on a $100,000 gain she paid a long term rate of only $20,000 whereas Tony had to pay over $50,000 on the same (but faster) gain. (As individuals, if their income was greater than $200,000 per year they also paid a 3.8% ObamaCare tax on any gains.)

And like so many others, both Tony and Terri liked the idea of trading up for a better property. But Tony, due to his accelerated activities, wasn't allowed to do so on a tax-free basis. Terri, on the other hand, by being patient and holding on for over a year, was able to use a 1031 transaction (discussed more fully in Chapter 10). She could trade up tax-free for a newer and better property every year or so. All in all, Terri greatly appreciated the slow satisfaction of real estate wealth building.

Like Terri, the Rich Dad philosophy is to keep a property as long as its value continues to appreciate and its cash flow is sufficient to at least cover the costs of owning the property. Again, everyone has a different style and agenda, but it bears remembering that when renters cover your mortgage payment and operating costs, they're in effect paying you to have your equity grow. That's why Rich Dad's preference is for cash flow over parking your money in paper. And "parking" is the operative word here. When you park your car, how much acceleration do you get? The same thing happens (or, really, doesn't happen) when you park your money in paper assets.

What you can charge and receive for rent is determined by what the market will bear, just as with any other good or service in the economy. Therefore, your cash flow and profit from a property are really determined by how much you paid for the property (and the rate of interest on your loan). As the old real estate adage holds: "You make your profits when you buy." Acquire the right property at the right price with the right financing, and cash flow and profit will follow.

Building up your capital gain—your growth in equity—and securing cash flow are both important to growing your wealth through real estate. As previously stated, the U.S. tax code is set up to reward property holders. The government knows that it can't properly or efficiently perform the service of housing. Which is why there are government-sanctioned tax advantages to investing in real estate. And financial institutions such as banks are eager to lend money to investors who can prove themselves good risks by being capable of generating cash flow from the properties in which they invest. This allows the knowledgeable investor to accelerate income with the OPM—$1:$9 accelerator.

As a knowledgeable investor you can put your money to work to build wealth fairly quickly. Time is our most precious resource. For you as a real estate investor, time is an ally.

Loophole #4

Real estate investing loopholes work best for you over a period of time. The sooner you implement them, the sooner they will start working for you.

Are you ready to get in the game? The next few chapters explain how this is done...

Part Two:
Get in the Game

Now that we have an idea of the advantages it is time to move forward. It is time to develop your real estate plan, create your team of advisors, set up the books and take action.

Chapter Four

Creating Your Real Estate Plan

We've all heard the expression, "Those who fail to plan, plan to fail." In real estate, this saying certainly holds true. It's essential that you develop a workable plan and start building a team of experts before you get started, so that you start off on the path to success.

Perhaps you already have these two vital components. If so, feel free to skip ahead to Part Three, where the meatier issues, such as taxes, are dealt with.

But for those of you just getting started, you're wondering where to begin. And the answer is, with taking a good, hard look at your financial affairs in order to develop an accurate, comprehensive financial report card.

Step #1: Preparing Your Financial Report Card

You can't move forward until you determine where you are right now. Unfortunately, this basic premise is overlooked by many investors, and it's a crucial foundation for success.

Start creating your financial statement by developing an income statement that lists your monthly income and expenses. Most of us are checkbook-driven; we put our paychecks into our checking accounts, pay bills with that income throughout the month, and, if we're lucky, we have enough income each month to pay those bills. The income statement will show you your monthly financial activity.

Next, you'll create a balance sheet, which lists your assets and liabilities. Your assets, as you'll recall, are the things that generate wealth for you, such as investments, savings accounts, stocks, 401(k) plans, mutual funds, real estate, or a business that you own. Your liabilities are all the things that take money away from you, which might include your credit cards, the remaining balance on your car loan, or the mortgage on your home. Your balance sheet will give you a picture of your current wealth.

Your personal financial statement will bring your financial goals into sharp relief. You'll see where your debt is concentrated or how to pay it down, and you might see where you could bolster your asset column. It may lead you to form a plan to decrease expenses or increase income. Some decide to downsize their homes in order to free up some money for investment, while others may opt to rent out their existing home and move to a smaller home to generate cash flow, increase passive income and decrease expenses. Only you can decide how to address your financial situation. Seeing your assets and liabilities in black and white will open up a lot of possibilities you hadn't considered before.

But unless you plan to increase your working hours, ask for a raise, or seek a better-paying job, your income options will be limited. The only real way to significantly improve your income will be to increase your passive or portfolio income.

Step #2: Setting Your Real Estate Goals

Passive income is the suggested method for growing wealth. It is not only the fastest method, but is also the easiest, because it means other people's money, time, and energy are working for you.

If you're like most people, your financial report card reveals that zero percent of your income is passive. So your first step is to determine what percentage of your income you'd like to make passive. Start with where you'd like to be one year from now, as well as a longer-term goal of five years from now. What would a reasonable monthly passive income goal be? $1,000? $5,000? $10,000? More than that?

Remember that your goals are dependent on what you're willing to do to make them happen. Know that you can also recalibrate your goals down the road as you learn more and determine what works and what doesn't.

A lot of people, once they've made up their minds to invest in real estate, decide to jump right in and figure things out as they go along. Some people learn best by doing and making the occasional mistake, while others do what they can to head off those mistakes by completely educating themselves first and consulting with advisors and investors. Everyone is different, and you should do whatever is most comfortable for you.

Essentially you'll want to determine something specific—how much you want to save, how much of an initial investment you plan to make, what you'll do with that initial investment, and over what period of time.

For example, maybe you've decided that within six months, you want to save $10,000, which you'll then turn around and invest into a piece of rental property by the end of one year. If this is doable for you, it's a worthy goal. From there, perhaps, you might decide that within ten years you want to have five rental properties.

Beyond that, you have other decisions to make: What kind of properties you'll invest in, where, and what to do with them.

The following are your numerous real estate options:

- Single-family homes
- Condominiums
- Duplexes
- 4 plexes
- Trailer parks
- Apartments
- Commercial office space
- Commercial industrial space
- Storefront retail
- Hotels
- Motels

Each of these has its own choices as well—apartment complexes vary in size, so are you interested in 20-unit complexes, 100, or more? Starter-market or high-end gated communities? High-rise office, strip-mall retail... your choices are plentiful.

Then you must decide where you want your properties to be. Are you looking for properties nearby in your town, in a neighboring town, in another state, near water, urban, rural?

Now, what will you do with the property? You could:

- Buy foreclosures cheaply, without intending to earn immediate cash flow from them,

- Fix and flip, intending to purchase cheaply, refurbish, and resell for a profit,

- Buy and hold, capitalizing on appreciation, or

- Buy, hold, and rent, earning both appreciation and cash flow.

The *Rich Dad* strategy is buying and renting, which maximizes short- and long-term income potential.

The Wisdom of Investment Specialization

Because the real estate world offers so many options, it's a good idea to focus on a particular area of specialization. For instance, you might become an expert in buying, holding, and renting small, one and two-bedroom apartment buildings in a particular area of town. Perhaps you used to live in an apartment in that area years ago and understand the needs of that community and that type of resident. Each geographic area has its own unique dynamic, its own zoning regulations and its own distinctive resident, so it's a good idea to focus on one particular area. As you become an expert in one investment area, you will be more apt to learn another area quickly.

Another word of advice: Start small. You will make mistakes, so make them early on, with low-risk, low-end properties in which there isn't as much at stake for you.

Case #2
Omar, Ashley, and Zeke

Omar was itching to get into real estate. He had read ten books and had bought (and later regretted buying) a $5,000 system from a get-rich-quick real estate promoter who, he later learned, had never actually owned real estate. Recovering from that lesson, Omar had talked to more than a dozen real estate brokers in his local area.

Omar had come to appreciate that real estate was not a get-rich-quick enterprise, but rather a slow process of growth and incremental success. Still, he was impatient to begin the process. He had saved $20,000, and it was definitely not appreciating in his savings account, which paid a measly 1% annual return. When inflation was factored in, he knew he was actually losing money.

So he was intrigued when Ashley was introduced to him by a local broker. Ashley was an attractive woman in her early forties who had put together a number of real estate syndications. Her typical deal was for five to ten investors to put up $20,000 to $50,000 toward the purchase of a large apartment complex. Ashley received a commission on the purchase of the real estate, a monthly management fee and 20 percent of the equity in the deal. When all the numbers were added up, Ashley was quite well compensated. But, as she freely admitted, many of her investors simply didn't have the time or inclination to be actively involved. And they were willing to pay for her assistance.

Omar was interested in Ashley's proposal. He could put his $20,000 into her investment and perhaps in five years, or whenever he and the other partners decided to sell, he could receive $35,000 to $40,000. At least, that's what the projections said.

Omar was seriously considering the investment until he spoke to Zeke, another real estate broker who had taken an interest in Omar and his investment path. Zeke questioned whether Omar really wanted to be a limited partner in a real estate syndication. While it was an excellent investment for some people, Zeke thought that it didn't seem to be a good fit for Omar. In the syndication as a limited partner, Omar would have no say in how the property was managed. He would have no control and no voice in the project. As such, Omar wouldn't really learn anything about real estate management and acquisition. He would be a passive investor instead of an active and involved real estate entrepreneur.

Omar appreciated Zeke's comments. He refocused his goals, which were to learn about real estate by starting small and then grow into larger properties as his experience and confidence expanded. He realized it was possible that a few mistakes might be made on his first investments and acknowledged that he would prefer to make them early on smaller properties, where the consequences wouldn't be so dramatic.

Omar politely declined Ashley's opportunity to invest. He explained to her that as a passive investor he couldn't learn real estate the way he wanted to learn it. Instead, Zeke found Omar an $80,000 duplex to buy with $16,000 down. Omar's remaining $4,000 was held in a reserve account in the event of any emergencies or vacancies.

Omar used this first opportunity to learn about what it took to manage real estate and to increase its value. This knowledge was extremely useful when Omar bought his next duplex, a 4 plex, and, eventually, larger properties.

And here is why it gets easier for Omar, and other investors like him. A system becomes a blueprint for investing. And the chances for making mistakes decrease as experience increases. There's yet another plus of repeating a successful formula: Once you get established in an area of investing—after you've become known as someone who buys a certain type of property—you gain momentum. For example, brokers will seek you out when good deals arise. You'll hear about these deals before the mob of other would-be buyers do.

Sticking With Your Game Plan

One final point about why it's a good idea to stick to the same game plan when you're investing in real estate: When you assemble your team of advisors, one of them will be your real estate agent. He or she will be an expert in one particular sector—the one you're investing in—but most likely won't be an expert in other sectors. For example, he or she might specialize in duplexes, but not strip malls.

So by sticking with one sector, you can retain the same team of advisors without having to seek others. And as far as your team is concerned, it's best to find them, understand their strengths and use them as your investment vehicle. This leverages experience. When you're ready to broaden your investment horizons, you can seek new team members.

Loophole #5

To fully master all of the real estate loopholes, consider specializing in one real estate sector at the start.

Now, let's get things in order...

Chapter Five

Getting Your Financial House in Order

It's tempting (especially as you're just beginning to build an investment portfolio) to save money by doing things yourself, such as property management or bookkeeping, and to keep things simple by using your own bank account for all transactions. But as you'll quickly see, keeping things "simple" may create some complicated problems.

Case #3
Pam

Pam owned a beauty salon and a 4 plex. Against the advice of her CPA and attorney, she held both her business and her rental real estate in her own name as a sole proprietor. Her attorney was concerned for asset protection reasons. A claim against the beauty salon (for even a bad hair day) could expose the 4 plex to a creditor's judgment, and vice versa. Meanwhile, Pam's CPA was concerned that the books were not being handled properly. All activities of the beauty salon business and the real estate business were mixed into the same bank account. It was a recipe for confusion, or worse.

One day, Pam's supplier for hair products came into her store and demanded he be paid $4,000 for back invoices before any beauty supplies were delivered. Pam was taken aback by this request. Her records indicated that the supplier had been paid already, but the supplier argued otherwise.

Pam knew she needed the popular and expensive shampoos, rinses, and styling products sold in her salon's retail department as that generated a significant portion of the salon's revenue. So she reluctantly paid the supplier, with the agreement that she had a credit on future purchases if she had indeed overpaid. The $4,000 payment left Pam's account with a balance of just $12.

That afternoon, two tenants at the 4 plex called to say that they were moving back to Guatemala. Pam was incredulous. "Why does it seem like my tenants are always moving?" Pam wondered. The tenants promptly requested the repayment of their $500 deposits. Pam was struck immediately by the coincidence in these events: She didn't have the money in her account at the exact moment it was needed to pay back the deposits.

While she may have had a credit on hair supplies, she couldn't very well offer the tenants repayment in the form of shampoos and conditioners. She knew that the state required that the deposits be repaid within three days. Pam told the tenants that she would get them the money in due time.

Pam was in a panic. She knew that both her business and real estate were profitable, but the books now indicated otherwise. And, worse yet, under state law, she now owed the deposit money in 72 hours. Failure to make these payments could result in fines, penalties, and interest.

Rather than run into trouble, Pam went to the bank and obtained an unsecured loan for $5,000. With the new money, she paid the tenants their deposits back and immediately retained a bookkeeper to keep track of her activities through separate bank accounts.

The Importance of Separate Accounts

You can see how easy it is for finances to get tangled up, even for the most well-intentioned and serious-minded of investors. That's why my advice is to do it right the first time. Set up your books so that your investment accounts are separated from your personal and business accounts. Treat your investments seriously, as you would any business, not only because you will be taken more seriously this way, but also so that you can closely track where the money is coming from and where it's going. It's easier to track how well your investments are performing if they have their own accounts.

Plus, each investment you make is its own separate business, its own legal entity, and a separate account enables transparency for your bookkeeper, your accountant, and the IRS, should you happen to be audited. (And know that if you operate a business as a sole proprietor and handle real estate in your individual name you have a five times greater chance of an IRS audit than if you operate through an entity.)

Once your accounts are set up, the tax savings can begin. Now it's time to bring your bookkeeper and accountant on board to ensure the health of your finances, so you can grow your investments.

A Bookkeeper is a Wise Investment

Pam's situation is a great example of the benefits of hiring a bookkeeper, not just in business but also in your investments. Pam's bookkeeper would have immediately recorded the original $4,000 payment to the hair-care supplier that was later disputed—preventing her from having to repay the supplier with money she didn't have. Not only that, but it's likely that other transactions slipped through the cracks and went undocumented, digging Pam into an even deeper hole. Pam believed her business and her investments to be profitable, despite what her books said: A bookkeeper's diligence might have helped Pam's books to actually reflect that profitability.

A bookkeeper is your eyes and ears in terms of tracking your cash flow in real estate investments. He or she will immediately spot oversights—a tenant's unpaid rent payment or a long-overdue utility bill, for instance—and will notify you before it becomes a serious problem. Bookkeepers not only process checks for deposit and payments to vendors, but they also, if they're good at what they do, keep a close eye on the money flowing in and out. This gives you a snapshot of your investments.

Plus, it enables you to focus on growing your portfolio and ensuring a continued positive cash flow, rather than managing the day-to-day administrative tasks that may not be your forte.

Sure, you can purchase bookkeeping software that performs many of the same duties, and for some people, this is a great, affordable alternative. Other people assign the duties of rent collection and vendor payments to property managers, rendering bookkeeping duties not quite so important. Your needs dictate the bookkeeping services required.

The point here is that too many investors don't keep a close enough eye on their investments, from watching where the expenses are going to looking at the income rolling in. A bookkeeper is the master of details, enabling you to make important decisions. Perhaps you need to cut expenses. (Have your utility expenses held steady, or have they increased? Is your landscaper charging you fairly?) You may need to look at ways to boost your income. (Do you have enough coming in each month? Perhaps you might consider raising your rents, or adding vending machines or laundry facilities.) Hiring a bookkeeper provides you with such performance information, allowing you to keep your eye on the big picture of making your investments lucrative.

A Tax Accountant or CPA Makes Sense

If your bookkeeper is in charge of maintaining the trees, the CPA is watching the overall health of the forest. Your accountant is one of the most important members of your advisory team, and this expertise is invaluable to you in making financial decisions. While a CPA's services can often be expensive, the advice you get makes this a crucial investment that could actually save you thousands of dollars. Meanwhile, the financial losses you risk in not having a CPA—or in using one that gives bad advice—could be even more costly. So be sure to spend quality time in hiring the right one.

Don't have an accountant do the day-by-day financial tracking, which a bookkeeper can do at lower rates. Bookkeepers are the masters of the minutiae. Rather, your accountant will analyze your financial records to form conclusions that help you make sound decisions: Should you get into that property or not? How will it affect your overall financial picture? Are you making the right quarterly estimated tax payments, or should you increase them?

He or she will also advise you regarding tax deductions, so you want to make sure that whoever you hire is taking advantage of all those options. Your accountant is your year-round partner in developing your wealth goals and creating the strategy to reach them.

Loophole #6
Accountants and bookkeepers can help you keep the tax loopholes open for your everlasting benefit.

Now let's talk about creating your team of advisors...

Chapter Six

Assembling Your Team of Advisors

You've probably heard before, "It's not what you know, it's who you know." This simple premise is the reason why networking is the number one way that people find jobs and clients, and it's a key *Rich Dad* principle.

Robert Kiyosaki's rich dad told him, "Business and investing are team sports." By their nature, E and S people—people on the left side of the CASHFLOW Quadrant—operate individually and autonomously. Their own efforts provide them with their own rewards. But B and I people, by their nature, capitalize on the power of teams, which can accomplish far more than can be accomplished by a single person.

Successful real estate investors realize the value of surrounding themselves with experts in a range of areas—taxes, the law, real estate, insurance, property management, etc. When these experts come together out of trust, respect, and a mutually desirable outcome, they learn from and support each other, effectively improving the outcomes and streamlining the process.

But how do you find the right people for your team?

Educate Yourself

Before you can begin assembling your real estate investment team, you have to start taking advantage of your own valuable real estate—your mind. You can't hire the right employee until you understand the needs of the company and the demands of the job, and you can't form an investment team until you understand the real estate investment landscape.

I'm not suggesting that you need to know everything. You don't. You'll continue to learn as you go. But you must educate yourself in the basics to get started on the right foot.

A little education goes a long way in accomplishing four essential goals.

Learning about real estate will demystify it for you, reducing your fear of the unknown. Without that fear, you're more likely to take the leaps necessary to progress to the next level and reach your goals.

It will show you that you don't need to have any innate real estate talent or know-how. You'll truly see that anyone can do this. You don't need a degree in law, finance, or real estate, and you don't need outrageous sums of cash. Ordinary people just like you, with ordinary reserves of cash, have achieved great results in real estate investment, and you can too.

It will help you to narrow down which area of real estate you'd like to specialize in. When you understand some of the unique qualities of each type of real estate, you're more likely to discover the type and location that best suit your investment style and needs. It will also help you to identify which experts might be best for your particular kind of investment strategy.

While you're learning the basics of real estate, you'll likely also discover who the players are, and it will enable you to cross paths with potential mentors or team members from whom you could continue learning.

Start educating yourself by asking a lot of questions. Learn the terminology of real estate. Read books that use the language of the industry and give you a foundation of the basics, such as *The ABCs of Real Estate Investing*. You could also subscribe to trade publications, or even take classes or attend seminars in your community. (See Appendix A for a list of valuable resource materials.)

Consider also scanning communities or towns where you're interested in investing for real estate signs. Do you see any names recurring? One mark of a savvy investor is noticing these sorts of patterns.

Once you've become familiar with the basics of real estate enough to talk about it with other people and ask the right questions, it's time to start figuring out who would be a good fit for your investment team.

Who Are Your Influences?

Is there anyone in your life right now who could mentor you, or who might even become part of your investment team?

In *Rich Dad's CASHFLOW Quadrant: Rich Dad's Guide to Financial Freedom*, there's an exercise that asks you to list the six people you spend the most time with on a regular basis. Then, next to each one, you're asked to mark whether each of those people is on the left or the right side of the quadrant.

Look at what you have, and compare that to where you want to be. If you are on the left but want to be on the right, shouldn't you be spending time with more "right-minded" people?

Recovering addicts are advised that if they want to stay clean, they should stop hanging out with the same friends they spent time with as addicts. The influence of those people, and all the memories and behaviors associated with them, make it more tempting to fall back into the same addictive tendencies. By surrounding themselves with good influences, it's not so easy to fall into those bad patterns.

It's actually not so different in the case of becoming a real estate investor. If the people you spend your time with are on the left side of the quadrant, it may be hard to find support from them as you make your transition to the right side. Their fear of the risks involved, or of simply veering off course from the standard plan we're all taught to follow, may cause them to be unsupportive of your plans, or to act as if you're making a mistake in pursuing your real estate goals.

Instead, if you want to be a B/I person, surround yourself with B/I people—people who not only believe what you're doing is possible, but who have done it themselves, and serve as living proof that it's a worthy goal. Seek people that you would like to model yourself after. They can share advice with you about what mistakes to avoid, what's worked and what hasn't. They'll support and teach you. And they can probably introduce you to others who might make great team members as well. The best people in your life will encourage change and growth, not argue against it.

Loophole #7

Who do you want to be with at your castle's loopholes? A person who has built and defended their own castle? Or the type who is mindlessly outside the castle walls trying to tear everything down, including your dreams of a better future?

A word of advice about mentors: Make sure there's an equal exchange taking place. Mentors usually become mentors because they want to give back, but if they're always carrying the heavier burden, doing the lion's share of the work, you might just lose them. It doesn't serve them well to go into business with you if they're sharing all their knowledge and doing all the work. If they're contributing their knowledge, make sure you're at least leveling the field with your sweat equity. Mentors won't want to go into business with you if they start to feel put upon. Make sure you don't take without giving or showing appreciation—even if all you can offer is lunch.

How to Build Your Team

After you've taken a close look at your existing circle, identifying those people who might serve as models and mentors, it's time to branch out and expand your circle.

These outlets could yield many mentors for you:

- **Real estate seminars:** Most communities have these on a regular basis. They're usually free, full of good information, located around town, and held by real estate agents and mortgage brokers, so they're a great way to meet experts. Check your local newspaper listings or visit individual brokerage websites.

- **Real estate clubs:** Just as many cities have stock investment clubs, in which people, some experienced and some beginners, get together and invest their money, there are real estate clubs in many communities as well.

- **Community colleges and city or county education programs:** It's somewhat common to find classes in real estate investment at the community college or local adult education programs, and, in addition to being insightful, they're often led or attended by insiders in the field.

- **CASHFLOW game clubs:** Clubs have formed around the country to get groups of people together to play this game. You can also play online with others at RichDad.com. It's a fun learning experience that could also help you to encounter experts and mentors.

- **Professional networking organizations and chambers of commerce:** Like with most things, attending networking events is an excellent way to encounter like-minded people in your area with a particular kind of expertise. This is a great way to meet people in a variety of fields, from accounting and bookkeeping to real estate, mortgage services, property management, roofers, landscapers, or even plumbers. You may be able to talk to others who know these experts, and who might give them good references. And it's a good way to let people know what your goals are and what you're looking for.

- **Ask for referrals:** As you start meeting people and gathering a group of advisors together, start asking them whom they would recommend. After all, they're familiar with the field and the people who are knowledgeable in certain areas. For example, real estate agents and mortgage brokers often ask escrow officers, appraisers, inspectors, and handymen that they like using for recommendations. Did your friend work with someone he or she liked? Start mining the resources you already have.

Once you have a list of people that you would consider for your team, it's important to conduct interviews to ensure it's a good fit. Questions you might want to ask include:

- How much experience do you have in this field, or in this particular type of real estate?

- Are you taking on new business?

- Is becoming part of an investment team appealing to you?

- Do you have clients investing in the same type of projects I'm interested in, and are they projects you would invest in yourself?

- What is your policy on returning messages? Do you typically return calls within 24 or 48 hours, or at set times of day?

- Will you be handling my account yourself or will you be passing it to an assistant or junior team member, and if so, does that person have experience?

- How do you charge—per hour, per transaction?

- Do you have references?

Call the references to make sure they're happy with the professional you're considering.

You'll want to make sure that the person understands you're looking for a long-term relationship, one that relies on mutual trust, respect, and experience. This is especially true of lenders, real estate attorneys, and accountants. They are intimately aware of your financial situation and they understand that a relationship like this could benefit you both, because the better you do, the better they do.

Also, be sure anyone you choose is very experienced in the particular kind of real estate you'll be investing in—you don't want him or her learning on your dime to get up to speed.

Finally, unless they're qualified, competent advisors, you may not want to include friends and family members on your team.

Who You Want On Your Team

Here's a typical list of advisors and experts that you might want to consider adding to your investment team:

- **Real estate brokers:** Realtors or other agents are your eyes and ears to the real estate market, so they're essential parts of the team. They know the trends, they recognize patterns, they know the market, they have access to information you need, and they can tip you off to deals.

- **Real estate lenders:** These people might be mortgage brokers or loan officers at financial institutions, or they may simply lend money as private individuals. Your lender can tell you what you're qualified to invest in, and, hopefully, is prepared to support you in your purchase. It's a good idea to get quotes from several lenders, to be sure you select the one best for you and your situation. On a side note, you may opt to find other sources of investment capital, including friends and family members. Sometimes this is a great solution, but sometimes it ends up making things worse. Money has a way of interfering with relationships. My advice is that if you're planning to go this route, you spell everything out in writing in a formal document that clearly defines the "exit strategy"— Would you sell the property? Buy the other out?—before you enter into the arrangement. Emotions can heat up during an investment, and it's a good idea to have a logical, peaceable agreement in place to govern what happens before that emotion overtakes sanity.

- **Real estate attorney:** Some states and jurisdictions require real estate attorneys to preside over all real estate transactions—the laws vary by location, so be sure you select an attorney who is familiar with the area and type of real estate in which you plan to invest, and who actually specializes in real estate.

- **Bookkeeper:** A bookkeeper is a valuable resource to have, as he or she will assist you with the day-to-day oversight and management of your books and records. You might opt to tackle this yourself as you get started, but what often happens is that investors quickly realize that they're spending valuable time on these administrative tasks that they should be devoting to their investment activities. Hiring a bookkeeper is an investment in accuracy, as well as your valuable time, and it is well worth it.

- **Real estate accountant:** Your accountant will analyze the records that your bookkeeper provides and ensure that your financial records are in order and compliant with the law.

- **Tax accountant:** This may also be your real estate accountant, but he or she will not only know the law as it pertains to your taxes, but also the tax ramifications and loopholes inherent in real estate investment. A good tax accountant is an invaluable member of your team, and in the case of an IRS audit, he or she will represent you. Ultimately, this person always has an eye toward minimizing your tax obligations.

- **Insurance agent:** You'll need to find an agent who specializes in real estate to make sure you have insurance coverage on your properties to cover risks and liabilities.

- **Property manager:** Although many people manage their own properties, especially as they just begin investing in their first properties, a property manager is a wise investment that can save you a lot of time and money.

Other valuable team members to include are:
- Escrow officer

- Appraiser

- Home Inspector

- Property management contractors, including handyman, cleaning service, landscaper, roofer, and plumber. The property manager may hire these people, and they may or may not become permanent team members. But if you find someone you really like, keep using them and develop a solid working relationship.

As you advance in your understanding of real estate investing and become more successful, your team of real estate brokers, attorneys, CPAs, property managers and the like may evolve and change. You may add team members, or replace members who simply aren't fitting with the direction of your investment team. And if you decide to branch out into other areas or types of real estate, you may find you need professionals with a new set of credentials and experience. Know too that if you grow to the point where you need a bigger mortgage company, for instance, or a larger accounting firm, you can expect to pay more for those services.

Case #4
Jacob and John

Jacob and John were both real estate investors. Jacob had managed within just a few years to take his investments from single-family homes and duplexes to apartment buildings of up to 50 units. His investment team consisted of many experts who gave him tips about available properties before they came on the market, so Jacob was able to grow his investment portfolio quickly, and get in on some of the best deals in town.

Meanwhile, John was envious of Jacob's success. John had struggled for a few years to grow his investments beyond the few duplexes he owned, and aspired to include apartment buildings similar to what Jacob had managed to find in his portfolio. He watched in amazement as Jacob landed deal after deal, seemingly effortlessly, while John slugged away and couldn't seem to make it to that next level.

How was Jacob hearing about these great deals? What was Jacob's secret? John had a great network of advisors who were very well respected in the area, yet despite the professional relationships they had agreed to, they didn't seem to be alerting him to the deals that came their way. John was determined to find out what Jacob was doing differently.

He called Jacob to invite him to dinner, intimating that he wanted to talk about business opportunities. Jacob readily agreed, and the two met a week later at a local steakhouse.

After the small talk had wrapped up and the two were enjoying their beers, John broached the subject of "business opportunities" by making it clear that he wanted to know Jacob's secret for finding these opportunities.

Despite the fact that John had lured him to dinner under false pretenses, Jacob smiled. He didn't have any problem revealing his secret— he thought it was about time he shared what he knew with John.

"It's very simple, actually," Jacob began. "I have an excellent team of people in my corner, friends that I respect personally and professionally."

"Well, I have that, too!" argued John, convinced that Jacob must be holding out on him. "But they're not tipping me off to the great deals! You must have some sort of inside track."

"No," reassured Jacob. "It's just that simple. Because we have a relationship, and because they know I'm easy and fair to do business with, they call me when they get wind of great deals. They know that when they call me, I'm going to act quickly, and protect their interests in the deal, as well as my own."

At this, Jacob looked John right in the eye. John grimaced—he understood what Jacob was referring to. In a few situations, John had openly complained about brokers' commissions, even haggling with a few of them, asking them to cut their commissions in order to push deals through. In their community's real estate circles, word had obviously traveled about John's tactics, and Jacob was letting him know that he'd heard about this.

Jacob continued, "I'm also a believer in the concept that if you scratch my back, I'll scratch yours. They refer business my way, but I frequently refer other people to them, too. So by doing business with me, we all win."

John was sheepish. He blushed as he remembered how, just last week, he had griped to a friend at a title company about how a broker he normally worked with had not been producing the deals he'd believed her capable of. Was it possible that this broker had heard about John's complaint from the title company, and intentionally held back potential deals out of resentment?

"As the old saying goes, it's not what you know, but who you know," Jacob commented, taking another drink of his beer.

John realized he had probably been hurting himself with his own behavior. Believing the idea that it's "every man for himself," he'd been acting in his own interests, while disregarding the interests of others. But ironically, if he had been looking out for his team, he might have found himself in a better position, investment-wise.

He confessed this to Jacob, who advised him to begin mending fences and embark on a good faith effort to do business differently. And, eventually, things began to turn around for John.

Loophole #8

Coaches love to say, "There's no I in TEAM," and the same goes for real estate investing. The team is always stronger than the individual. The castle is not defended by just one archer. The sooner you embrace the concept of working with your team and relying on their collective experience and knowledge, the sooner you'll find yourself successful in growing your portfolio.

Okay, you are ready...

Chapter Seven

Time to Jump In

Now comes the exciting part. You've made the decision to jump into the real estate pool with both feet. You've done a little research; you've put your financial house in order and have funding for your initial investments; you've educated yourself on the essentials of real estate investment; you've put a great team of colleagues, advisors, and mentors in place; and you now have some prospective properties in front of you.

There's nothing left to do but...invest!

It's an invigorating time, but it's also full of challenges and potential risk, which can be scary.

I liken this phase to being a baby again. Think about it: Infants don't just go from lying down to walking. First they crawl, slowly getting across the floor any way they can. Pretty soon, once they've figured those skills out, feel more confident in their strength, and become more anxious to get from place to place, they pull themselves up and begin learning to walk. They take a step, falter, fall down, and then brush themselves off and do it again, and before the parents know it, that child is running at full speed.

And young children have a fearlessness that enables them to try new skills without worrying about whether they'll hurt themselves. Babies don't have anxiety about trying to walk. They get a few bumps and bruises along the way, but each time they try, they get better, so they keep at it.

Well, investing in real estate isn't all that different, believe it or not. You have to crawl first—you'll have to start small, get lots of help and support, make a few mistakes and get a few "bumps and bruises," but before long, you'll be off and running. But you can't be afraid to jump in there and take a calculated risk; you'd never jump in blindly, but assuming some risk that you've accounted for and counteracted with education will eventually pay off.

This all goes against our natures. We were taught growing up, by our parents and teachers, how to avoid mistakes, that mistakes were bad. We worked so hard to avoid them, and for the most part that's a good thing. It keeps us healthy. But mistakes are also how we grow. What if we never let babies fall down? They'd never gain the strength it takes to get up, would they? Mistakes are where the lessons are, and they're invaluable.

Bottom line: You WILL make mistakes. Count on it. All you can do is minimize them by starting small, asking a lot of questions, and learning from your mistakes, and you will grow stronger as a result.

Tips, Tricks, and Traps to Avoid

To get started, you'll begin hearing about properties, start writing offers with the appropriate loopholes and contingencies, and begin getting comfortable and familiar with the process as you go. Only write offers for investments you're serious about; there's plenty of time to gather experience, don't rush it or waste people's time by jumping in too quickly for the sake of practice.

Your first step, after an agent brings you a prospective deal, should be to ask for "comps," or prices on comparable properties in that area.

You'd ask all the same questions you'd ask a Realtor if you were buying a home for your family to live in: What schools is it zoned for? How's the school district? Is it near any amenities, major thoroughfares, or a bus line? Is it a safe neighborhood? You'll need to know all this in order to speak to prospective tenants.

Of course, you'll also need to ask about the condition of the property, just as you would your own home. You need to know whether it needs any major repairs, or if any have been done. How's the roof? Are there cracks in the walls, and are they a sign of anything important? Is there, or has there ever been, mold? Has the HVAC system been serviced, and is it in good working condition? Are appliances included, and do they work? What does the yard look like? Is there an easement on the property? Any liens?

Most importantly, you should always ask your agent, broker, appraiser or other advisor, "What questions haven't I asked that I *should* ask?" This is how you learn, and you may get some expert insights that help you to make an informed decision.

And here's a tip about real estate professionals: They love when you ask questions, because it gives them an opportunity to tell you how much they know. So ask away. They may not always know the answers right away, but they'll know who to ask in order to find out.

And ask yourself some important questions, too, such as:

- Is this a good investment? (Your gut and early education on the subject should help you answer this.)

- Do I have the risk tolerance necessary to take on this investment?

- Am I doing all I can to educate myself and understand what's involved?

- Can I trust the people I'm working with?

- Are all the necessary contingencies built into the contract (things like having an inspector come to survey the property)?

- Should I consider forming a limited liability company to hold the asset? (See Chapter 23 where we cover such legal matters in greater detail.)

You may frequently find that even good deals aren't easy; they don't always come together smoothly, and there are a lot of moving parts to keep track of. But you may be surprised to learn that not only can this process pay off in a significant financial way, but also that you enjoy it, hard work and all.

Putting together a great deal can be invigorating, even fun, and having one will give you the confidence and sense of accomplishment that you need in order to get into the next one, and the next. And even when the occasional deal proves troublesome, you'll learn and grow from the experience.

It's all part of what we at Rich Dad embrace in our philosophy of lifelong learning. Don't expect to get rich right way. Like all things worth waiting for, it takes time. But what you learn, and the joy you take out of the experience, will be a great reward. So get out there and get started.

Case #5
Charlie and Matt

Charlie wanted to get into real estate. His parents had been afraid of investing, which made Charlie even more interested. With limited reserves, Charlie asked his best friend, Matt, if he would be interested in partnering with him on an investment.

Matt agreed to the idea, and the two formed an LLC. They identified a 4 plex just right for their purposes—small enough to manage, large enough to get several renters into it quickly, and located in a regentrified part of town that many young couples and families would find appealing. As college roommates, the two had occasionally done odd jobs to earn some income, so they felt sure they could take on the property management themselves.

But almost as soon as the property became theirs, problems began cropping up. First, there was the tenant who picked up bed bugs on a recent trip, and before long had a full infestation in his bedroom. Charlie and Matt now had to immediately pay for expensive bed bug abatement services.

Then on a particularly cold night, the building's old pipes burst, flooding tenants' leaseholds. Not only did they have to pay for the clean-up and plumbing fixes, they had to put tenants up in a nearby hotel while the work was being done.

On top of everything else, Matt was regretting his decision to partner with Charlie on this investment, and wanted out.

It was very fortunate that there was an uptick in the real estate market, with demand and sales prices rising for homes in this up-and-coming area.

Charlie and Matt managed to get the repairs on the building completed, sell the 4 plex within one year's time, and dissolve the LLC somewhat amicably.

Charlie didn't give up on his real estate goals, though. He had learned some expensive lessons through this first experience, and in his next investment—a 12-unit apartment building—he took care to ensure that he had cash reserves for such last-minute emergency repairs. He brought on a property manager. And he never again partnered with a friend, opting instead to partner only with other like-minded professionals who shared his goals, responsibility for the investment, and a contract detailing every aspect of the working relationship.

Loophole #9

Real estate investment can complicate friendships and family relationships. Be sure your friendship can survive the ups and downs of investing. If it can't, let your friend escape through a loophole in the wall. You both will be better for it.

All right, on to everyone's favorite topic...

Part Three: Tax Strategies

If the word "taxes" strikes terror in your heart, you're going to want to pay careful attention to this next section. I'm going to share some tips for making sense of a property's financials, turning depreciation to your benefit, and capitalizing on the tax code by considering making real estate your business. When you educate yourself about real estate investing and make it a priority to learn the ins and outs and the not so hidden loopholes, you might just find that when you hear the word "taxes," you'll simply smile to yourself as you wonder what all the fuss was about.

I want you to remember this key concept: Real estate investing is good for the economy.

This is an important mantra for you. It means that the government (yes, even the IRS) wants you to invest in real estate. Your investment provides housing to a large portion of the population, it promotes continued development and community improvement, and, through construction, rehabilitation, maintenance, and management, it provides jobs for thousands of people.

In short, the government not only supports investment, it needs it to stimulate and grow the economy.

I emphasize this point to explain why the tax code favors investors, and why real estate investment can be such a financial boon for you. It's truly a win-win: You can earn passive income, while also saving money on your taxes.

But in order to achieve such positive results, the investment has to look good on paper. How do you know what to look for? What will the numbers show? And what are the tax strategies used by successful investors that you can put into practice? That's what we'll cover here.

It is important to note that there is a new tax on net investment income. If you have an adjusted gross income (at this writing) of $200,000 as a single person or $250,000 as a married couple you get to pay a Medicare surtax of 3.8% on gains, interest, dividends, royalties and passive rental income. So when we talk about a 20% capital gains rate in this book, know that for upper income earners it is really a 23.8% rate. Please remember this in all your calculations.

Of course, you shouldn't make any major decisions without consulting your tax accountant, and this section certainly won't take the place of having an accountant that keeps his or her eye on your particular financial picture. But you'll know what to ask and what's possible, and hopefully these tax strategies can help your own portfolio grow.

Loophole #10

The government has opened up tax loopholes to encourage all citizens to consider real estate investing. Not one person is excluded from these rules. Whether you decide to take advantage of them or not is up to you.

Chapter Eight

Analyzing the Numbers

Unfortunately, there's no crystal ball or magic wand that can reveal to you whether a property will earn you a lot of money. If such a tool were available, you wouldn't be reading this book, and everyone would be wealthy.

But even without a crystal ball, you have a few tools that, if examined carefully, can at least provide an indication as to which way the wind is blowing for any property you're considering.

The first of these tools is called a *pro forma*. The Latin term *pro forma*, literally translated, means "as if." (Or, as real estate veterans like to think of it, "*As if* you expect me to believe those numbers!")

It's not an encouraging name for a document that is supposed to present all the correct information about a prospective property. But nonetheless, a pro forma provides details at a glance about a property's selling price, operating costs, utility charges, property taxes, repairs, insurance, and more. It also offers projections of the property's future value and potential income if at full occupancy.

However, because it's developed by the seller and the seller's agent, based on their idea of what prospective buyers want to see, it could be slightly exaggerated at best, and pure fantasy at worst. It's an important document that provides a starting point for your analysis and determines whether you're even interested in pursuing the property, but it's by no means gospel in terms of making a real estate purchase.

This is where your own due diligence plays a key role. You'll need to draw upon your own experience and knowledge about the real estate market in your area, as well as the expertise of your team of advisors, who can shed light on aspects of the prospective property and community as well as on your own financial picture.

Once you've determined that you want to sign a contract on a property, you'll be given access to the actual financial figures (usually referred to as "the financials") on a property. Typically, the language a buyer will use when reviewing a property's financials will say something like this: "This offer shall be contingent upon Buyer's complete review and acceptance of the financial records associated with the subject property." So if the financials aren't to your liking the contingency is a loophole allowing you to escape the deal.

Upon receiving the financials, you're going to look at the following:

- Selling prices of comparable properties in the area ("comps").

- Rents on similar properties in that area.

- Number of rentals in the area. (Is the market saturated? Is there a market for rentals here?)

- Utility bills for the property.

- Property tax bills.

- Recent expenses for repairs on the property.

Additionally, due diligence on any purchase must include a building inspection, which will reveal the actual condition of the property. Will you need to make major repairs, and if so, when? Can you do any of them yourself, or will it involve hiring outside help? Will you need to hire maintenance help on a contract basis, for things like landscaping, etc.? Do you have enough cash reserves to cover such costs?

All of this information will reveal whether the asking price is fair, or whether you need to ask for a bit of a price reduction (a "haircut") to close the deal.

In addition, you'll need to figure out the actual debt involved in taking a loan on the property (principal plus interest). And don't forget that your property might remain vacant for a period of time after you purchase it.

It may be unrealistic to expect to collect money from day one. Are you prepared to weather such a vacancy with your cash reserves?

All of this analysis, when taken in combination with the pro forma and the actual financials, will give you a clear picture of the potential risks and returns associated with the investment ... if, indeed, it actually is an investment at all.

How a Real Estate Purchase Affects Your Financials

If the property appears to be a good investment, one that will produce positive returns, then it's time to think about the impact this purchase will have on your overall financial picture.

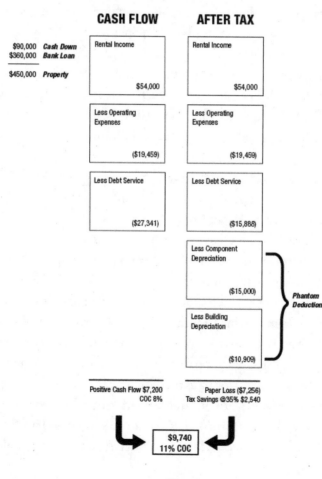

The property's positive cash flow will only be part of your cash-on-cash return. We previously used a cash flow chart in Chapter 3. We're going to use a new one here, which involves a purchase of a five unit apartment building for $450,000 with 20% down.

The IRS considers your rental property as a business, and gives you several deductions. One is the payment you make on the interest (but not the principal) of your debt service. In addition, there are the "phantom deductions"—the "passive loss" from component depreciation and from building depreciation, which are computed at an annual rate (discussed later in this chapter). So after you take your rental income (five units at $900 per month or $54,000 per year) and subtract operating expenses ($19,459), you also subtract the interest payments ($15,888) on debt service, and you subtract the component and building depreciation ($15,000 and $10,909, respectively). You multiply this "paper loss" ($7,256) by your tax rate (35 percent), and determine your tax savings ($2,540).

You add the tax savings ($2,540) to your net cash flow from the property before taxes ($7,200) and come up with your true cash-on-cash return: $9,740, or 11 percent. Your true cash-on-cash return will show you how good (or not so good) a particular real estate investment will be for you.

In this case, the investor put down twenty percent of the $450,000 purchase price of the property. So that $90,000 investment yielded a cash-on-cash return of nearly 11 percent.

Obviously, real estate enjoys a distinct tax advantage over the stock market. If your projected paper loss in a rental property is $7,256, you can claim $2,540 in tax savings. But if you lost the same $7,256 in the stock market (and it would be a true drop in value, not a paper loss), you would only be able to claim the maximum for a capital loss—$3,000—on your annual tax return. To claim the entire loss would take you three years.

By now you've learned that passive income, earned from such sources as rentals or stock, is superior to earned income. Earned income is earned because you had to work for it, and second, earned income is taxed at the IRS' highest rate of all income (it could reach more than 50 percent in some cases, when you consider payroll taxes). But for a rental such as the example above, the passive income can actually come to you tax-free, thanks to the write-offs from depreciation. Our example showed a $7,200 positive cash flow that was not taxed, because the depreciation eradicated that income on paper.

This is why it's critical to determine your depreciation on a property as part of assessing whether or not to invest in it.

Calculating Depreciation

The concept of depreciation is one that warrants a thorough discussion. This is because it has a tremendous impact on your cash flow and the overall financial benefits of a real estate investment.

When we talk about real estate investment, there are four types of property we are referring to:

- Land, which cannot depreciate (at least, not on paper),

- Land improvements, such as sidewalks or landscaping,

- Personal property, which refers to those items that can be removed without harming or affecting the structure's operation and maintenance, such as furniture or large appliances, and

- Buildings or structures on the land.

Though land cannot depreciate, improvements made to it, as well as all other types of property, have relatively short life spans, and therefore are subject to depreciation.

The U.S. Internal Revenue Service (IRS) defines depreciation as "an income tax deduction that allows a taxpayer to recover the cost or other basis of certain property. It is an annual allowance for the wear and tear, deterioration, or obsolescence of the property."

Included within this general definition would be, of course, the normal wear and tear that comes with regular use of a piece of property. But it also includes physical deterioration that comes from weather and the elements, lack of regular maintenance, or damage that may occur from natural processes, such as pest infestations or dry rot. "Obsolescence" refers both to features of the property that may be inadequate, outdated, or lacking in modern equipment or functionality, or to a property that may have been subject to economic restrictions, such as zoning restrictions or simple changes in supply and demand as a result of economic conditions or market changes.

The federal tax code designates items of personal property with a "class life" for each item, which is generally either five or seven years. While desks and fax machines may be considered seven-year items, computers, furniture, and even carpeting are considered five-year items; and you'll need your tax accountant to determine what items in your possession fall into which category and what your rate of depreciation will be for them—it's usually accelerated for the first few years.

Personal property's depreciation rate is better than that for building depreciation, which the IRS has assigned in a seemingly arbitrary fashion to be a 27.5-year period for residential rental property and a 39-year period for commercial real property.

That is, unless you apply cost segregation.

The Magic of Cost Segregation

Cost segregation is an important component of any discussion on depreciation, and is an extremely important tool in enhancing the value of any real estate investment. Which is why I have asked Tom Wheelwright, CPA, a Rich Dad Advisor and author of *Tax-Free Wealth* to share his insights about cost segregation with you here:

Cost Segregation

In my book, *Tax-Free Wealth*, I spend an entire chapter explaining the "magic" of depreciation. Why is it magic? Because this is a deduction that the IRS gives to you without requiring you to put in any cash. Your property can rise in value and you still get a deduction for depreciation. Of course, depreciation is simply a deduction for the cost of a building and its contents over a period of time. The idea in the tax law is that you will have wear and tear on the building, so you should be able to deduct the cost of the building as that wear and tear occurs.

Part of the magic comes because you don't have to pay for all of the building. The bank will pay for 80 percent of it. And your tenants pay the bank with their rent. Even though the bank is paying for most of the building, you get 100 percent of the depreciation deduction. In essence, you get the bank's depreciation.

Pretty cool deal, huh?

Well, it gets even better with a cost segregation. While you may get a deduction for depreciation equal to anywhere from 2.5 to 3.6 percent for the cost of the building each year, you can get an even higher depreciation deduction if you do a cost segregation. So let's talk about what a cost segregation is, and how you do it.

Think about what you actually purchased when you bought your building. You purchased land and a building, of course. But you also purchased the contents of the building, such as the lighting, flooring, cabinetry and window coverings, as well as the land improvements. Your land improvements include the landscaping, outside lighting, fencing and covered parking spaces. The IRS has determined that the contents and the land improvements will wear out more quickly than the building itself. So you get a higher depreciation deduction for these items than you do for the building itself. Of course, even the IRS understands that land doesn't wear out, so you don't get a depreciation deduction at all for the cost of the land.

So how does cost segregation work? It's pretty simple, actually. You merely have to determine what portion of your purchase price you paid for the land, the building, the contents, and the land improvements. While you may get a depreciation deduction of 2.5-3.6 percent for the building, you will get a depreciation deduction of 15-20 percent or more for the contents and 5-10 percent for the land improvements. Some commercial buildings will end up with 50-60 percent of the cost of the project being allocated to contents and land improvements, creating much more depreciation in the early years of ownership.

When I talk about cost segregations to a group of real estate investors, I invariably get comments that many of their CPAs don't like cost segregations. They say they are risky. They also talk about the downside to a "recapture." What these CPAs are really saying is that they are lazy. Cost segregations take work. But let's discuss these objections one at a time.

First, let's address the idea that cost segregations are risky, aggressive, or even that they are not allowed. The IRS has an audit guide that specifically addresses how to handle cost segregations and what the IRS requires in a cost segregation. Obviously, they are allowed. In fact, by definition in the tax law, they are required. The IRS just doesn't enforce this requirement. Let me explain.

When you do a cost segregation on a building that you acquired several years ago (yes, you can even do one years after you purchased the building—which is good news if you're one of the folks who got bad advice from your accountant about doing a cost segregation), the change in depreciation is called a change in accounting method.

There are two types of changes of accounting methods. The first is a change from one acceptable method of accounting to another (like changing from the cash method to the accrual method of accounting). The second is a change from an incorrect method to a correct method of accounting. Cost segregations are this second type. This, by definition, means that not doing a cost segregation is an incorrect accounting method.

Still, you must do it the way the IRS instructs you to in its audit guide. It requires that you either use a CPA or an engineer to do the cost segregation for you. So just estimating the cost of the contents and land improvements won't fly. At my CPA firm, ProVision, when we do cost segregations for our clients, we use both a CPA and an engineer.

The other primary objection to a cost segregation is recapture. Depreciation recapture can occur when you sell the building. Portions of the depreciation you took could be added back into your income when you sell the property. How is this bad? You received a deduction for the depreciation early and then paid back some of the taxes you saved later on. It's not so different from a pension, profit-sharing plan, or 401(k), except that, unlike these plans, you will never have to pay back all of the depreciation because contents and land improvements really do wear out. So when you sell the building, those things will be worth less than what you paid for them, and a smaller portion of the sales price will be allocated to these items.

You can also avoid depreciation recapture in total with good tax planning combined with a good wealth strategy. You can avoid recapture by doing a proper 1031 exchange (also called a "like kind" or "Starker exchange") which is covered in Chapter 10 ahead.

So don't be afraid of doing cost segregations. In fact, you should embrace them. Do them on all of your properties and you will pay far less in the way of taxes. And if you are a serious real estate investor, cost segregations could, and should, result in you never paying taxes on your rental income. Combined with a 1031 exchange strategy, this means that a good investor should never pay taxes on his or her rental income or on gains from rental real estate. This is the best tax advantage in the entire tax law. Don't let it pass you by just because you have a lazy or fearful accountant.

Loophole #11

Certain tax loopholes exist which scare less experienced CPAs. Be sure to work with a professional willing to exploit all of the loopholes that the law allows.

Cost Segregation in Action

As Tom Wheelwright has just explained, cost segregation enables you to deduct depreciation from each of the components that relate to the operation and maintenance of a building. These may include ceilings and roofs, HVAC systems, bathroom fixtures like tubs and sinks, stairs, doors, floors, landscaping, and paving.

Let's take an example from the U.S. Tax Court case of *Hospital Corporation of America v. Commissioner* to illustrate how this works, and why cost segregation can have greater benefits to you than a simple building depreciation. The Tax Court permitted Hospital Corporation to use the cost segregation technique on building improvements.

The company could depreciate these components over a 5-year life span:

- Accordion doors and partitions
- Carpeting
- Conduit, floor boxes and power boxes
- Electrical wiring relating to internal communications
- Kitchen wall pipings and steam lines
- Patient corridor handrails
- Primary and secondary electrical distribution systems
- Vinyl wall and floor coverings
- Wiring and related property items in the laboratory and maintenance shop, as well as other wiring and related property
- Wiring to television equipment

The rest of the building, since it was a commercial property, was depreciated over 39 years. These elements included the following:

- Acoustical tile ceilings
- Bathroom accessories and mirrors
- Branch electrical wiring and communications special equipment
- Overhead lights
- Steam boilers

Without cost segregation, or the application of component depreciation, the building would be subject to "straight-line depreciation," in which the value of the building or structure is divided by the term of depreciation (27. 5 years for residential; 39 years for commercial) to arrive at your rate of annual depreciation. Know that such rate will remain constant for the duration of the 27.5 or 39 years, whichever standard applies.

Here's a basic formula for calculating the value of personal property, as well as a building or structure:

1. **Determine the value of the land.** Begin with the purchase price of the property, and then contact your tax assessor for a statement of value for the land and building. The statement will indicate the ratio of the land value to the building value. You'll apply that ratio to the actual purchase price to determine the actual value of the land in relation to the building. (Note: Some accountants use a simple 20-80 rule, in which 20 percent is land value and 80 percent is building, but I recommend a more authoritative, precise approach if possible.)

2. **List the items of personal property and assign values to each.** Hopefully, you have an appraiser among your advisory team members—it's a good idea to turn to this person for help with this task. A word of caution here: The IRS is likely to be skeptical of a tax return in which personal property accounts for more than 30-40 percent of a building's value.

3. **Subtract the value of the land and personal property from the purchase price to arrive at the structure's value.** At this point, a cost segregation study will appoint costs to either structure or personal property (components).

To illustrate this point, the personal property depreciation in my early example in this chapter about the $450,000, five-unit apartment building was $15,000, while building depreciation was $10,909. This "phantom deduction" (deduction on depreciation, which is neither tangible nor an asset) meant a paper loss of $7,523 and an ultimate tax savings of $2,540 against your other income. All this together is what makes real estate investment lucrative.

There are other instances in which your cash-on-cash return could be increased. In the case of an interest-only loan, in which your entire debt service payment is interest, the entire payment is deductible, which then increases your return. Additionally, by reducing your down payment—say, from 20 percent to 10 percent—this would also increase your rate of return.

The 2017 tax act added a major improvement to depreciation for real estate. Under the new law, land improvement and personal property can be depreciated entirely in the first year, even if the property is used. This means that in the example above, the personal property depreciation could be $75,000 in the first year and the land improvements (typically about 10% of the purchase price, or $45,000 in this example) could also be deducted in the first year. This results in a huge tax benefit the first year if the taxpayers wants to take all of the personal property and land improvement depreciation in that year.

As you can see, there are a lot of ways to analyze and affect the numbers to suit your unique situation. Talk to your CPA about the possible strategies that you could use, or what suits your needs best to achieve the results you want.

Understanding Passive Loss

Investing in rental real estate offers a wonderful safety net to offset your income from nonpassive sources (such as wages or dividends) on your tax return. If your adjusted gross income is under $100,000, you can offset up to $25,000 of your ordinary income from losses in real estate (which would be "passive losses," since real estate gives you passive income). This is true for both single taxpayers and married individuals who file jointly. In order to take up to the $25,000 deduction, you (or your spouse if you file a joint return) have to have "actively participated" in the passive real estate rental activity. What does that mean? Active participation is not a stringent standard (and should not be confused with "material participation"). For example, you may be treated as actively participating if you make management decisions such as approving new tenants, deciding on rental terms, approving expenditures, and the like. So be careful: If you have a property management company taking care of your rental, be sure that you are still involved at some level.

Of course, there are certain exceptions to this allowance. You must be single or married and filing jointly in order to reap the full benefits of this rule. And if your adjusted gross income exceeds $100,000 per year, the offset begins to decrease until your adjusted gross income reaches $150,000, at which point there is no real estate passive loss offset allowed.

How, then, can you enjoy the full benefit of passive losses? By reading the next chapter...

Chapter Nine

Real Estate as a Business

In the last chapter, we covered how depreciation and passive loss help to make real estate income, a form of passive income, an effective method for building wealth.

As I explained, in terms of the U.S. Tax Code, passive loss refers to losses absorbed through ownership of a rental property. It's reflected as an amount of money, up to $25,000, that an individual (or a married couple filing jointly) may use to offset other passive income earnings, as long as that individual or couple has an adjusted gross income of $100,000 or less. Claiming passive losses can provide you with a significant tax deduction.

Now, imagine that you could claim the entire depreciation amount, along with all business deductions (discussed later on in this book), against your household's combined earned income.

If real estate were your business, that's exactly what you could do. I've asked Rich Dad Advisor Tom Wheelwright for his thoughts on this important strategy:

Becoming a Real Estate Professional

The biggest tax challenge for real estate investors are the passive loss rules. Under these rules, passive losses can only be used to offset passive income. A business activity is passive if the owner does not spend much time (typically less than 500 hours per year) participating in the business.

The challenge for real estate investors is that losses from rental real estate are generally considered passive regardless of how much time the owner spends working on the real estate. There are two exceptions to this rule.

The first, which is very easy to achieve, is referred to as the "active participation" exception. Any owner who spends some significant time on his/her real estate investments during the year qualifies, at least where the owner directly owns the real estate (that is, not as a limited partner in a partnership). This could include reviewing reports from the property manager, researching properties to buy, or handling the financing of real estate purchases. The IRS has been pretty generous in allowing this exception. The active participation exception allows up to $25,000 worth of losses during the year from rental real estate to be treated as ordinary deductions not subject to the passive loss restrictions. This exception only applies, however, when the owner's "adjusted gross income" (AGI) is not more than $100,000. If your AGI exceeds $100,000, then the $25,000 limit is phased out by 50 cents for every $1 the AGI exceeds $100,000. So, for example, if your AGI is $110,000, then the limit for that year will be $20,000 (or $25,000 minus $.50 x $10,000).

The second exception to the rental real estate passive loss rule is the real estate professional exception. The real estate professional exception is the "get out of jail free card" for real estate investors. If you meet this exception, then none of your rental real estate income and loss are subject to the passive loss rules. This is a much tougher exception to get than that for active participation, because you actually have to meet two criteria: 1) You spend more than 750 hours per year (which comes to about 14 ½ hours per week) as a "material participant" in a real estate business, which could include management, brokerage, construction, development, leasing, rental, and operation; and 2) You must spend more time in real estate businesses than all other businesses (including employment) that you're involved in, combined. If you meet both of these criteria, then you qualify as a real estate professional.

The good news is that for a married couple, only one of the spouses has to qualify. But one trap here is that you still have to meet the passive activity rules for each property as if it were a regular trade or business. In other words, the real estate professional status only gets you out of the rental real estate trap. You still have to meet the 500-hour criteria for each property.

This could be a problem, since most people don't spend 500 hours on a single property. The tax law provides a simple way around this. On your tax return, you may elect to treat all of your properties as a single property. This is called a Section 469(c)(7) election. The election is made on your personal income tax return. Doing so is permanent (and there can be some unintended consequences of electing to do this), so be sure to meet with your tax advisor before you make this decision.

Thanks again, Tom.

Loophole #12

The Section 469(c)(7) election is a classic tax loophole. Not that many people know about it, but it is there for everyone to use.

Now, let's apply the lesson...

Case #6
Sandy and Bob

Bob is a successful dentist in his community. In the 15 years since he established his own practice, he has established a reliable base of patients and has built a thriving business in a great location.

A couple years ago, he brought his wife, Sandy, a business expert with an MBA, on board to help him oversee the business end of the dental practice. She had recently left her job at a financial services firm, and Bob knew that Sandy's business acumen would be helpful in getting his administrative house in order. She brought on new employees, developed effective new processes, and enhanced the office's marketing efforts. Within a few months, Sandy's improvements had managed to make the dental practice a well-oiled machine.

Now she could turn her attention to their real estate portfolio. Bob and Sandy owned three small apartment buildings around town, as well as one small commercial center that was home to a nail salon, a chiropractor's office, a coffee house and a wine shop.

Fortunately, Bob's dental practice was a success and their investments earned a nice passive income for them. Unfortunately, because Bob earned on average $250,000 per year, the couple couldn't use passive loss, which in their case came to about $100,000, from their investments to offset his high earned income.

Eventually, they would be earning sheltered profits—when the mortgages on their properties were paid off and the rentals made pure profit, or if they were to sell a property. When those things eventually happened, they could use their losses to shelter those profits. But until that time, the losses were going unused.

Sandy made an appointment with their CPA to discuss the situation and see how they might improve their tax situation. The CPA asked, "What about becoming a real estate professional?"

He explained to Sandy that if she spent 750 hours per year, or about 15 hours a week, on the couple's real estate investments, she would be considered a real estate professional by the IRS. This would enable the couple to write off 100 percent of their passive losses against Bob's high income, which would bring his taxable income down to $100,000. This $100,000 deduction brought Bob and Sandy into a lower tax bracket, saving them roughly $31,000 in taxes.

Sandy already devoted a large percentage of her time to overseeing their investments, and when she saw the tax advantages, her decision became clear: She would file the Section 469(c)(7) election and become a real estate professional.

The Work of Being a Real Estate Professional

It's important to mention here that if you're married and filing jointly, like Sandy and Bob, only one of you needs to meet the two criteria for becoming a real estate professional.

You don't need professional licensure as a developer, contractor, or other specialized real estate service in order to be considered a "material participant" in those activities by the IRS. Your involvement in these services may be rather broad. They are as follows:

- **Acquisition:** As you've likely already determined, the business of acquiring real estate can be quite time-consuming and involved. Whether or not you use a Realtor, you're going to be meeting with various people, consulting professionals in areas of finance or real estate, traveling to see properties, drawing up offers and counter offers, arranging inspections, and more. Even without actually closing on a property, those hours spent in acquisition mode count toward your material participation.

- **Brokerage or Sales:** As much time as acquisition takes, you can expect an equally long amount of time preparing and executing a sale on a property. Everything from cleaning and repairing a property to arranging showings, advertising, addressing issues that arise during inspections, responding to offers, and, of course, signing closing papers takes considerable time and counts toward your real estate professional hours.

- **Construction or Reconstruction:** This category is fairly narrow and is often included within development/redevelopment. It pertains to actual work you perform on the building, as well as time spent hiring, firing, or meeting and working with those involved in actual construction.

- **Conversion:** Similar to redevelopment, conversion activity may involve going through the rezoning process, or turning, for instance, an old Colonial-style home into an inn.

- **Development or Redevelopment:** This category includes any time spent on real estate improvement. You may perform the work yourself, but you don't have to, in order to qualify as a "material participant" in the process. It might mean hiring contractors, reviewing architectural plans, dealing with financing, filing plans with cities or counties or discussing the plans with any professional as part of the project. "Improvements" might include building additions, dividing up a property, adding new structures, or removing features that are not wanted.

- **Operations or Management:** These activities are likely things you're already doing. It involves actually managing the operations of the property yourself or working with a property management company. All administrative tasks—including paying bills, replacing appliances or equipment, arranging repairs, collecting rent and other landlord activities—are part of this category.

- **Rental or Lease Activity:** The activity in this category is part of any overall effort to find, secure, and maintain tenants in a rental. This includes advertising and showing the property to potential renters, reviewing applications and lease agreements, and conducting walk-throughs.

Whether you perform these activities yourself or devote time to finding other professionals who can do these things, this is valuable time that can be applied toward being classified as a real estate professional.

Tracking your time spent on these activities is fairly simple: Just keep a log or journal in which you record the dates and time spent, and what tasks you performed. (For example, "Met with property manager, Judy Green, to review rental applications.")

There's also another way to earn this designation: Work as an actual, licensed professional in one of these covered trades, such as a contractor or broker. As long as you own at least a 5% interest in the real estate company employing you, your activities will be considered nonpassive. Without this share of ownership, you cannot qualify as a real estate professional in the eyes of the IRS.

One final note: If you're a real estate agent who works as an independent contractor, you also have the option of forming an S-corporation (or an LLC taxed as an S-corporation), which your brokerage firm can then contract with. Commissions are paid to your entity. Your entity then pays you a salary. In this way, you own at least 5 percent (likely it's 100 percent) of the business paying you, thus qualifying you, under the rule above, as a real estate professional. Work with your tax advisor to discuss whether this option is a good one for you. As well, know that the IRS does scrutinize the real estate professional designation. So keep good records and stay up to date on the rules with your tax professional.

The Professional Flipper

Many people approach real estate purchases with different goals. Some have the desire to earn quick returns. These people purchase properties with the intention of fixing and flipping—buying an inexpensive property, fixing it up and selling it when the market is ripe for gains. Flipping can seem a lucrative strategy, especially if you're handy and can put your own sweat equity into the property, saving on your improvement costs.

However, if you do this frequently, you won't be considered a real estate professional. Instead, flipping may be viewed as your trade and business and you will be classified as a broker/dealer. As such, you'll be generating ordinary earned income doing this. It's considered your salary, and this means paying regular income taxes, plus employment taxes, which have some of the highest tax rates. And as a broker/dealer, you can't take advantage of passive losses or the real estate professional strategy.

Be sure to consult your tax advisor if you are flipping properties or are interested in doing so, in order to be sure of your tax obligations.

Other Tax Write-Offs

No matter what category you fall under—investor, real estate professional or broker/dealer—real estate is likely still a business for you, and with that comes certain business deductions on your tax return that can be quite beneficial to you.

Like with any home-based business, you can write off a portion of your utility bills and mortgage (based on the square footage of your work space). Additionally, you can usually write off such business expenses as cell or internet service, fuel or gas mileage, subscriptions to industry publications, membership fees to networking or professional organizations, office supplies and more.

According to the IRS, Section 162(a), "There shall be allowed as a deduction, all the ordinary and necessary expenses paid or incurred during the taxable year in carrying on any trade or business."

The terms "ordinary" and "necessary" are intentionally vague—they're open to interpretation so work with your tax accountant about whether any expense is a truly viable deduction in your situation. As well, my book *Run Your Own Corporation* deals with home office and other business deductions you may want to use.

The Section 179 Deduction: Depreciation

The U.S. Tax Code, Section 179, allows for a certain amount of depreciable business expenses to be deducted as business expenses each year. The deduction limit as of this writing is $1,000,000. This means that rather than depreciating your qualified business assets over several years, you can write off 100 percent of the purchase price up to $1,000,000. Beginning in 2018, Section 179 also applies to residential real estate.

The section 179 deduction is available for most new and used capital equipment, and also includes certain software. See your tax accountant for information on how to do this properly. As well, since the dollar limit changes check www.corporatedirect.com for the most recent amount.

The following is a list of typical personal expenses that you could feasibly write off as business expenses, if they are legitimately used for business. As always, consult your tax advisor about your unique situation:

Personal Expense	Potential Business Expense
Art	Artwork for your office
Automobile	Your auto payments, or, if owned by business, your repair expenses, plus depreciation, including bonus depreciation under the 2017 Act
Cell phone	Business equipment/service
Child care	Child care provided by the business
Children's allowance	Spending money for your child (must be tracked carefully, including descriptions, times, and reasonable wages)
Computer/software	Business equipment
Dining out	Business meals (50 percent deductible; must have receipts and notation of who attended)
Dry cleaning	For out-of-town expenses
Furniture	Business furniture (if appropriate; includes desk, etc.)
Home costs	Home office or business rental (must measure square footage, follow guidelines for a home office, and track all home expenses in order to be reimbursed)
Internet service	Utility

Magazines/publications	Subscriptions (for your use, or for customers to peruse while they wait)
Medical/vision	Medical reimbursement (use a medical reimbursement plan to pay all medical, vision, dental, and orthodontia costs)
Seminars	Education (authorize employee/owner and document applicability for your business)
Tuition	For education (authorize employee/owner education)
Vacation	Business trips (only if they have a business purpose as the primary reason for the trip; some limitations apply)

Loophole #13

Using business expenses that happen to benefit you personally are well within the law and a widely utilized strategy. Use them to your advantage too.

Now, let's review another key tax strategy...

Chapter Ten

Tax-Free Exchanges

Case #7
Blake

Blake was an auto mechanic who knew that the way to wealth was through real estate investing. As an auto mechanic, he could only get paid when he repaired a Range Rover or tuned a T-bird. If he wasn't working, he wasn't getting paid.

But by owning real estate, by collecting rents from tenants, he got paid whether he showed up to work or not. And knowing this, Blake set out to acquire real estate according to the most tax-efficient means possible.

Blake had acquired two properties in the last four years. One was a two-story, tan-colored 4 plex in a strong rental neighborhood. Blake had used deferred maintenance issues (the need for a new roof and air-conditioning units) to obtain a below-market price for the property. The 4 plex, even after the improvements were made, provided Blake with positive cash flow each month.

His second property was a duplex in a transitional neighborhood. Blake had hoped that the area would improve at a faster rate and that the tenant mix would improve as well. But this was not happening quickly enough for Blake.

So Blake decided to sell the duplex and acquire another property in an area with greater appreciation potential. He was concerned about having to pay taxes on the tidy gain from the sale of the duplex, so he met with his CPA to better understand his tax situation.

The CPA was glad Blake had come to see him. By doing so, he was able to let Blake in on an incredible tax strategy that would save him $10,000. Blake was intrigued and asked for more information.

The CPA explained that by selling his old property using a "1031 exchange," Blake could defer taxes if he reinvested all the proceeds from the old property into a new property. Blake liked the sound of this strategy and, following his CPA's advice, engaged in the following:

- First, Blake sold the duplex for $100,000. With just $7,500 down, he had only paid $50,000 for it four years ago. So with the sale, he had a nice profit of $50,000 on it. Because he had held it for over one year, the capital gains tax (at this writing) was 20 percent (or $10,000 on a $50,000 gain) plus any depreciation recapture. That is, if he had sold the property (instead of exchanging it as he is doing in this example) he would have to pay a higher tax on the amount he had previously depreciated. (Again, because of the exchange, the capital gains and depreciation recapture are deferred.) Blake's property and residence were in a state that didn't have a state capital gains tax, so all he had to deal with was the federal capital gains tax. The CPA noted that if Blake moved to, or held property in, a state with a capital gains tax, he would have to factor that state tax in as well. But, again, the point of the transaction was to defer capital gains taxes and depreciation recapture until a later day.

- The CPA instructed Blake to line up a "qualified intermediary" to handle the monies received from the escrow closing. Blake couldn't touch the money or the 1031 transaction would fail. The money had to go straight to a qualified intermediary.

- The CPA then indicated that Blake had 45 days to identify a new property and 180 days to close on it. So Blake set about promptly locating a new property. After two weeks of searching, he found a 5 plex in an appreciating area for $300,000. With the $50,000 held by the qualified intermediary and new financing of $250,000, Blake purchased the 5 plex. The $10,000 in capital gains (again, plus depreciation recapture) he would have had to pay the IRS in a traditional sale situation was deferred and could be used tax-free to buy a bigger property.

Blake liked this real estate strategy. He learned that he could continue to trade up to bigger properties as long as each one was held for a year and a day.

Over the next five years, Blake traded up three more times. At the end of this run, he owned an immaculate 24-unit apartment building as well as the original two-story, tan-colored 4 plex. Both properties had positive cash flow, giving Blake hope that someday soon he could retire from the auto mechanic business with a nice, continuing income stream.

And Blake had to pinch himself when he thought about the benefits of 1031 transactions. After all, he had started out buying a duplex with just $7,500 down, and without putting in any more money along the way, or paying taxes on any gains, he now owned a cash-flowing, 24-unit apartment building for essentially $7,500. What a great country!

The 1031 Exchange

To understand the 1031 process is to understand six key rules. And to explain these rules, we are pleased to include a section written by 1031 exchange expert Gary Gorman. Gary is the author of *Exchanging Up! How to Build a Real Estate Empire Without Paying Taxes…Using 1031 Exchanges* (SuccessDNA, 2005):

What is a 1031 Exchange? A 1031 exchange rolls the gain from your old investment property over to your new. It's called a "1031" exchange because 1031 is the IRS Code Section that governs this rollover. The fact that it is an IRS Code Section means that it is law, and if you follow the rules the IRS has to allow your exchange.

So, what do you have to do to have a valid exchange? There are six basic rules that you have to follow, which is another way of saying that there are six things the IRS will look at if they audit your exchange. And before we review the six rules, there is one very important point to know: Section 1031 is a form-driven code section. You must follow all of the rules exactly. Failure to follow one small rule can result in your exchange being disallowed if you get audited. Every form and document that is part of your exchange must be exactly correct.

RULE #1—IT MUST BE INVESTMENT PROPERTY.

A 1031 exchange is available only for property held for investment or used in a trade or business. Used in a trade or business means that if you own a bicycle shop, and you own the building that your bicycle shop is in, that building is used in your (bicycle) trade or business. A 1031 exchange does not apply to your personal residence, meaning the house you live in.

The new tax law repealed personal property exchanges as of 2018. No longer can patents, vehicles, aircraft, boats, livestock, artwork, collectibles, and the like be exchanged.

While people do exchanges on property used by their business, the vast majority of real estate exchanges are done by people that own other investment property. Under the law that has been in effect since 1991, you can exchange any type of investment property for any other type of investment property. For example, if you sell a purple duplex, you could buy an office building, an apartment building, a warehouse, or even bare land. Or you could sell bare land and buy income-producing property in order to increase cash flow, which is a popular investment strategy.

After Section 1031 was first written in 1921 (it had a different code number back then), people commonly thought that if you had a purple duplex, you had to find someone else who also owned a purple duplex and swap deeds with them. You might find Adam, who had a purple duplex and was willing to sell it, but he didn't want yours—he wanted Barb's. Barb wanted Chris's, and he wanted Debby's. Debby, luckily, was willing to take yours. This is what we used to call a five-legged exchange, and the problem with them was that if any one of the parties to this transaction backed out, or wasn't able to complete his/her leg of the transaction, the entire exchange fell apart for everyone.

In the 1970s, this concept was challenged by a man named T.J. Starker and his family, who sold some expensive timberland, got the money, and then bought their replacement properties over the next year or two. The IRS challenged their exchanges and the matter ultimately ended up in U.S. Tax Court, which is the Supreme Court of tax law. Starker and his family won, and people immediately began doing "Starker exchanges," which were, essentially, very unstructured transactions. In order to bring some order to the exchange process, Congress rewrote Section 1031 in 1991, and these transactions are now called 1031 exchanges rather than the archaic "Starker exchange" label, although you will still occasionally hear someone call them that.

Section 1031 does not allow you to do an exchange on property you hold for "resale," although the IRS does not define that term. Essentially, it means property that you buy with the intent of immediately selling it rather than holding it for investment. A classic example of property held for resale is "fix-and-flips." A fix-and-flip is where you buy a distressed property with the intent to quickly fix it up and then sell it. As you can imagine, there are people who are adamant that their fix-and-flip property, which they owned for mere weeks, was investment property. And, not surprisingly, some of these cases end up in U.S. Tax Court. Most of these people lose, although occasionally someone will win one of these cases.

The tax court opinions typically require a "two tax year" holding period. This creates a problem because January 1 of year one to January 1 of year two is two tax years. So is July 1 of year one to January 1 of year two, as is December 1 of year one to January 1 of year two. The last two examples are not fair if you are the one that bought your property on January 1, so to level the playing field the IRS seems to favor a "year-and-a-day" test, meaning that a year and a day from any point in time, even leap year, will get you to a new tax year.

The more probable reason for the year-and-a-day rule is that it forces all exchange transactions to be long-term capital gain transactions. Long-term gains apply to property that has been owned for at least 365 days, and are typically taxed more lightly than short-term gains, which apply to property owned less than a year. The IRS doesn't want you turning short-term capital gains into long-term capital gains by doing an exchange. They don't want you, for example, buying a distressed property, fixing it up, and then selling it two months later and doing an exchange. The reason, of course, is that the IRS, in that case, is losing out on higher tax revenues.

Let's say that you do a 1031 exchange and buy another distressed property and do it again. You do this on ten properties and now it is three years after you bought your first property. You're tired of the fix-and-flip business and so you decide to sell your last property and cash out. Because of all the exchanges you've done, you've built up a large accumulated gain and it's time to pay tax on it. Would this gain be taxed as a short-term gain (at a high tax rate), or as long-term capital gain (at a much smaller tax rate)?

The correct answer is that it should be taxed as a short-term gain, although it would be easy for you to convince yourself that it ought to be long-term, because of the three-year time frame between the purchase of your first property and the sale of your last. This is why the IRS doesn't want you doing exchanges on short-term transactions.

The taxpayers who have won court cases where they held the property for less than a year were able to convince the court that their "intent" was to hold the property for more than a year, and that due to circumstances beyond their control, they had no choice but to sell the property sooner. In other words, they were able to convince the court their hearts were pure.

Our firm gets calls daily from people wanting to do exchanges on properties that they've only owned for months, or even days, before they sold them. We got a call once from an attorney that wanted to do an exchange on a property he was going to sell five minutes after he bought it, because he believed that he could prove his heart was pure. (Of course, this involves a higher standard for attorneys.) The facts of the case are that he got a good deal on the purchase, and had listed it for sale at a higher price before he closed the purchase. His buyer was buying the property from him five minutes after the closing of his purchase (on a sales contract that was entered into well before he even owned the property). The so-called "proof" of his investment intent was the fact that he was a successful stock market day trader, which he considered a form of investing, and he didn't see any difference between day trading and what he was doing with this property. The IRS would have disallowed this exchange.

There are so many so-called exchange professionals who preach that you can do fix-and-flip-type exchanges if you can make some type of intent argument. They will tell you that taxpayers have won these types of cases in tax court. The problem with their argument is that the IRS has an unwritten policy of disallowing exchanges of less than a year. Yes, there are a few people who've won short-term exchange cases in tax court. But the problem is that getting to tax court could easily cost you in excess of $50,000, and once you get there your chances of winning are not good. Play it safe and stick to a holding period of at least a year and a day.

One last thing before we move on to the next requirement, and that is "vacation homes." Do they qualify for 1031 exchanges or not? You could make an argument, as many do, that they are not held for investment or used in a trade or business (unless they are rented) and therefore do not qualify for a 1031 exchange.

In 2007, the IRS issued guidelines on doing 1031 exchanges on vacation homes. According to these guidelines, to automatically qualify for a 1031 exchange, your vacation home has to have been rented for at least two weeks in the last two years before you sell it, and you can't have used the property for personal enjoyment for more than two weeks during the same time. If you buy a vacation home you also have to follow these guidelines during the first two years you own it.

These are guidelines, not an all-or-nothing test, meaning that if you fail to meet the test you haven't lost any hope of doing an exchange on the property—it simply means that if your exchange is audited you'll have to prove that your intent was to hold the property for investment rather than personal enjoyment. I don't think that it's any accident that there is a two week rental requirement and a two week use limit—I think that the IRS intends that your personal usage not exceed your rental period. In other words, I'm comfortable with our clients who use their properties for a month but rent it out for four or five months that same year.

Note that the two weeks in the IRS guidelines are personal use days. Maintenance days are not considered in calculating the two weeks. Maintenance days are days that you perform maintenance on the property: Painting walls, repairing or replacing faucets or window coverings, etc. It is your responsibility to keep track of your personal use and maintenance days. Obviously the IRS can't easily verify what days you occupied your unit, or what you did on those days, so the key to surviving an audit on this issue is to have great records. If the IRS sees that you've kept a log of the use of your property, and that obviously the log was updated as you used the property (as opposed to being created the night before the audit), they really have no choice but to accept your records. However, if they think that you prepared the log specifically for the audit, they may make you prove the details of your log which might be almost impossible for most people to do.

As I said, maintenance days don't count against your two week personal use allowance, so document the maintenance wisely—if you paint a wall, you should have a receipt for paint you bought at Home Depot. Likewise, if you shampooed the carpet, you should have a receipt for a carpet cleaner. And, as with your usage log, don't play games with your maintenance claims—the IRS knows that it doesn't take a week to shampoo the carpets in a 1,000 square foot condo.

RULE #2—45-DAY IDENTIFICATION PERIOD

From the day you close the sale of your old property, you have exactly 45 calendar days to make a list of properties you might want to buy. You typically want three properties, or less, on the list. The reason for this is that there are no limits on your list if it has three properties or less.

If you put more than three properties on your list, you become subject to the "200-percent rule" of Section 1031, which says that, since your list is more than three (whether it has four, or ten, or forty properties), the total combined purchase price of everything on the list cannot be more than twice the selling price of your old property.

Let's say that you sell your purple duplex for $100,000 and you list three properties worth $10 million each, for a total list of $30 million. Is this okay? Yes—because your list only had three properties in it. But what if your list shows four properties for only $75,000 each—is this okay? No. Because your list has more than three properties on it, you can only list $200,000 worth of properties (twice the $100,000 selling price of the old property). Since four times $75,000 is $300,000, which exceeds your 200 percent limit, your exchange is toast. And your whole exchange is toast even if you bought one of the properties. So be smart; keep it simple and keep your list to three properties or less.

How do you complete your list? You have to list each property in terms that are clear enough that an IRS agent could take your list and go directly to the door of the property. This means, for example, that if one of your properties happens to be in the Phoenix Condominium Towers, you have to list Unit 203—you can't simply say 123 Camelback Road, which is the address of the towers.

You will give your list to your qualified intermediary, a person we will discuss in Rule #4. Just make sure that it is in your intermediary's hands before midnight on the 45th day.

RULE #3—180-DAY REINVESTMENT PERIOD

From the day you close the sale of your old property, you have exactly 180 calendar days in which to buy your replacement property, and whatever you buy has to be on the 45-day list. This means that you can buy one or all three of the properties on your list. Just make sure that you actually close the purchase, because "closing in escrow" does not meet the requirements. Title to the new property has to be in your name before midnight of the 180th day.

And like the 45-day requirement, these are calendar days, and there are no extensions—if the 180th day falls on a Saturday, a Sunday, or a holiday like the Fourth of July, then that is the day. One exception to this requirement that you have to be careful of is that if your 180th day falls after the due date of your tax return (such as April 15), and you have not purchased your replacement property, you will need to extend your tax return. The reason for this is that if you file your tax return without reporting your exchange, then your exchange is toast. And obviously you cannot properly report your exchange if you haven't purchased your new property.

RULE #4—QUALIFIED INTERMEDIARY REQUIREMENT

You cannot touch the money in between the sale of your old property and the purchase of your new property. By law the money has to be held by an independent third party called a qualified intermediary. Intermediaries have two primary roles: They prepare the exchange documents that are required by Section 1031, and they hold the money during the exchange.

The problem is that almost anyone can be an intermediary. To be sure, the law excludes certain people from being an intermediary (people like your own personal or business attorney, your CPA, or anyone that is related to you). But essentially, virtually anyone can be an intermediary. And this creates potential problems for you and your exchange. There are three potential problems you need to be aware of.

The first is that very few intermediaries have backgrounds in taxation or real estate law. Section 1031 is a very complicated code section with lots of potential traps, yet most intermediaries lack the knowledge or sophistication to really help their clients stay out of trouble. They cover this by inserting "hold-harmless" wording in their documents, or making you sign a separate hold-harmless agreement. A hold-harmless agreement says that you can't sue them no matter how badly they screw up your exchange. You should never sign such an agreement and you should make sure that you delete similar provisions that might be buried in the exchange documents. When intermediaries won't let you remove the hold-harmless wording, what they are telling you is that they don't have confidence in their knowledge and abilities, which means that you need to find another intermediary.

The second problem is that Section 1031 is a form-driven code section, meaning that all of the forms and documents have to be perfectly prepared and completed for you to have a valid exchange. There is no room for error in this code section—you either get it exactly right (dot the "i's" and cross the "t's") or your exchange is disallowed. There are a lot of bad exchange documents out there, and you can't assume that because you are paying your intermediary a large fee, their documents are correct, which is another reason why you don't want to sign a hold-harmless agreement.

The last problem is the most important, and that is that they must hold your money in between the sale of your old property and the purchase of your new property. Since virtually anyone can be an intermediary, there is really no reason why a convicted felon can't be your intermediary and hold your money. Make sure you know whom you are dealing with.

Related to this is the fact that most intermediaries hold their clients' money in commingled, or pooled, accounts. This means that they hold everyone's money in the same account. This is tremendously risky for you. A recent court case has ruled that such an account is available to any creditor of the intermediary. If one of the intermediary's employees is on his way to the bank on intermediary business and happens to hit a school bus, killing some kids, their parents could sue the intermediary and get your money.

Commingled accounts are also very tempting to less scrupulous intermediaries. In recent years, there have been a number of intermediary losses—two of them by intermediaries who were day trading with the money in a commingled account.

In the recent court case mentioned above, the court stated a number of times that money held in a separate account for the intermediary was protected from the intermediary's creditors. So, if you get nothing else out of this discussion on 1031 exchanges, please know that you must insist that your intermediary hold your money in a separate account just for you. This is critical; do not let your intermediary commingle your money with anyone else's money. Insist upon a separate account.

RULE #5—TITLE REQUIREMENTS

In simple terms, how you held title to the old property is how you have to take title to your new property. This means that you have to stay within the same tax return—the same tax identification number or Social Security number.

In other words, if Fred and Sue hold title to their purple duplex in their own name (Fred and Sue Jones, for example), they cannot take title to the new property in the name of their corporation (Jones Investment Corporation), because the corporation files a different tax return.

There are several exceptions to this rule dealing with what the IRS calls "disregarded entities," which are things like revocable living trusts and single-member limited liability companies. While a complete discussion of disregarded entities and 1031 exchanges is beyond the scope of this book, you can obtain more information at www.expert1031.com, or ask your qualified intermediary to explain it to you. If he or she is a good intermediary, they should be able to do so easily.

RULE #6—REINVESTMENT RULES

In order to pay no tax, you must do two things: First, you must buy equal or up. If Fred and Sue sell their purple duplex for $100,000, they must buy their new property for at least $100,000 in order to owe no taxes. If they buy down and only pay $90,000 for their new property, it does not mean that their exchange is defective—they simply pay tax on the $10,000 buy-down. And in a 1031 exchange, the entire $10,000 buy-down would be taxable.

The second thing you have to do is reinvest all of the cash from the sale of the old property into the new property. If there was $40,000 of debt and closing costs when Fred and Sue sold their purple duplex and their intermediary received the balance of $60,000, they must reinvest all of the $60,000 in the new property in order to avoid paying tax. This is true even if they put $5,000 of their own cash into the original purchase of the duplex.

If Fred and Sue are buying their new property for $150,000, they do not have an equal or up problem since they sold for $100,000 and are buying for $150,000. However, if they get a new loan for $100,000 (which would mean that they would only need $50,000 of the $60,000 that the intermediary is holding), then they will pay tax on the leftover $10,000 because they did not reinvest all of the cash. And, as stated above, the entire $10,000 would be taxable. One thing that Fred and Sue could do to avoid this problem would be to reduce their loan to $90,000 so that they use the entire balance of $60,000 held by the intermediary.

Another way that Fred and Sue could have avoided paying tax in both of the examples above would be to buy a second property, which would get them to their required equal or up computation and use up any unspent cash. The second property would have to be on their 45-day list, of course.

Finally, contrary to the belief of most tax advisors, there is no requirement that the debt on the new property be equal to or greater than the amount of debt on the old property. You only need to buy equal or up and reinvest all of the cash to avoid having to pay any taxes. Many tax professionals, as well as most exchange advisors, are confused about this, but it's true—there is no debt replacement requirement.

What happens to the gain that gets rolled over? This is a common question, and the answer most people want to hear is that it disappears, but it doesn't. Your rollover gains are aggregated until you finally sell your last property and don't do a 1031 exchange. For example, if Fred and Sue roll over a $30,000 profit on the sale of the purple duplex, and buy their replacement property for $150,000, they have a $30,000 built-in gain on that property. If they then sell that property for $200,000 and decide not to do an exchange, their taxable gain will be $80,000 ($30,000 from the first property and $50,000 from the second). In the real world, their gain will actually be greater than this because of something called depreciation recapture, but you get the idea. If Fred and Sue decided to do an exchange on the second property, their built-in gain on the third property would be $80,000 and they would continue from there.

Thanks to Gary Gorman for that clear explanation of 1031 exchanges. Now, let's put it to use...

Transferring Property to Your Heirs, Tax-Free

Case #8
Ron and Betty

Ron and Betty had been successful real estate investors throughout their lives. In fact, they had been so successful that it was now time to plan distributions in such a way that their children, and not the IRS, were the proper beneficiaries.

Ron and Betty purchased a strip commercial center many years ago for $100,000. The center was now worth $500,000, and their mortgage had been paid off. Knowing that they wanted to transfer assets to their two children, Kenji and Cindie, they met with a 1031 exchange expert to devise a plan.

The first step was to sell the strip center for $500,000 and enter into a 1031 exchange whereby Ron and Betty acquired a 50-percent interest in New Property A. The new property was worth $1 million and was 50 percent owned by the children, Kenji and Cindie. Ron and Betty's contribution was the $500,000 in cash from the sale of the strip center, while Kenji and Cindie's contribution was a promissory note secured by a first deed of trust on the property for the remaining $500,000.

The 1031 exchange expert explained that even if Ron and Betty owned 100 percent of the strip center, it was acceptable for them to only own 50 percent of New Property A. There were two key points to consider in the transaction. The first was that for Ron and Betty to defer capital gains taxes, they had to buy a property equal to or greater in value, which they did; the strip center was worth $500,000, and New Property A was worth $1 million. The second point was that they had to take title in the same name with which they held the strip center. Ron and Betty always used limited liability companies (LLCs) for asset protection purposes. For New Property A, they used a tenants-in-common structure whereby Ron and

Betty's LLC and Kenji and Cindie's newly formed LLC were listed in title as tenants-in-common owners. As long as these points were satisfied, Ron and Betty were okay and ready for the next step.

After a year and a day of holding on to New Property A, the family began looking to trade up to New Property B. In another six months, they located the right property in a desirable area. New Property A had appreciated, and it sold for $1.2 million. New Property B was purchased for $2 million. Ron and Betty's contribution was their $600,000 share of New Property A. Kenji and Cindie, meanwhile, bought from their $600,000 share of New Property A a $1.4 million interest in New Property B. As such, in the new property, Kenji and Cindie own a 70-percent interest ($1.4 million of $2 million), while Ron and Betty's interest is reduced to 30 percent ($600,000 of $2 million).

Obviously, one can appreciate where this is headed. After two more exchanges, Ron and Betty could, for example, own 12 percent of a $5-million New Property D. Kenji and Cindie, on the other hand, would own 88 percent of such a valuable property. And remember, neither the parents nor the children have paid capital gains taxes as this transfer of wealth has occurred.

And because Ron and Betty own such a small percentage of New Property D, their ownership interest may be subject to IRS-sanctioned discounts. This is because the IRS prudently recognizes that even though 12 percent of a $5-million property may be worth $600,000 on paper, no investor is going to pay that kind of money for a property in which they have no say in management or control over major decisions, such as selling the property. So the IRS generally agrees that such a lack of control may account for a 10- to 40-percent discount—let's say, in this case, a 30-percent discount, meaning that Ron and Betty's 12 percent is really only worth $420,000.

This discount gives Ron and Betty the option of gifting their interests tax-free (at $15,000 per year, at this writing) to Kenji and Cindie over a period of years. With Ron able to gift $15,000 each to Kenji and Cindie, and Betty able to do the same, a total of $60,000 per year ($15,000 per gift times two parents, times two children) could be given away. Assuming

New Property D didn't wildly appreciate, thus driving up the value of Ron and Betty's 12-percent interest, the giving could be accomplished over a seven-year-plus period. (That is $60,000 per year in gifts, to give out a mildly appreciating $420,000 discounted interest in New Property D.) For a more detailed discussion on gifts and discounts, see my book, *How to Use Limited Liability Companies and Limited Partnerships* (Success DNA, 2017).

Or, Ron and Betty could decide to wait until their passing to bequeath the remaining 12 percent to Kenji and Cindie according to their wills, living trusts, or other estate-planning vehicles. With the tax-free exemption for federal estate taxes at $11,400,000 for each of their estates (as of this writing), Ron and Betty, assuming they had no other significant assets, could pass the remaining 12 percent in New Property D to Kenji and Cindie tax-free.

Of course, you will work with your own tax and legal advisors on your own situation. But the point to take away here is that Ron and Betty, starting with just a $100,000 investment in their original strip center, were able to pass along a $5-million asset, tax-free, to their children through the effective use of 1031 exchanges and estate-planning strategies.

You can, too.

Loophole #14

You can't ask for a better tax loophole than one that allows you to defer capital gain taxes forever. Become familiar with 1031 Exchanges.

Now, let's focus on a tax-savings strategy that hits close to home.

Chapter Eleven

Your Principal Residence

Case #9
Emily and Jack

Emily and Jack were a happy couple. Married for several years, they had inherited from Emily's mother, Helen, their small, quaint bungalow in an older part of town. The house had been purchased for $50,000 many years ago. When Helen gifted the house prior to her passing, that amount—the $50,000 Helen paid—became Emily's tax basis for the house. The homes in their neighborhood were distinctive and had character. Over the years young couples discovered the area. Inevitably, the boutiques and small restaurants followed and just as inevitably home prices increased in value over the intervening decades.

After the financial collapse and subsequent rise in prices, homes were in the $400,000 range. Accordingly, if Emily and Jack sold the house their taxable gain would be $350,000 (or the $400,000 home value less their $50,000 tax basis.)

Emily and Jack's daughter Sarah was one year old and a second child was on the way. After learning the space demands of one child they realized that with two they would need bigger quarters. But Jack worried they could not afford a larger house.

Then Emily learned of a friend in the neighborhood who was selling her house tax-free. The friend had moved into the area many years ago when the prices were lower. The appreciation on her house had been significant. Emily called to wish her friend well in her new house and in the process learned about how to sell your house tax-free.

When Jack heard about the strategy he immediately called his CPA to confirm whether it was accurate. To his surprise, it was.

Jack learned from his CPA that the IRS allowed married couples a significant tax benefit if they lived in their primary residence for two of the last five years. The benefit was an exclusion of capital gains of up to $500,000 for married taxpayers upon the sale of the house.

So instead of a tax on the gain of $350,000 (again $400,000 sales price less $50,000 tax basis) because it was their primary residence that they had lived in for two out of five years, there was no tax.

With that, Jack quickly calculated that they could move into a larger house. They would have $350,000 tax free to put down on a new house. Jack felt comfortable in his financial life to now be able to afford a $200,000 mortgage. Together, Emily and Jack found a beautiful $550,000 new home with four bedrooms and a large backyard for their growing brood to play in. It was hard to believe that, when all was said and done, they had obtained this new house, with just their original gift from Emily's mother. The tax fee capital gains rule made all the difference for their family.

The Primary Residence Exclusion

One of the greatest tax gifts is the principal residence rule for capital gains on the sale of your home. So great is the principal residence tax exclusion that even married couples filing jointly are benefited to the same, if not greater, extent as single taxpayers. While some may argue that there've been greater gifts, not much beats the simplicity of the rule. The basics of it are easy to grasp: You own a house, you live in it for at least two years, you sell it and you don't have to pay any taxes on the first $500,000 in gain. Gone are the days when the young homeowner had to save every receipt for every upgrade, every repair, every minor item bought at the hardware store. If you have lived in your own home for two years you probably don't have to worry.

Of course, there are some technical points associated with the general rule. They are pretty simple so first let's bullet-point the main ones:

- If you are single your capital gains exclusion is limited to $250,000.00

- If you are married your capital gains exclusion is limited to $500,000.00

- You have to own the home and it has to be your "primary residence" for two of the previous five years

What is your "primary residence"? Basically, it is a home that you personally live in the majority of the year. If you have a house in Palm Beach and one in Lake Tahoe and you spend 8 months of the year at the Tahoe home then that is your primary residence. But, keep in mind the two year out of five year part of the rule. Let's say that the next year you spend 7 months at the Palm Beach house. Then the Palm Beach home is your primary that year. Do you see where this is headed? You can primary more than one home at once over a five year period so long as each is your main home for at least two years during that five year period. Temporary absences are also counted as periods of use – even if you rent the property during those absences.

Now don't let the five year requirement confuse you – it only takes two years to achieve the tax exclusion. The five year part is a bonus, allowing you some freedom. You don't have to personally use the home as your primary residence for two consecutive years or for the two years immediately before you sell, you just have to use it as your primary residence for two of the previous five years. But, it is also a limitation. You cannot live in a house for two years and then rent it for four years and then get the exclusion. You could live in it for two years and then rent it for three years and then sell it (as long as it is sold within the five year mark from when you first lived in it as your primary residence).

Also, bear in mind that married couples do not have to live together. So long as one spouse lives in the primary residence for the two years then the couple can take advantage of the $500,000.00 exclusion. But, they cannot create a primary residence for two homes at once and get the $500,000.00 exclusion for both. If they live apart during the two year period and each sell their primary residence then they are each limited to the single taxpayer exclusion of $250,000.00 for each house.

If you have a home office or rental as part of your primary residence or run a business out of a portion of your property, your ability to maximize your capital gains exclusion largely depends upon whether the home office, business or rental was part of your home (in the same dwelling unit) or a separate part of your property (a separate building or apartment). If the business use of your home was contained within your dwelling unit then upon the sale you will need to recapture any depreciation taken for that part of the home. But you will not lose any of the allowable capital gains exclusion ($250,000.00 for single taxpayers and $500,000.00 for married filing jointly). If the business use of your home was not a part of your dwelling unit then you need to bifurcate the sale by allocating the basis of the property and the amount realized upon its sale between the business or rental part and the part used as a home.

Remember, only one home can be sold in any two year period unless you and your spouse live apart, and even then you can each only take the single payer exclusion of up to $250,000.00. But what if you need to sell a home that you have not lived in for the full two years? The IRS tells us that in special circumstances you can sell a home before you reach the two year mark and get a pro-rated exclusion. An example of a pro-rated exclusion is, if you are a single taxpayer and have to sell your primary residence for a qualified reason after living in it only one year then you could exclude up to $125,000.00. In other words, you lived in a home 50% of the requisite time so you can take 50% of the allowable exclusion. The special circumstances that qualify you for this safe harbor and allow you to take the prorated exclusion have to do with health (yours and certain qualified individuals such as close relatives), change of employment, or what the IRS calls "unforeseen circumstances" (examples include death, natural or man-made disasters, multiple births from the same pregnancy, divorce). These circumstances also have to cause you to sell your home. Factors used by the IRS to determine causation include:

- Your sale and the circumstances causing it were close in time,

- The circumstances causing your sale occurred during the time you owned and used the property as your main home,

- The circumstances causing your sale were not reasonably foreseeable when you began using the property as your main home,

- Your financial ability to maintain your home materially changed, and

- The suitability of your property as a home materially changed.

Be sure to work with your accountant in this area. Also review IRS Publication 523 as rules and regulations do change.

Loophole #15
Your home is your castle. It also features one loupe, one window, for significant tax savings through the Primary Residence Rule.

Now, let's try and combine two loopholes to save taxes on your personal fort.

1031 Exchanges and the Primary Residence Rule

What happens if you do a 1031 tax deferred exchange of rental property or other property held for investment and then later decide to live in (and later sell) the property that was purchased? Can you take advantage of both tax benefits?

As discussed in Chapter 10, it is crucial to your 1031 exchange that both the sold and purchased property are held for investment. The property purchased must undergo a holding period before it is resold or converted into a non-investment property. After you have complied with the "held for investment" requirement by, for example, renting the property if it is rental property, then what? Well, you could sell the property and pay your taxes on that sale and all previous sales that were perhaps in a series of exchanges or exchange and defer the tax once again. Or you could live in the house as your primary residence. If you have had a series of gains that you have deferred this is a way to extinguish your tax debt forever – all you have to do is move into your investment property once the holding period for it qualifying as an investment is over.

Gaining the primary residence exclusion for property that was 1031 property isn't as easy as the simpler primary residence rules talked about above, but it does allow you to take advantage of two loopholes at once. The main difference when primary residencing a 1031 exchanged property is that you actually have to hold the property for 5 years. The 5 year part here is a main rule. You can't sell after only 2 years of ownership as if you were simply primary residencing a home that was not exchanged into. But that first year you had to hold onto the home for investment goes towards the five year calculation. So, you rent it for two years and live in it for three, or vice-versa, so long as you start with a one year rental period and live in it two of the remaining four years.

After buying a commercial building at $150,000, you now realize that it is worth $300,000 and you do a 1031 exchange into a nice single-family home worth $350,000 (you have to put in an additional $50,000 to complete the purchase). You've deferred $150,000 worth of gain. You then choose to rent the home for the first two years that you own. Then you later decide to move into the home. You live in the house for three years, at which point it is now worth $700,000, and you sell it for this amount. You and your spouse have now effectively wiped out not only the $350,000 gain from the sale of your primary residence but the previous $150,000 gain as well, utilizing the $500,000 exclusion on gains from the primary residence.

Loophole #16
With careful planning you can use the Primary Residence Rule and 1031 Tax Free Exchange Rule for significant tax savings.

1,000,000
350,000 taxes

Rent 2 years
they live in

HELOCs and Personal Residences

Have you ever tapped the equity in your home to pay for a new car or a college tuition? With a HELOC, also known as a home equity loan or line of credit, you could do so. Better yet, you could deduct the interest you paid on those loans on your tax return.

The new tax law has changed all of this (at least through 2025, when this portion of the tax law expires). With over 14 million HELOCs borrowing over $500 billion the new rules effect many Americans for the tax year starting 2018.

You can still tap into your home's equity for whatever you want. But under the new tax law you can't deduct the interest in every circumstance. And there are limits on how much you can deduct even if you are using the money correctly.

Borrowings used to "buy, build or substantially improve" your home are accepted. Fast cars are not. (But again, you can still buy the car and just not deduct the interest.)

The borrowing must be used to improve the house securing the loan. So you can't use a HELOC on your primary residence to improve a vacation home.

Interest can only be deducted on the total debt of up to $750,000 for up to two homes. If you had a debt of up to $1 million on one or two homes before December 15, 2017 (the last date before the tax law changed) you can still deduct the interest if the money was used to improve, build or buy a home.

Let's say John has a $700,00 mortgage on a primary residence and borrows $100,000 on a HELOC to make improvements on that property. His total borrowings are now $800,000. John can only deduct interest on the first $50,000 of the HELOC. The remaining $50,000 in interest is over the $750,000 limit.

Mary has a primary residence and a vacation home. Her residence has a $300,000 mortgage on it with the vacation home having $200,000 mortgage. Her total borrowings are $500,000. Mary then borrows $100,000 against each property. The money borrowed against her primary residence goes for improvements on that property. Likewise, the $100,000 vacation home borrowing is used for a landscaping project on that property. Mary's total borrowings are now $700,000. Because she used the money the right way on each property she can deduct the full amount of interest on the $700,000 in loans.

There is another wrinkle to be aware of here. You can only deduct interest on a HELOC of up to $100,000. And that HELOC deduction is limited to the price you paid for the property.

Let's say you bought a Detroit fixer upper for $50,000. Somehow, you are able to get a HELOC on it for $75,000 so you can completely remodel it. You can only deduct interest on the first $50,000 of the loan, because that is what you paid for the place.

Once again, the tax law benefits single persons. Two singles could deduct a combined $1.5 million in mortgage debt ($750,000 each) if they bought a home together. Married couples are limited to the $750,000 amount.

Of course, record keeping becomes important in the arena. You've got to be able to prove all of this up to the IRS. Track your spending and save all of your invoices. If you don't already have one, consider using a bookkeeper to assist with it. Save these records for a good long time. The IRS may take years to get at any audits on this. You may need to be prepared into the distant future.

Now let's consider tax savings on equally important real estate...

Chapter Twelve

Vacation Homes

For many people their second purchase of real estate will be a vacation home. And while vacation homes can offer a much needed retreat from city life and a reservoir of family memories, as well as appreciation in well located areas, they can also offer an under-appreciated benefit: Tax savings.

There are four basic scenarios to understand regarding how vacation home tax rules can be utilized. The best way to review these rules is through a case study, as detailed below. (Of course, if you don't own or ever want to own a vacation home feel free to jump to the next chapter.) But if you are staying, please note that the rules apply whether your vacation home is a condominium, home or other type of residence.

Case #10
The Edgar Family

The Edgar family was a well-liked group of competitive brothers and sportsmen from Buffalo, New York. The four brothers had hunted, fished, brawled, boated and camped together since their youth. And now, even with wives and families, they vowed to continue their family heritage. Although each brother had a different profession and they all made different amounts of income on an annual basis, the brothers were able to scrape together enough money for a down payment on a vacation property.

Of course, due to their competitive natures, the brothers, and even more so their wives, realized that they could not own a vacation home together.

The beauty for the Edgar brothers was that their proposed purchase was for four cabins right next to each other on Seneca Lake, one of the prime lakes in the Finger Lakes region east of Buffalo. They could hunt, fish and boat together during the day without combusting under the same roof after cocktails in the evening. The wives were in agreement and the four cabin Edgar compound was purchased.

The cabins were right on the lake and each was well appointed with four bedrooms, two baths, and a large living and dining area. They were in a desirable area and could be used for both vacations and rentals. Because the cabins were on four separate parcels and each brother was in a different financial situation all four vacation home tax scenarios were utilized:

Scenario One: Brother Al
Rent to Others for the Entire Year

Al was a machinist. While a talented individual with a mix of skills combining artistry with science, the American economy no longer rewarded machinists.

After purchasing the cabin, Al's job was outsourced to China. Al knew it would be some time before he found another job. But he vowed to keep the cabin in order to be with his brothers. Still, at his wife Amy's urging, he decided to rent the cabin to others during his period of unemployment.

Renting the vacation home for the entire year provided Al with some excellent tax benefits. He could receive tax sheltered personal cash flow and a tax loss for sheltering other income. Renting out the cabin for the full year put Al in the real estate business, which thus provided the tax benefits.

Let's look at how Al's rental of the cabin provided him with a tax shelter. Of course your own situation will depend upon the rents and expenses you generate, but Al was able to rent the cabin for $20,000 a year to a wealthy family from Manhattan.

Profit

Income from Rent		$20,000
Expenses		
Advertising	$200	
Property tax	$5,500	
Mortgage interest	$9,500	
Insurance	$400	
Maintenance & Repairs	$1,500	
Total Expenses		$17,100
Cash Profit		$2,900

Tax Loss

Income from Rent	$20,000
Total Expenses	$17,100
Depreciation	$6,200
Expenses plus Depreciation	$23,300
Tax Loss	($3,300)

In Al's case, the vacation cabin provides a cash profit of $2,900 that is tax sheltered by depreciation, plus a tax loss of $3,300 from depreciation. Thus Al pays no tax on the $2,900 in cash flow and he can use the $3,300 tax loss to shelter other income.

As we've discussed, if you have less than $100,000 in adjusted gross income you can deduct up to $25,000 in rental activity losses against your nonpassive income including salaries. (The exemption phases out and is inapplicable after your adjusted gross income reaches $150,000 unless, as we discussed, you are a real estate professional.)

In Al's case the loss could be utilized. Al was out of work and Amy's teacher salary was less than $100,000. So the $3,300 in tax loss on the cabin sheltered taxes Amy would have otherwise paid on her income.

When Al did get another job and their combined income on a joint return was over $150,000 any tax losses would be "suspended" and carried forward into future tax years. These losses could be used to offset future passive income or be deducted against gain when the property was sold.

This scenario worked for Al and Amy on a tax basis, but still left them missing all the fun with the other brothers. However, in speaking with their CPA they learned of a little exception in the law they could use to their benefit. As long as they personally used the cabin for no more than the greater of 14 days or 10% of the days the cabin was rented during the year their tax shelter would not be blown.

As it turned out, the family from Manhattan was going to be out of the country for the 4th of July holiday. They agreed that Al and his family could use their cabin during that week. All four brothers were together, and Al still received the much needed tax relief the cabin generated for him.

Scenario Two: Brother Bob
Vacation Use and More than 14 days Rental

Bob was a mountaineer and a CPA. This was a good thing because when it came to renting out the cabin for 15 or more days and also using it personally for the greater of 14 days per year or 10% of the number of days the cabin was rented one needed a Sherpa guide to get through the tax regulations.

The four steps to be discussed can get complicated but there is a silver lining at the end of the process. And while Bob would certainly suggest you see your own tax professional to discuss your specific situation, as a general rule Scenario Two prevents obtaining a tax loss if personal use limits are exceeded. As such, home ownership expenses can't exceed rental income, meaning there is no great tax-loss shelter as in Scenario One.

In Bob's case he liked renting the cabin for 90 days during the year. With kids in youth baseball and bowling programs the family couldn't get to the lake every weekend. Still, during the summer he wanted to spend as much time as possible on the lake, and the family logged at least 60 days a year at the cabin.

Accordingly, the applicable percentage for use here is determined by dividing rental days (or 90 days) into 150 days (the total days used-rental plus personal). The resulting rental percentage is 60 percent.

Loophole #17

If you discount your daily or weekly rental rate to friends and family certain fair share rules can come into play which may limit the effectiveness of such rental days. Be sure to work with your CPA in attempting to utilize the complicated loopholes in this area.

In Bob's case, he rented his cabin out 90 days for $140 per day. The first step is to then calculate direct expenses incurred for the rental.

Gross receipts:
90 days at $140 per day

Total Rent	$12,600
Less: advertising fee	$900
Limit on deductions	$11,700

In this case Bob can write off the $900 fee to find renters since that expense is directly related to the rental. The remaining $11,700 is the amount Bob can use for vacation ownership expenses. If his expenses exceed this amount he is unable to deduct them, thus preventing a tax loss from being created.

In step two, Bob deducts the interest and taxes allocable to rental uses.

	Allowable	Rental Allocation (60%)	
Limitation deductions (from above)			$11,700
Property tax	$5,500	$3,000	
Mortgage interest	$5,000	$3,300	
Allowable amount			$6,600
Deduction limit amount remaining			$5,100

So, the amount of property tax and interest deductible as a cabin rental expense is $6,600. The remaining balance of $3,900 can be treated as a regular itemized deduction Form 1040. The deduction limit has now been reduced to $5,100.

In step three, Bob figures out the remaining home ownership expenses that may be allowed as rental deductions.

	Allowable	Rental Allocation (60%)	
Limit on deductions (from above)			$5,100
Utilities	$2,000	$1,200	
Repairs	$1,600	$960	
Insurance	$400	$240	
Total Rental Allocation Expenses			$2,400
Deduction limit amount remaining			$2,700

As such, the home ownership expense that may be deducted is $2,400 (or 60% of the $3,000 in actual expenses.) The deduction limit is now reduced to $2,700.

In step four, Bob calculates the amount of depreciation that can be used as a rental deduction.

	Allowable	Rental Allocation (60%)	
Limit on deductions (from above)			$2,700
Depreciation	$6,200	$3,720	
Allowable amount			$2,700

The amount allowed is the $2,700, not the higher $3,720. If the allowable amount had been above the $2,700 a tax loss would have occurred and, again, the intent of the tax is to limit deductions to rental income actually received. So the remaining $1,020 of depreciation ($3,720-$2,700) is disallowed as a deduction and carries forward to future years.

Remember we mentioned there was silver lining in all of this? While the detailed calculations prevented Bob from taking a tax loss, the deductions did allow for one positive benefit: Bob was able to offset his $12,000 in rental income. And that is why Bob, ever the CPA, liked Scenario Two. It operated as a vacation home tax shelter.

For more information on this topic consider reviewing IRS Publication 527, "Residential Rental Property."

Scenario Three: Brother Casey
Vacation Use and 14 days Rental

Casey owned a picture framing and art supply store in Buffalo. His was a decent business that provided income for the family and enough time off to enjoy the cabin on Seneca Lake. It was not Casey's intent to ever rent the cabin but a situation came up where Casey felt compelled to assist.

The family from Manhattan who had rented Brother Al's cabin for the year needed a favor. They were planning a two week family reunion at the end of August and needed an extra cabin to accommodate all the cousins coming to visit. Brother Bob's cabin had already been rented out and so Al talked to Casey on behalf of the Manhattan family.

Given that the family had let Al use his own cabin for the 4th July weekend so that all the brothers and their families could celebrate together Casey felt obligated to return the favor. It was agreed that the family would rent Casey's cabin for the two weeks at $145.00 per day.

Casey was worried about the tax situation he had got himself into. He spoke to his CPA brother Bob about how to account for the $2,030 in income he would be receiving.

Bob told Casey not to worry. While Bob's situation was complicated by the amount of personal and rental use of the cabin, Casey's case was easy. The government provided a tax exemption for short term rentals.

The rule was that if you rented your vacation home for less than 15 days in a year your rental income was tax free. Thus Casey could keep the $2,030 without paying any taxes on it. As well, he could still deduct all of his mortgage interest and taxes on the property. Bob called this tax free scenario "the Masters Exemption" because it was used by Augusta National Golf Club homeowners who earned as much as $20,000 during the Masters Golf Tournament. Homeowners in Super Bowl cities also frequently used this exemption to their tax free benefit.

Casey liked this scenario, and was open to renting the cabin out for two weeks a year into the future. An extra $2,000 tax free never hurt.

Scenario Four: Brother Don
Exclusive Vacation Use

Don owned a concrete contracting company. He did work throughout upstate New York and was quite successful. Don and his wife Jeanne did not need to rent out the Seneca Lake cabin, nor did they want to do so. Don's work took him throughout the area and sometimes he would spend the night at the cabin while on the road. Don and Jeanne liked the flexibility of using the cabin whenever they wanted and on a whim, and were not keen on being constrained by obligations to renters.

But while there was no rental income to worry about Don could still utilize certain tax deductions his other brothers all received. Mortgage interest and real estate taxes were fully deductible for Don. As such, with $9,500 a year in mortgage interest and the $5,500 in real estate taxes, Don could write off $15,000 a year for the major costs associated with the cabin. Even though he never rented out the cabin.

This was such an incentive to vacation home ownership that Don and Jeanne looked into acquiring another property. The couple and their two children enjoyed a ski vacation in Colorado every year. Don found a condo at Breckenridge for a reasonable price and put in an offer.

It wasn't until Don was talking to his CPA brother Bob about the tax aspects of the transaction that he learned the bad news. The mortgage interest deduction is only available on your personal residence and one designated second home. The mortgage interest on a third (or fourth and on up) personal residence was nondeductible personal interest, and thus of no tax benefit.

Bob offered Don two solutions. One was to analyze whether the interest expense on the Breckenridge condo would be greater than the Seneca Lake cabin. If so, the condo could become the designated second home. The second option was to have one of the properties be used year round as a rental property, in the same way Al was treating his cabin. In that case Don could take the mortgage interest deduction on all three properties.

But Don was more interested in vacations than taxes. He decided to leave things the way they were and bought the Breckenridge condo for his own exclusive use. While he couldn't write off the mortgage interest he more importantly could enjoy excellent vacations with his family.

As a summary of the four scenarios involving vacation home ownership and their tax treatment, the following chart may be useful:

	Scenario One Rent to others all year	Scenario Two Vacation Use/More than 14 days rental	Scenario Three Vacation Use/ 14 days or less rental	Scenario Four Exclusive Vacation Use
Tax and Mortgage Interest Deductions	Yes	Yes	Yes	Yes (but not for third or more properties)
Rental Cost Deductions	Yes	Yes-but not over rental income amount	No-but rent is not taxed	N/A
Rental Loss Deductions	Yes (subject to passive loss rules)	No	No	N/A

Please work with your tax advisor to properly utilize these deductions. And remember that vacation properties may be (or may become) some of the most valuable real estate you will ever own. And not just in terms of dollars, but also in terms of family memories and shared experiences. You will want to do what is necessary to protect this important asset, so be sure to consider holding this property in a protected entity as discussed in Chapter 25.

Loophole #18

Along with the emotional and recreational benefits, be sure to appreciate the tax benefits of vacation homes.

And so you can enjoy your vacation home into your golden years, let's review real estate and retirement planning...

Chapter Thirteen

Real Estate and Retirement Plans

Most Americans are now concerned that company pension plans and Social Security will not adequately provide for them in their retirement years. This fact is keenly underscored by Congress – not in their flowery words and grand pontifications on the stability of Social Security, but in their contradictory legislative actions.

Over the last 40 years, Congress has approved increasingly beneficial retirement options designed to encourage Americans to save on their own for their golden years. While no Congressman will dare utter the fact that with mind-numbing trillions and trillions of unfunded obligations, Social Security and Medicare are now regarded by many as Ponzi schemes that can never be fixed, Congress has covered itself with retirement legislation. So that twenty years or so from now when the government system inevitably breaks, Congress, the institution, will be able to shake its finger at the American people and point to the IRAs, 401(k)s, Roth IRAs and the like they have created. And the message will be that the benevolent Congress gave the masses a way to save for their own retirement years ago. What will not be addressed is why the government continued to take 15.3% in payroll taxes from workers and businesses for a failed system. But that's an issue between you and the ballot box.

The point is that to provide for your own retirement, it is prudent, as it is in all facets of life, to rely on yourself and not on the government.

When it comes to planning for the future, some real estate investors use their real estate portfolio to provide for retirement.

We have many clients using this strategy. As an example, Denny is a dentist who owns a 40 unit apartment building financed on a 15 year note. While his mortgage payments are higher for now he will own the building free and clear upon his retirement. Denny will receive $12,000 a month or more once the mortgage is paid off. Better yet, because of depreciation and the suspension of losses until real estate gains are offset and realized, Denny's $12,000 a month profit will be tax free for a good many years. That monthly income will cover his needs throughout his retirement.

But what about real estate not just for retirement but purchasing real estate through your retirement plan? For one very definite opinion on this topic, our friend, Tom Wheelwright, the Rich Dad's Advisor on taxation, wrote the following section:

Why Only an Uneducated Taxpayer would buy Rental Real Estate in an IRA

I confess. I am not a big fan of 401(k)'s and IRA's. There are 5,800 pages of tax savings in the Internal Revenue Code. Of these, 400 relate to postponing taxes through IRA's, 401(k)'s, pension plans and profit sharing plans. The other 5,400 pages explain how to permanently reduce your taxes. So why waste time on postponing, or deferring your taxes when you can permanently reduce or eliminate them?

The reality is that IRA's and 401(k)'s presume that you are going to retire poor. Think about it. If you have the same income when you retire as you do when you are working, your taxes will be higher the day you retire. You won't have your business deductions, you probably have your house paid off and hopefully your children have moved on and are no longer dependents. The argument, of course, is that you won't have as many expenses. True, if you don't want to travel, play golf or enjoy life when you retire. For those of you who want to live more when you retire and actually make more money when you retire, read on.

Let's say that like most people, you bought into the idea of a 401(k) and you were diligent in putting money in and you received your match from your employer and, despite all of the turmoil in the marketplace and all of the fees taken out of your account by the mutual fund companies, you actually have a nice little nest egg. You quit your job or retired and so you can roll over your 401(k) into a self-directed IRA and have more control over your money. Then, you started reading this book and figured that you could have an even better lifestyle if you got out of your mutual funds and started investing in real estate.

You find that your savings are all tied up in your new IRA. So you listen to the pundits who tell you that you can invest your IRA money into rental real estate. Wow! What a good idea, right? Wrong. This is a terrible idea. Not a mediocre idea, not an okay idea, but a downright terrible idea! The reason is simple math.

When we were young we all learned the simple fact that $(-1) \times (-1) = +1$. Remember this? Two negatives equal a positive. The same equation works in the tax law. When you put a tax shelter (rental real estate) inside another tax shelter (IRA) you end up with a tax expense. In the Chapter 8 section on cost segregations, I explained the magic of depreciation. With a cost segregation, depreciation should be high enough that you don't pay any tax on the rental income from your property. On top of that, when you sell the property and use a 1031 exchange, you don't pay taxes on the gain from your property.

Unless, of course, you own your property inside an IRA. Then all of these tax benefits go away. When you eventually sell your properties and pull the money out of your IRA, you get taxed on 100% of the money at your ordinary income tax rates. Even if you didn't use a 1031 exchange, when you sell your property outside of an IRA, you are taxed at the lower capital gains rates. And since you want to retire rich, you are going to be in a very high tax bracket and pay maximum taxes on that IRA money.

Even worse is that you lose the substantial benefits of leverage when you buy your real estate inside an IRA. Banks don't like to lend to IRA's because you cannot personally guarantee the loan. And we all know that real estate is only a mediocre investment without debt. Debt is what makes real estate work.

What about a Roth IRA, you ask? Better but not ideal. You still have the leverage (debt) issue because banks don't like to lend to Roth IRA's any more than they like to lend to regular IRA's. You also lose much of the tax benefits in a Roth IRA. While you won't pay taxes on the distributions from the IRA, you also won't get the tax benefits of depreciation while you own the property.

On a well-leveraged property, not only should depreciation totally offset your rental income from the property, it will in fact produce a loss for tax purposes. With good tax planning, you can use that loss to offset other income, such as income from your salary, your business or your other investments. That can be a huge tax benefit that puts thousands of dollars in your pocket.

So what's the solution? You have all of this money tied up in your IRA and if you pull it out to directly invest in real estate you are going to pay heavy taxes and perhaps even a penalty. The answer is "it depends." It depends on what you want to use the money for. If your wealth strategy is such that you need your IRA money for real estate investing, you may want to go ahead and pay the taxes and penalties, pull the money out of your IRA and then invest in real estate. Chances are, you will make up the tax in a few short years, just because of the tax benefits combined with the additional leverage you get outside of the IRA.

Don't let an uneducated tax advisor or financial planner convince you to buy rental real estate inside an IRA. Unless you don't need or want the tax benefits from real estate and are uninterested in producing the returns that you get from leveraging your real estate, rental real estate inside an IRA is just a bad idea.

Thank you, Tom, for your very clear thoughts.

Loophole #19

A tax shelter (retirement plan) owning another tax shelter (real estate) negates both loopholes. The windows are closed.

But because some people are going to use their IRA monies anyway (because that is where their money is) let's look at another case study.

Case #11
Jeremy

As an enrolled agent and tax preparer, Jeremy knew the rules about retirement plans. And he knew that since Congress kept raising the amounts one could set aside each year he knew that he should take care of himself. The message was clear that no one else (and certainly not the government) would.

So, over the years, Jeremy had amassed an IRA account valued at $125,000. The account was invested in mutual funds and bond funds which, in the past few years, were only generating a four percent return. After factoring in the effects of inflation it was not a stellar return. Granted, the returns were accumulating tax free into his IRA account. But Jeremy knew he needed a great deal more money to retire on, at least $1 million. And he knew because this was a traditional IRA (and not a Roth IRA) he would be taxed on the monies when he started withdrawing them from his IRA for his retirement needs, thus further increasing the money needed.

Jeremy started looking for a better investment return. Many of his friends had done well by investing in real estate. And his good friend Terry had even successfully invested in raw land using his IRA. This was intriguing and it led Jeremy to his first real estate investment.

Jeremy knew his market and decided to stay local with his investing. He also knew that when the new freeway to the northern suburbs was eventually built, land values would skyrocket. But because people had talked about the project for years and nothing had been done, land values were still surprisingly affordable. And yet it didn't take 20/20 vision or a crystal ball to see that the road would someday be built. The traffic on surface streets during commute hours was getting worse. Quiet neighborhoods were not so quiet anymore. Political pressure for a freeway into downtown would certainly increase.

Jeremy found two acres of land near a proposed off ramp for the proposed freeway. It was selling for $100,000. He arranged for a trust company to set up a self-directed IRA, which is an IRA that can invest in a wide variety of assets. The trustee then set up an LLC to hold title to the property for asset protection purposes. (This will be discussed in greater detail in Chapter 23.) For now, please note that if the IRA took title to the real estate in the name of the IRA and a claim arose involving the property, a judgment creditor could reach not only the real estate but the remaining $25,000 in Jeremy's IRA account. By using an LLC the remaining IRA assets are protected from attack.

Jeremy purchased the two acres and waited.

In year one, he heard some people claim that because everything was tax free in an IRA that meant he did not have to pay property taxes on the two acres. But in checking with his advisors, Jeremy learned that was not the case. If the LLC owned by his IRA didn't pay the taxes he could lose the property in foreclosure. So with the $4,000 in annual contributions he used to fund his IRA each year he had the trustee pay the $1,500 a year in annual property taxes. The remaining $2,500 went into his IRA and was held in an interest bearing cash account as a reserve for any expenses that came up on the two acre property.

It was Jeremy's strategy to contribute the maximum amount possible to his IRA. The current maximum for any IRA, be it Roth or traditional, was $6,000. When Jeremy reached age 50 he could put in an additional $1,000 a year. These amounts, Jeremy knew, would increase over time.

Jeremy knew he needed a lot of money for retirement and funded the maximum amount each year. Jeremy's patience was well rewarded. Six years later the freeway was built through the northern suburbs. Jeremy's acreage was very well located and eventually sold for a million dollars. That money went tax free into his IRA account.

At age 59½ Jeremy began to pull money out of his now $1 million plus IRA account. Because he had used a traditional IRA, and the initial contributions were made with pretax dollars, he had to pay tax at ordinary income rates when he took the money out. (The Roth IRA, as we'll discuss later, is the opposite: Contributions are made with after tax dollars, but the withdrawals are tax free.) So if Jeremy's tax rate at age 60 was 35% he would pay the IRS $3,500 on every $10,000 withdrawal from his IRA account.

Jeremy's case illustrates the advantages of using IRAs to invest in real estate. But it also highlights a tax disadvantage.

What if Jeremy had used his own money instead of his IRA money to invest in the land? Or what if he used money from a Roth IRA? Would there be any tax difference?

The answer is yes.

If Jeremy had purchased the property using his non-retirement after tax dollars he would be subject to capital gains taxes (as of this writing) of just 20%. Remember, he held the property for over one year so that lower capital gain rate (vs. the ordinary income rate for a less than one year hold) would apply. As we've seen this 20% capital gain rate (even with the extra 3.8% for certain high earners) is less than the ordinary income rate that an IRA is taxed at upon withdrawal. So in many cases you'll consider using your own money to buy highly appreciating real estate.

Which raises the question: Why would anyone use an IRA given the tax difference?

The answer, of course, is that IRAs are where the money is held. Millions of Americans have been besieged by stockbrokers, mutual fund companies, financial planners and all stripes of investment advisors to set up Individual Retirement Accounts. And almost as many millions have done so.

When it comes to investing in real estate, many Americans, despite the later tax consequences, are going to use their IRA because that is where their money is held.

So how can you use an IRA too in a more tax advantaged way to acquire real estate?

The answer, which we've alluded to, is to use a Roth IRA. A self-directed Roth IRA, with a trustee investing in real estate through an LLC, can be a useful tax vehicle. Remember, we said that a Roth IRA is made up of after tax contributions. And because you paid tax on the money going in you don't have to pay tax on the money going out.

If Jeremy had used Roth IRA money to buy the two acres, the million dollars upon sale would not be taxed. And when Jeremy began to pull the money at retirement there would be no tax. It was almost too good to be true.

Of course, when we hear those words we are all trained to ask: What's the catch? There used to actually be a catch. Prior to 2006, there were income restrictions on how much money you could make when contributing to a Roth IRA. At the start high income earners were excluded from the generous tax benefits of a Roth IRA.

But remember how we said that Congress was getting more and more generous with retirement legislation as it became clearer and clearer that Social Security was beyond repair. As of 2006, anyone at any income level can contribute their after tax dollars to a Roth 401(k).

This is big. Now anyone can contribute after tax dollars and pull money out at retirement tax free. Plus, 401(k) plans, whether Roth or regular, allow contributions at this writing of $19,500 per year with 50 or older workers able to contribute a total of $26,000 per year. And while a Roth 401(k), as an ERISA plan, does not allow for investments into real estate, you can in many cases roll your Roth money from a 401(k) plan into a Roth IRA plan. Once there, you can use your Roth IRA to invest in real estate.

And from there you are given some excellent planning opportunities, such as allowing your beneficiaries, like your children, to draw money out tax free from your Roth IRA after you have passed on. (But know that inherited IRAs offer no asset protection under recent case law.) Still, with all the benefits available it is important to know the landscape of plans. Here are some key questions and answers:

Which Retirement Plans Can Invest In Real Estate?

Retirement plans such as IRAs, Keoghs, SEPs and Roth IRAs are not subject to the same limitations as ERISA [Employment Retirement Income Security Act of 1974] plans. These more restrictive plans include 401(k)'s and many corporate defined benefit pension plans.

ERISA plans, such as the popular 401(k)s, cannot invest in real estate, but IRAs can. IRAs may also be self-directed, meaning that you can retain an independent trust company to serve as IRA trustee and direct them where to invest your retirement monies.

What Can't IRAs Invest In?

IRAs cannot invest in S corporations, life insurance or collectibles (such as paintings, antiques, gems, coins and oriental rugs). Almost all other investments are fair game so, for example, you can invest in real estate, bonds, trust deeds, notes, annuities and limited partnerships.

What Type Of Real Estate Is An Acceptable IRA Investment?

Your plan can invest in raw land, subdivided or improved land, single family homes, apartment buildings, multi-unit homes, co-ops and commercial property. If your plan purchased real estate for cash (no loan) from an unrelated party and you never use the property for personal reasons (nor do certain family members), then the investment is rather simple.

Can An IRA Use Debt To Acquire Real Estate?

Yes, but there are several restrictions.

First, the loan must be non-recourse, meaning that the lender may only look to the IRA-owned property as security for the loan. If the loan isn't paid back, the lender can only proceed against the property. They have no recourse, or right, to proceed against any other assets, meaning your other retirement monies.

Which is good for you, the borrower, but is also a reason why not many lenders make non-recourse loans. They want as much security as possible. (You would, too.) So then how do you obtain financing?

There are several ways. You can have the seller carry back a note. Seller financing is a good way to proceed. You can also have a friend make the loan using their own funds or IRA funds. Remember that if you fail to make the payments your 'friend' can end up with the property. Finally, if you put enough money down (say 50% or more) some banks may make a non-recourse loan. With a large down payment some lenders will feel comfortable in having only the property as security.

Another restriction is that you, as the plan beneficiary, cannot personally guarantee or even sign for the loan. As such, the plan and your plan trustee must sign the loan papers. Not all trustees are going to do this, so check ahead of time what your trustee is willing to do to assist in the securing of financing.

Another issue is that any income or profits related to the loan are subject to UBIT taxes.

What Are UBIT Taxes?

UBIT stands for Unrelated Business Income Tax. It is the tax on income and profits related to your leveraged, or financed, part of the transaction. So if you purchase a property for all cash (meaning there is no financing involved) you will not have a UBIT issue.

If financing is involved the tax is based on net income after all expenses and deductions are taken into account. As well, your first $1,000 of net income is not subject to the tax.

Assume your IRA buys a 4 plex for $400,000. You put $200,000 of your IRA money in as the down payment and the seller finances the $200,000 balance. Your net annual income is $10,000. The UBIT is calculated according to the relationship between the property's tax basis (purchase price plus improvements less depreciation) and the average amount of debt on the property during the preceding twelve months. (As the debt decreases each year so will the UBIT rate.)

Thus, in our example, with a 50% debt to tax basis ratio the UBIT is calculated as follows:

Net Income	$10,000
Less Exclusion	$1,000
Taxable Amount	$9,000
50% UBIT Ratio	$4,500 of $9,000
Trust Tax 37.5%	$1,687.50 ($4,500 x .375)

Remember that once this tax is paid, the balance (in this case the $10,000 income less the trust tax of $1,687.50 or $8,132.50) remains in your IRA tax free and can accumulate tax free.

What Are The Disqualified Person And Prohibited Transaction Restrictions?

Your plan cannot buy real estate from a disqualified person or enable an investment for yourself or another disqualified person.

Your plan may also not purchase real estate and then have a disqualified person use it while the plan owns it. A disqualified person includes:

- The owner of the plan
- The owner's spouse
- The owner's children or parents
- The spouse of a descendent (daughter-in-law or son-in-law)
- A fiduciary of the plan or person providing services to the plan
- An entity where at least 50% of the beneficial interest is owned by a disqualified person or an aggregate of disqualified persons
- A 10% owner, officer, director or highly compensated employee of such an entity

Remember, because the property must be purchased for investment purposes only, your business, your family members (except siblings) or you may not live in or rent the property while it is in the plan.

Beware of promoters who state that family vacation homes and other family use properties can be purchased with your IRA. Buying property with IRA funds for personal use is a prohibited transaction. As such, the IRS will treat the account as if all assets were distributed to the owner at their fair market value on the first day of the applicable tax year. If the value is greater than the owner's basis in the IRA, a tax on the gain will be due.

Steer clear of promoters who would put you in a prohibited transaction. These include:

- Using your IRA as security for a loan
- Borrowing money from it
- Selling property to it
- Buying property for personal use
- Receiving unreasonable compensation for management of it

What Are Checkbook IRAs?

Checkbook IRAs are offered by promoters who have no idea about (or, because they charge large fees, don't care about) the rules and restrictions associated with IRAs. With an IRA you cannot have control of or place any of the monies in an IRA account. You can, however, have an IRA trustee do this for you in a self-directed IRA. The trustee, not you, places the money for you. (Of course, you will pay a fee to the trustee for this service.) The promoters take this one step (one very costly step) further by allowing you to save on trustee fees by writing checks for the LLC that is owned by the IRA, hence the term checkbook IRA. The problem is that if you ever manage the money in your own IRA account (which a checkbook IRA allows you to do) you are subject to very high penalties and fees. The IRS position is that by managing your own IRA monies you have in essence withdrawn the monies and are now subject to early withdrawal penalties. You have also lost your tax free accumulation status. The point here is to stay away from the lures of the checkbook IRAs offered by promoters. With a checkbook IRA you will eventually be writing penalty checks back to the IRS.

What Are RMDs?

RMD stands for Required Minimum Distributions. While you *may* start to withdraw monies from your IRA account upon reaching age 59 ½ you *must* start receiving RMDs by April 1st of the year following the year you reach age 70 ½.

The RMD changes each year and is determined by dividing the account balance as of December 31st of the previous year by the applicable IRS life expectancy tables. As a general rule, the older you get, the more you must withdraw. Your IRA trustee or administrator can assist with calculating your RMD.

It is important to note that Roth IRAs are not subject to RMDs during the participant's lifetime. They are, however, subject to RMDs after the owner's death.

Loophole #20

If your IRAs are invested in real estate properties consider your situation as you approach age 70 ½. If your real estate is illiquid and you are facing the requirement of minimum distributions it may be time to sell one or more of the properties.

Now let's consider another excellent tax strategy for purchasing real estate...

Chapter Fourteen

Using Pre Tax Dollars to Buy Real Estate

Case #12
Carlos

Carlos owned Something Fishy, Inc., an aquarium sales and service business. He sold the expensive angelfish and koi and the less expensive goldfish and guppies to fish lovers throughout the city. And then, for the large percentage of his customers who didn't want to actually deal with cloudy water and its causes, he provided a mobile tank cleaning service. Business was good and he used after tax profits from his S-corporation to buy duplexes and 4 plexes around town. He knew he didn't want to be in the aquarium business forever and his goal was to build passive income from real estate for his retirement years.

While Carlos had been good at acquiring real estate for his own account he, like many others, had never known about a tax advantaged strategy for buying business real estate. This secret was revealed to him when he met with an attorney about asset protecting his properties.

The attorney asked about protecting his business real estate, assuming that Carlos owned the stand alone aquarium retail building he used. When Carlos said he leased the building from crusty old Hector who would never fix anything on time, the attorney smiled and said he had the last tax advantaged real estate acquisition loophole for him to consider.

Carlos was interested.

The attorney explained that Carlos, like virtually all business owners, needed a location for business operations. A location – be it a retail store, an office building, a warehouse or even an equipment storage yard – was a business necessity. As such, rent was a necessary business expense that had to be paid first before profits were calculated.

With rent as a write off then why not rent to yourself? Or, as the attorney further explained, why not let your business, which used pretax dollars for rent, buy you, the new landlord, a piece of real estate.

The light was coming on for Carlos. He had never considered such an option and he asked the attorney to chart it all out.

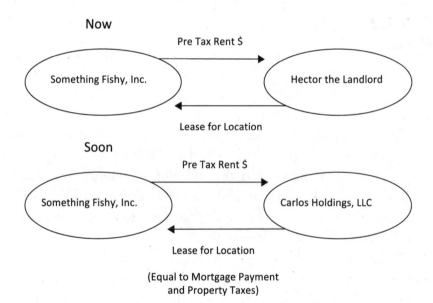

The attorney explained that Carlos would find a new location to purchase for the aquarium business. (He could also try and negotiate with old Hector to buy the existing location.) Once the new spot was located, Carlos would form an LLC or LP to acquire the property. He would use after tax dollars for the down payment on the building. Using pretax dollars from the business for the down payment would be inappropriate and could lead to a finding that the business owned the building. The attorney explained that for asset protection purposes you wanted the real estate to be separately owned. In this way, if the business was sued the real estate would be better protected, since it would be an asset owned in a single purpose LLC separate and apart from the business.

It was further explained that after Carlos paid the down payment with his own funds, the rest of the payments—the mortgage, utilities, property taxes and the like—would be paid by the business. That is, after Carlos' initial down payment, all other expenses would be paid by the business. The beneficial use of pre-tax dollars was underscored by the attorney. These were monies that the business could write off before calculating profits and before the payment on any profits of federal, state, local and payroll taxes. These were full one hundred cent dollars (and not after tax fifty cent dollars) put to good use, increasing Carlos' real estate portfolio.

The attorney further noted that there was no limit to the number of locations the business could buy for Carlos. If he wanted a second location on the west side of town, after paying the down payment the business could pay the mortgage and buy him another commercial property.

The attorney then explained that the U.S. Small Business Administration had loan programs to assist business owners in acquiring real estate. Known as the SBA 504 loan program, typically a bank and a Certified Development Company work to help small businesses with a net worth of less than $15 million and a net profit of less than $2 million. The program provides access to long-term fixed rate financing usually only available to larger companies. The business must occupy at least 50 percent of the space in the building to be acquired.

An SBA 504 loan allows for down payments as low as 10 percent versus 25 percent down required by most conventional lenders. After the 10 percent down, the bank in this type of transaction makes a loan for 50 percent of the cost of the real estate, and the SBA 504 loan will be for the remaining 40 percent.

The bank's loan will be in first lien position on the acquired real estate with the 504 loan being in second position. The maximum 504 loan portion is generally $5 million but the SBA does not limit the bank loan amount. SBA 504 loans have allowed business owners to purchase buildings valued at up to $15,000,000.

Some banks will only offer 10 year maturities, requiring owners to renew and pay renewal fees. (And if the market turns renewals can be difficult.) It is best to shop around for a bank that offers a 20 to 25 year fully amortized first lien position loan for peace of mind. For more information on SBA loans see my book *Finance Your Own Business*. The attorney said it was best for Carlos to talk to several SBA lenders about their programs.

Using your business to acquire real estate for your own personal portfolio is a strategy any business owner can pursue. And not only do smaller entrepreneurs like Carlos pursue it, some of the world's largest corporations do the same thing. There was no better example of this strategy than McDonalds. In fact, it could be said they weren't in the hamburger business but rather the real estate acquisition business. For while being known for flipping burgers, they didn't flip properties and McDonalds now owns billions and billions of dollars in real estate around the world. And what works for McDonalds can work for you.

Carlos liked the whole strategy. The attorney suggested that a lease between the business and the LLC owning the property would be appropriate. He also suggested that the business make one payment to the LLC each month. The LLC from its own separate bank account would then pay the mortgage, utilities and property taxes. The attorney noted it was important for the LLC to be seen as a distinct and separate entity.

Carlos found a new location for his business, and started having his business buy him real estate.

Loophole #21

The tax laws allow your business to buy a property for you using tax advantaged pre-tax dollars.

Now let's review some miscellaneous tax strategies...

Chapter Fifteen

Three Extra Tax Strategies

There are three extra tax strategies for real estate that are often overlooked. In the right situations they can work quite well for investors.

Installment Sale

There are several methods through which one can sell property now and be taxed on it later. We have already discussed one of the main tax deferral strategies, the 1031 Exchange. Another method is the installment sale.

An installment sale is a sale of property where the sale price is paid in installments and at least one payment is received after the tax year of the sale. So, for example, an installment sale could involve receiving a 10% down payment on a red brick duplex in December and a 90% full payment of the balance in January.

Through this method, a taxpayer can avoid paying the entire tax on the gain in the year of sale. So that in our red brick duplex example not all of the taxes on any gain would be due in December when only the 10% down payment was made. Instead, any taxes on gain would be spread out over the two tax years in which the payments were received. This can be a valuable technique, especially when, as in our example with only 10% down received in year one, not all the money is received the first taxable year. It is not pleasing or painless to pay taxes on profits you haven't yet received.

The installment method not only allows you to defer taxes, it can help with the marketability of your property as well. Because sellers have the flexibility to defer a substantial part of their gains, they may in turn be more flexible with the structure of an offer to their ultimate benefit. For example, accepting only a small cash down payment at the start may allow more buyers to get into the property. Thus, sellers have increased the market of potential buyers of their property. And, since price and terms are interrelated, a low down payment allowing the buyer in may provide the seller with the negotiating leverage to obtain an overall higher sales price.

Under current tax law the capital gains rate is 20% on properties held over one year. (This may include an additional 3.8% for upper income earners.) So by deferring from one year to the next, you may not save a great deal of money when the tax rate is constant. But what if the tax rate was to go down in future years? (It does happen.) Under that scenario, deferring taxes into future lower rate years would be beneficial. Similarly, what if you have short term capital gains on the sales of properties held less than a year? These gains are taxed at your ordinary income (i.e. salary) rate. Consider the consequences if you retired in two years so that, with no salary income, your tax rate dropped from 35% to 20%. You certainly could save money by deferring gains into future, lower tax rate years.

On the other hand, if you elected not to be taxed under the installment method then you would pay tax on the entire gain in the year that any money is first received. Again, if your current tax bracket is lower than it will be in the future years then paying the taxes now at a lower rate may be an option. For most people, however, deferring any tax may be the better choice, especially since paying taxes ahead of gains can be a difficult, out of pocket expense. Be sure to work with your tax professional to analyze which scenario is best for you.

Under the installment method, the seller typically accepts a promissory note from the buyer to pay the balance of the purchase price off in future years. (Hopefully, this promissory note is secured by a deed of trust against the property.) Any gain from the sale of property is pro-rated and based upon the ratio that the gross profit from the sale bears to the total contract price and taxes are then due on the pro-rated gains in each year in which the payments are received.

Case #13
Joe and Jane

Joe purchased a duplex for $148,500 and two years later sold it to Jane for $180,000. Jane paid Joe a down payment of $50,000 and Joe took back a purchase-money mortgage in the amount of $130,000 to be paid over 30 years beginning the following year.

Joe's gain from the sale (assuming he had no other expenses) would be $31,500 (or $180,000 less $148,500). By using the installment sale Joe only has to claim 17.5% of the down payment as capital gain. This percentage reflects the ratio between the $31,500 total gain Joe will realize from the sale and the $180,000 contract price (or $31,500 is 17.5% of $180,000). Thus Joe only has to claim $8,750 (or 17.5% times the $50,000 down payment) as capital gain the first year. Assuming a capital gain rate of 20% and no other offsets Joe will owe $1,750 in taxes in the first year (or 20% of $8,750 equals $1,750).

Each year thereafter whenever Joe receives payment he will only have to report 17.5% of the sales price payment as capital gain. As a separate matter, if you receive interest from the loan on the property such monies will be taxed at your ordinary income rate. Of course, if you do not charge a reasonable interest rate (generally in the 3% to 4% range) the IRS will impute (or assert) a rate for you.

Those classified as "dealers" by the IRS may not use the installment method of reporting sales. If you are a dealer and you sold your property through an installment sale you would have to pay tax on the gain up front, regardless of when or whether you actually received the money. As a general rule dealers are those who are in the trade or business of selling property, meaning they are active and consistent sellers of property. Be sure to work with your tax professional to analyze if dealer status applies to your specific situation.

Incomplete Contract of Sale

A dealer is permitted to defer his tax obligation if the contract for sale is incomplete. It is important to note that just because a contract for the sale of real property has been entered into does not mean that a "sale" for tax purposes has occurred. In order to be a taxable event the property transfer must be a completed sale. Whether a contract is a completed sale depends upon the obligations of the parties to the sale and the contract language. If the sale is considered to be incomplete, then the seller does not have to pay any tax on his gain until the entire contract is paid off and the title is transferred. This tax strategy can be useful for dealers of real estate.

So what determines if the sales contract is completed or not completed? In a Private Letter Ruling the IRS summarized when the sale is complete:

1. Whether the amount of and right to the purchase price is fixed and unqualified.
2. Whether the obligation to convey title on final payment of the purchase price is absolute.
3. Whether the buyer has taken possession or has the legal right to possession.
4. Whether the buyer has otherwise assumed the benefits and burdens of ownership.

It is clear that the presence of all these factors would compel the conclusion that a sale has occurred; moreover, since a single factor is not controlling, the absence of any one of them would not compel the conclusion that a sale had not occurred.

Let's review each of the factors individually as none but number 3 is terribly self-explanatory.

Whether the amount of and right to the purchase price is fixed and unqualified.

If you are selling a piece of property you are going to have a fixed price, otherwise there would be nothing to enforce should there be a default in payment. So, this is one factor you will certainly want to meet. But fear not, there are three others to beat.

Whether the obligation to convey title on final payment of the purchase price is absolute.

This requirement essentially refers to whether or not the contract has non-recourse language. With no-recourse language the seller may never receive the payment of consideration and therefore is under no absolute obligation to deliver the title. In a relevant case where the contract at issue specifically said that there was no recourse, the Tax Court stated that the sellers did not have an "unqualified right to recover the consideration for their old residence...until they were paid in full." The Tax Court then upheld the sale as incomplete based upon this one factor. Unfortunately, the appeals court disagreed and overturned the decision saying: "the 'no recourse' paragraph of the contract should be looked on as only one of the conditions of the total transaction." So having the no-recourse language will help you on your way to an incomplete contract, but you will need at least one additional factor to get you there.

Whether the buyer has taken possession or has the legal right to possession.

Does the buyer have possession of the property? Most likely, yes. It would be very difficult indeed to get a buyer to agree to pay you for possession when they have to live elsewhere. One more factor is met.

Whether the buyer has otherwise assumed the benefits and burdens of ownership.

You need to have this question answered in the negative in order have the incomplete contract. Make sure when you draft your contract that all or most of the following are true:

- The buyer is not responsible for insuring the property
- The buyer does not have the right to rent the property and keep the profit
- The buyer does not have the duty to maintain the property
- The buyer is not obligated to pay taxes, assessments and charges against the property
- The buyer does not have the right to improve the property without the seller's consent
- The buyer does not have the right to obtain legal title to the property by paying off the contract at any time

If the majority of the above are true and there is no-recourse language in your sales contract then for federal purposes you most likely have an incomplete contract.

It is important to bear in mind that the incomplete contract for sale strategy also relies on state law. How each state defines title transfer is important. Do not try to put this strategy into effect without a complete understanding of its rules and the laws of the state in which the property is located. Be sure to work with your legal and tax advisors to make certain the incomplete contract of sale will work for you. If it works, dealers may be able to defer taxes into future years.

Charitable Remainder Trust

Another tax strategy involves charity.

A charitable remainder trust (CRT) is a way for a philanthropic-minded owner of a property that has greatly appreciated in value to earn an income-tax deduction, contribute to a worthy charity and provide an income stream for beneficiaries—all at the same time, and while the property owner-donor is alive.

There are two notes of caution surrounding CRTs. First, it is imperative to know that once a CRT is formed, it is irrevocable. The property will remain in the trust and out of your reach. You can't change your mind once the trust is formed and funded. However, the charitable beneficiary—the charity you want to benefit—can be changed, if desired.

Second, you must have a charitable intent. Beware of promoters selling CRTs as a way to avoid taxes. Unless you don't want the assets working for you in the future, do NOT set up a CRT. If charity is your intent, here is how a CRT can work:

- You donate your property to the CRT, receiving a tax deduction calculated on the current value of the interest the charity will receive. (And because the property is no longer considered part of your estate, it will not be subjected to estate taxation after your death.)

- The CRT can sell the property without incurring tax on the sale.

- The CRT will invest this principal, and while you're alive the profits will go to specified beneficiaries (such your children), based on the amount of income the assets generate and the payout percentage the donor has specified. (As of this printing, the IRS requires a minimum distribution of 5 percent of fair market value of the assets).

- After your death, the charity will receive the principal. Again, the principal will not be there for your children or other beneficiaries upon your passing. Still, for some a CRT is a good tax strategy.

Case #14
Tyson

Tyson thought that he had it all: a great job, a big and ever growing stock brokerage account, a fat 401(k) plan and the vision and means for a luxurious retirement in paradise. But with the financial collapse, everything had changed. The great job was grating with worthless stock options offering no incentive, the brokerage account was broke, the 401 (k) plan was thin and retirement was a distant vision. Tyson would be working for a lot longer than he ever anticipated.

But Tyson had made one smart and totally unintended investment decision along the way. He never thought about it during his hectic work years. It was almost more of a nuisance then. But now, with real estate values rising again, it was becoming his biggest asset.

Tyson lived in Albany, a quaint, small and desirable city north of Berkeley along the east side of San Francisco Bay. He had purchased his two bedroom bungalow style house in 1982 for $95,000. He was single, the house was comfortable and he liked the neighborhood and his neighbors. Until the rowdies moved in next door.

They were students at the nearby University of California. Six of them lived, laughed and yelled in the adjoining two bedroom bungalow. The wild neighbors consistently proved that the music of Aerosmith and ZZ Top did not get any better the louder it got. The neighborhood was kept awake every Thursday, Friday and Saturday night as well as Monday nights during football season. All of the neighbors, led by Tyson, complained to the absentee landlord, the police, the community board, the city council and to whoever would listen.

Finally, a city councilman dropped by Tyson's house as an all-night party was being held next door at the Animal House bungalow. With this shocking revelation of rowdy neighbors the government wheels began to move.

The owner of the bungalow had moved to Southern California. He was getting sick and tired of the nasty neighborhood letters and police complaints. When the city councilman called demanding a solution to the problem the landlord offered to sell the house for $125,000, a price that was $15,000 above market in 1985. When this high handed solution was offered to the neighbors no one bit. Except Tyson.

He realized that by controlling the house next door he would better be able to enjoy his own property. He was a not a real estate investor. Instead, he considered the purchase a necessary quality of life expense.

Over the years Tyson rented the bungalow to quiet professors and solitary writers. The neighborhood revered him as the neighbor who stepped up for everyone's peace and tranquility. But then a funny thing happened. As Tyson's old high tech options and retirement plan began to fade, the bungalow began to appreciate. More and more families and professionals wanted to live in Albany at the same time prices throughout San Francisco Bay Area had recovered and were now rising again. The bungalow was now worth $900,000 and with the mortgage long since paid off Tyson owned it free and clear.

With no stock portfolio to speak of the bungalow was now his most valuable asset. And as Tyson neared retirement he considered ways in which to tap into the totally unintended pool of equity that sat next door. Tyson looked into a 1031 exchange but that did not appeal to him. He was an accidental real estate investor and he did not really want to own more real estate. He looked into selling the house but didn't quite like the idea of paying a capital gains tax.

Then Tyson learned from a lawyer friend about charitable remainder trusts, or CRTs. By placing the house in a CRT the house could be sold tax free. While the sales proceeds pass into a charity upon the donor's death the trust pays the individual an income in the form of annual fixed-dollars or a fixed percentage of the asset or proceeds' value.

Tyson liked the sound of this strategy. Because he was never married and he had no children to consider for estate planning, he liked the idea of being able to benefit his favorite charity. And because charity begins at home he also liked the idea of a fixed annual income through his retirement years.

The lawyer made certain Tyson understood the key downsides to using a CRT. Once established the trust was irrevocable, meaning that the principal was beyond his control. If Tyson had a medical emergency or wanted to send his nephew to college the trust monies (absent his annual payments) could not be reached.

Tyson acknowledged his understanding that the trust principal would be placed irrevocably beyond his control. And with that Tyson's lawyer friend set up the CRT and the house next door was contributed into the trust. The house was sold by the CRT to a quiet family without having to recognize any capital gains. The proceeds were then invested into low-risk bonds and index funds. The CRT provided that Tyson would receive a 5 percent annual payment based on the total value of the trust's assets.

The result was that Tyson received $45,000 a year from the Trust. This money was subjected to income tax, but when Tyson was fully retired he was of course in a lower tax bracket.

Tyson appreciated the annual income he received and the irony of how his retirement plan came about. Once a year, at the annual 4th of July picnic, he and the old neighbors turned up the head banger music real loud and remembered the rowdies and the rich rewards for getting rid of them.

Loophole #22

Charitable remainder trusts are an excellent tax loophole in the right circumstances. But beware of promoters selling them as a way to avoid taxes. And be sure to work with a tax professional as the rules can be complicated and onerous.

Now that we have maximized our tax advantages let's explore the legal side of things...

Part Four:
Legal Strategies

You have just learned many of the key tax advantages to owning real estate. Now it is time for an equally important task in today's litigious society: Learning the legal advantages necessary to protect the property, as well as you and your family, from the risks of ownership.

It is important to note that the legal strategies to be used, just like the tax strategies previously discussed, do not happen automatically. There is not some benevolent protector out there who instinctively structures everything for you to maximum advantage. Instead, if you want maximum advantage, you need to take two affirmative steps. First, you and your advisors must understand and appreciate the strategies. Second, and more importantly, you and your team must move to implement these strategies on your behalf. As the architect of your own defense plan, you must put into place your own legal loopholes to limit liability.

So as soon as you are in contract to buy that first piece of property, you need to start thinking about how to protect it. And if you already own real estate in your individual name, you must immediately consider the many risks of such ownership and the legal advantages our legal system offers to better protect you. Please note that when we speak of protection, we are speaking in very broad terms. We want to protect not only the property you will (or have) acquired but also all of your personal property, your other real estate, and your other assets as well. We are building castle walls here. We are creating a structure to defend you and your family.

The concern for protection is basic. Real estate involves risk. And when risk is not properly managed, demands, litigation, and money judgments can arise. These can lead to the exposure (and loss) of your personal assets.

What are some of the risks associated with owning real estate? First and foremost is the risk of injury. If a tenant or a tenant's guest falls at your property, you can be held liable for allowing a dangerous condition to exist. (Whether or not you knew of the problem may or may not be determinative.)

You'll want to have insurance coverage in place to cover such risks. Insurance is your first line of defense. But insurance companies don't cover every claim. Many insurance companies deny coverage for hurricanes on the basis that it was water, and not wind, that caused the problem. (What's the difference? Besides millions of dollars in denied claims?) If you can't rely on your insurance company in every case, what can be done? Read on and learn the legal loopholes our system offers the rich (and all of us) to better protect valuable assets.

Real estate also involves obligations. You will sign contracts and agreements and mortgage documents. And there is a risk that you may not be able to perform all of the promises you have made. Will you be personally responsible for all your obligations? It depends on how your affairs are structured, and how well you have utilized the legal advantages and strategies that exist.

Another underappreciated risk comes from environmental liability. If there are toxins on your property, whether you put them there or not, you can be held liable for potentially huge remediation costs. Innocent landowners, whose only misstep was to be involved in a toxic property's chain of title, have been wiped out, both financially and emotionally, from environmental liabilities.

For these and related reasons, it is imperative that you know the legal and financial risks before you buy a property. And once again, equally important is knowing, appreciating and actually implementing the legal advantages our laws and courts afford you.

These strategies have been used for centuries by the rich to protect themselves. Which is why the singular term 'loophole', over half a millennia ago, came to mean a defensive or escape maneuver used by those well connected people in the know. And these strategies are now available to all of us today, by taking affirmative steps forward.

So in using the legal system to our advantage, let us start by protecting your primary residence...

Chapter Sixteen

Personal Residence Protection

Case #15
Ogelthorpe

Ogelthorpe was wrongly accused. He had been framed. The tabloids said he'd killed his wife. He was nowhere near the scene of the crime.

But Oglethorpe was a celebrity, a public figure. So the tabloids could say whatever they wanted about him. Even if it bore an inexact relation to the truth. Live in the spotlight. Die in the spotlight.

Ogelthorpe had been a star athlete and had used that fame to get into the movies. He was a likeable lug and got his fair shot at roles where he played the buddy to the main lead. His celebrity led to endorsement deals and a comfortable, if frenetic, lifestyle on Hollywood's A circuit.

And then murder. He swore to everyone he didn't do it. He loved his wife, in spite of her infuriating, fetishistic love of thousands of lit candles that, on numerous occasions, had almost burned the mansion down.

A jury of his peers found him innocent of murder in a criminal trial. The evidence wasn't there—it didn't fit, so they had to acquit. But his wife's family brought a civil action against Ogelthorpe for the loss of their daughter.

The new jury didn't have to worry about whether Ogelthorpe, the well-known celebrity, should go to jail or not. Their issue was just whether the deceased wife's family should get some money. Ogelthorpe bitterly predicted that in today's blame-everyone-else society, the jury would throw cash at the poor, hurt family. If the money is there, you've got to share. True to Ogelthorpe's prediction, millions of dollars were awarded to the family.

But Ogelthorpe knew some good attorneys. He had partied with the best of them in his years in Hollywood. And these guys knew every trick in the book.

Move to Florida, they said. Use Florida's incredible homestead laws to protect your assets from these ridiculous claims.

Ogelthorpe wondered what a homestead was. His big-dog lawyer explained that it was a way to protect the equity in your house. Homesteads were governed by state law and each state had a different limit.

In California, for example, the homestead exemption was $75,000 for a single person and $100,000 for a married couple. Ogelthorpe was now single. The attorney explained that if your house was worth $500,000 and your mortgage was down to $425,000, you had $75,000 in equity in your home.

But Ogelthorpe pointed out that $75,000 wouldn't help much. His house was a full-scale mansion, valued at $9.5 million, and he held it free and clear.

That's why you move to Florida, his lawyer explained. They have an unlimited homestead exemption. As long as your house sits on a lot no larger than one acre, no one can take your home in Florida, no matter how many millions of dollars of equity you have in it.

And so Ogelthorpe exchanged his expensive home in California for an even more expensive home in Florida. He filed a homestead on his new home and was protected to the maximum extent by Florida law. And in Florida he joined a unique collection of stockbrokers, corporate executives, and other unfortunates who had been severely mistreated by the United States system of justice.

Using the Homestead Exemption to Protect Your Primary Residence

As our case points out, homesteads can be an extremely valuable technique for protecting a very important real estate asset–your personal residence–from the claims of others.

Homestead exemptions were started in Texas in the late 1830s, as a way to induce settlers to leave the United States and come to the then independent Republic of Texas to develop the land. Of course, the Texans wanted the Americans as a hedge against the Mexicans. And the homestead worked like a charm. The incentive was powerful for farmers and ranchers who wanted to protect their land from creditors, and homestead laws soon spread to other states as a useful economic development tool. The benefits of homesteads were used to attract European farmers to the United States in the 1870s and 1880s.

Because each state had (and has) different economic development strategies, each state's homestead law is different. Although the size of the property in acres is usually limited, Texas, Florida, Kansas, Iowa, and Oklahoma allow homesteads for an unlimited dollar amount. Pennsylvania, New Jersey, and Delaware offer no homestead exemptions. A chart detailing each state's homestead exemption laws can be found at www.corporatedirect.com/homestead-exemptions/.

As a general rule, a person can only have one valid homestead at a time. Also, homesteads usually only apply to real estate owned and occupied as a principal residence. Subject to that constraint, condominiums and co-ops are generally protected and in some states so are mobile homes.

While each state may have variances, generally a homestead does not protect one against debts secured by a mortgage or deed of trust on the property, IRS liens and the payment of taxes, mechanics' liens, child support, and alimony payments. If you file bankruptcy, a lower bankruptcy homestead rate may apply. But for other general claims–business and personal loans, credit card debt and accidents–a homestead can preclude the seizure or forced sale of your personal residence.

In Florida the policy protects homeowners to the greatest extent. The Florida Supreme Court has ruled that converting nonexempt property (cash or other property subject to immediate seizure) to an unlimited exempt homestead (a multimillion-dollar home situated on one acre of land or less) is quite all right, even if the purpose is to defraud an existing creditor. Which is why Ogelthorpe was seen running through airports in a rush to Florida.

Using Qualified Personal Residence Trusts To Protect Your Home

A second protection (and tax savings device) is the Qualified Personal Residence Trust, or QPRT, pronounced Q-pert and rhyming with Hubert. Because the QPRT is such a creature of complex regulation it can be difficult to explain it simply. So if you don't completely get this next passage, don't worry. You are not alone. If you can just get a sense of what the QPRT does–passes the home from mom and dad to the kids with some real tax savings–you will be fine.

Okay, let's get technical.

A Qualified Personal Residence Trust (QPRT) is a special type of trust allowed by IRS regulations. (See, 26 C.F.R. 25.2702-5.) It basically is an estate-planning device used to transfer mom or dad's (or both's) residence out of their estate at a low gift tax value. (From here on, mom or dad or both will sometimes be called the settlor, meaning they are setting up the QPRT.) A gift to the QPRT of their home (usually to family members) removes all residences from the settlor's estate, thereby reducing potential estate taxes upon the settlor's death.

Under a QPRT, the settlor transfers his or her personal residence to an irrevocable trust, while retaining the right to live in the residence for a fixed number of years. Although the settlor makes a taxable gift when the property is transferred to the trust, if mom or dad survives until the end of the trust term, the ownership of the residence is transferred to their beneficiaries (most often their kids). Once the trust is funded with the settlor's residence, the residence and any future appreciation of the residence is excluded from their estate, which can be a big help if the value of their home is gaining value over the years.

Under the regulations, an individual is permitted to create two QPRTs: (1) one for a principal residence; and (2) one for an occasional residence (a vacation home). Again, once the parents transfer title to the QPRT they still retain the right to live in the residence for a specified period of time ("fixed year schedule"). During that fixed year schedule the parent would pay no rent, but would be responsible for all the expenses of the home. If the parent is still alive at the end of that period of time, then the residence would pass to their children free of estate tax. Once the kids take title, the parents can still live in the house, but they have to pay rent at the going rate.

Importantly, if mom or dad passes away during the fixed year schedule then the entire value of the property would be includable in their estate. In that case, nothing would have been accomplished. The QPRT would not have passed title to the kids. But know that nothing would have been lost either. You are in the same boat if you hadn't used a QPRT to begin with.

The tax advantage of a QPRT stems from the fact that, when the residence is transferred, the taxpayer (read mom or dad) does not pay gift tax on the full fair market value of the property. Instead, the gift is computed on the value of the property, reduced by the value of the interest that the taxpayer has retained. If the taxpayer dies before the trust has terminated, then the residence will be included in the taxpayer's taxable estate, and estate tax will be paid on it, because the settlor retained the use of the property for a period that did not end before his or her death. Again, the purpose of the trust will have been defeated. On the other hand, if the taxpayer does not die during the trust term, then the property will be distributed to his or her children without further taxation.

Thus, when the trust term is relatively long (i.e. 10 years) the value of the gift to the remainder beneficiaries will be relatively low, and the gift tax cost of transferring the residence to the trust will be correspondingly low. On the other hand, when the trust term is relatively short (i.e. two years) the value of the gift to the remainder beneficiaries will be relatively high, and the gift tax cost of transferring the residence to the trust will be correspondingly high. However, the lower gift tax cost that results from a relatively long trust term must be weighed against the greater risk that the residence will be included in the settlor's gross estate if he or she dies before the expiration of the trust term. In summary, this is definitely the time to work with a tax professional.

The next question becomes: Can a QPRT be used as an asset-protection device?

A QPRT is an irrevocable trust. Consequently, a gift of a settlor's personal residence (or vacation home) to a QPRT is a gift to a separate person (the trust). A judgment against the QPRT's settlors (mom or dad) would not encumber the property transferred to the QPRT, provided that the transfer to the QPRT was made prior to mom or dad being sued.

Even so, a creditor of the settlor conceivably could argue that the transfer to the QPRT was a "fraudulent transfer" made to "hinder, delay or defraud" the creditor, within the meaning of the Uniform Voidable Transactions Act (UVTA). However, if the transfer to the QPRT was made prior to the entry of the judgment, a creditor's argument is not guaranteed to work. Mom and dad will be able to argue that the primary reason for the transfer to the QPRT was to reduce the estate taxes, and that they used a substantial portion of their uniform estate and gift tax credit in order to transfer their home to the QPRT. The argument of 'I did it for estate planning and not asset protection' is always a good one.

However, mom and dad's fixed year schedule to stay in the house rent free has some value. Could a creditor go after mom's right to stay in a Beverly Hills mansion rent free for five years? Sure they could. That would be a valuable asset. A creditor could turn around and rent out the house for a significant sum of money. So in high dollar matters, sometimes the fixed year schedule of rent-free use of the house is held by a separate LLC. Set up in the right state, which discussion lies ahead, there would be no monetary distribution to receive, and thus no reason to go after the LLC. Frivolous litigation denied.

For asset protection and tax savings a QPRT is a good strategy for a personal residence.

Loophole #23

Homesteads and QPRTs are protective loopholes allowed by statute. And because legislatures meet, laws change. So be sure to work with your up-to-date professional advisors when considering and implementing these strategies.

With your primary residence protected to the greatest extent possible, it is appropriate to shield yourself from personal liability in all of your other real estate dealings. To fully understand why this must be a part of your future, it is useful to look back in time...

Chapter Seventeen

Land Ownership and Notice Requirements

As with the historical meaning of loopholes, the legal relationship between landlords and tenants can be traced to medieval Europe, where the king reigned over all the land. The king would allow a select group of lords to each take control of a parcel of land in return for their contributions of money, military service, favors and loyalty. The lord was given absolute control over his parcel of land, and answered to no one except the king. This is the origin of the term landlord—the idea of one being the lord of his land.

The lord would often give others the right to live on his land as long as they performed all of the necessary maintenance. These people that worked the lord's land were called serfs in feudal times, referring to their service to the lord. They would work the land, care for animals and construct homes and other buildings to make the land valuable, but received no rights -- or respect. They were never in the position to actually own the land they worked. This is the origin of our modern idea of tenancy. In order to have the right to use a piece of land, there are certain responsibilities expected of the tenant. The word tenant comes from the Latin word *tenere*, which means to hold. Today, the legal meaning of the word tenant refers to the person who holds certain legal rights to the land.

During England's feudal times, lords only owned their land until their death, at which time the land would revert back to the king's ownership. If the lord's family wanted to continue holding the land, they were charged a hefty fee. It wasn't until 1290 that owners gained the right to freely sell or transfer their land. This change made families even more protective of their land because they had the opportunity to hold it for generations and even centuries.

Fortunately, for habitability purposes, the relationship between landlords and tenants has evolved over the years. Landlords are expected to keep their rentals at least up to code and habitable. Tenants no longer are expected to rent a place "as is." Mechanical skills have become less valued by society, thus making it harder to demand that tenants make all their own repairs and perform all maintenance. Therefore, landlords are now responsible for many aspects of property maintenance. Tenants have also gained the right to quietly enjoy their property. This means in part, at least in most jurisdictions, that the landlord cannot come on to the property without notifying the tenant in advance.

So while most of the laws concerning the landlord/tenant relationship have evolved with time, they can all be traced back to the feudal model of kings, lords, and serfs as practiced in medieval times. So, in order to lord over your real estate, it is important to know the following:

Four Types of Ownership

Modern times have brought four types of ownership. These four types and their characteristics are as follows:

- **Fee Estates**: This type of estate provides absolute ownership for an indefinite period of time. Though use is somewhat limited by governmental land use restrictions, a fee owner has the right to do whatever he or she wants to do with the land. This also allows the owner to sell, lease or give the land away as they see fit. When buying an estate, this is the most desirable type of ownership since it allows you to do what you want with your land.

- **Life Estates:** This interest occurs when the titleholder grants the tenant possession of the property, lasting the tenant's lifetime. The lifetime tenant is responsible for taxes and repairs until their death, at which time the possession of the house reverts back to the titleholder.

- *Estates at Will:* Occurs when a fee owner allows a tenant to use the property for free. Estates at will terminate at the will of the fee owner once they have given the tenant proper notice.

- *Leasehold Estates:* This occurs when a fee owner grants a tenant the right to possess the property for a pre-determined amount of time. This is the typical landlord/tenant agreement in which the fee owner retains the title while the tenant possesses and uses the property for the term of the lease.

There are different types of leasehold estates, characterized by their measure of time and term. These variations include:

1. *Fixed-Term Tenancy (or a Lease):* This is tenancy for a fixed term. At the date of termination, the tenant's possession automatically comes to an end. However, entering into a new lease at this time can extend the agreement and continue the tenancy.

2. *Periodic Tenancy (or a Rental):* Rental or periodic tenancy agreements can be year-to-year, month-to-month, or week-to-week. The time period is determined based on the time between rental payments. The most common type of periodic tenancy is a month-to-month agreement. These types of agreements can only be terminated with timely notice. In the case of a month-to-month rental, a thirty-day notice of termination from either the landlord or tenant is considered to be proper notice.

3. *Tenancy at Will:* This is similar to an estate at will when a tenant possesses the property for an undetermined amount of time without making payments. Unless otherwise specified, the agreement terminates with the death of either the tenant or the landlord. When terminating the agreement before such an event, the landlord must give the tenant proper notice.

Since the terms of each leasehold agreement are so different, each type also has a different definition of what characterizes proper notice should either the landlord or tenant wish to terminate the lease.

For example, the Fixed-Term tenancy agreement expires on a certain date. No notice must be given in this situation since the terms of the agreement specify this date as the date of termination. If a tenant stays past this date without negotiating a new lease, procedures to evict the tenant can proceed.

Notice for Periodic Tenancy agreements is given in accordance with the period between rental payments. This means that a tenant making weekly payments requires only a week's notice. A tenant on a month to month agreement must be given thirty days' notice. If the tenant remains on the property after the period of notice has run out, the landlord may evict the tenant.

While all these periods of notice may vary according to state law, the general rule is that thirty days' notice must be given to a tenant at will.

Once a lease, rental or at-will tenancy agreement expires, either automatically or by giving notice, the tenant is considered to be holding over. This results in tenancy at sufferance. Once a tenant is holding over, they do not require any notice because any agreement you made no longer applies. These tenants can be evicted.

As a landlord, you most certainly will have to evict a tenant at some point. While this is not something that anyone likes to do, it may become necessary. Owning rentals is a business. Any tenant that is not paying what they owe, or is otherwise hurting your business, must be removed. It is incredible to me that some in our society see their cable television bill as more important than rent. They wouldn't ever let their cable TV be turned off for failure to pay the bill. But they are quite willing for you to keep paying the mortgage so that they have shelter and can watch their cable. Always remember that this is a business, and that you must do what is in your best interests.

It is recommended that you recruit a knowledgeable local attorney who represents landlords in eviction cases before you even buy your first property. Ask people you trust, such as your CPA, friends, and others who own rentals for an attorney they would recommend. While most times you will be able to handle an eviction on your own, it is reassuring knowing that someone is behind you if things ever turn ugly.

Now you know that there are many types of lease agreements, and that each of these tenancy types requires a different notice requirement. Knowing the notice requirement for your agreement is key in evictions. Some requirements can even differ by state. As a landlord, it is important that you are knowledgeable about eviction laws in order to properly serve your tenants and to protect yourself against lawsuits.

Case #16
Cari and Chad

Cari owned an old Victorian house located near the University. The house had been renovated so that it now contained two apartments. A professor who just moved to the area with his wife and two young daughters lived on the top floor. He loved the location because of the proximity to his classroom. And he was always timely with his rental payments.

Chad, an absent minded herpetologist, lived on the first floor. He was forgetful with his rent and forgetful about whether his reptiles, snakes and various other crawling creatures were in their cages or not.

Needless to say, the professor, his wife, and especially their children did not enjoy the creepy crawlers on the stairways and the porch. They had complained more than once to Cari about Chad's behavior. She began to realize that Chad was a problematic tenant and she would have to do something about it.

Chad's lease was a periodic month-to-month agreement, yet he usually forgot to pay the rent on time, if at all. Cari knew from her previous experience with rentals that Chad's periodic lease only required her to give him thirty days' notice in order to terminate the lease. If he did not move out by the time the thirty days was up, she would be able to evict him.

However, Cari knew if she didn't do something sooner than that, she might lose the responsible tenants she really wanted to keep: The family living upstairs. Once Chad was late with his next payment, Cari contacted her attorney to see if there was anything she could do.

He advised Cari to serve Chad with a three-day notice to pay rent or to leave the property. The notice stated the exact amount of rent Chad owed, which is a requirement in most states for such a notice. The notice also stated that if the rent was not paid within three days, the landlord would forfeit the lease and take hold of the property.

After four days, Chad contacted Cari and said he was ready to pay the rent. Cari refused to take the rent, telling Chad that he had missed the deadline and he now must vacate the apartment. Chad hung up the phone while hissing expletives.

Cari went to her attorney and asked him to file an unlawful detainer action to evict Chad. He claimed that he had tried to pay Cari the rent he owed, but she would not accept it. However, the court noted that Chad's lease agreement was terminated only after he had not paid the rent within the three days outlined in the notice and that Cari had opted to forfeit Chad's right to possession.

Chad and his creepy creatures were evicted from the building.

This example is used to show you that sometimes you do not have to wait the required thirty days or more to end a lease agreement. However, a three-day notice like the one given to Chad cannot be used if a tenant fails to pay late charges. This is considered only a minor breach. But if a tenant has not paid rent, conducts criminal activity on the property, or is destructive to the property, the lease agreement can be promptly terminated. The three-day notice is delivered and the lease is terminated, thus restoring possession to the landlord.

If a tenant still refuses to leave the property, eviction proceedings must follow. If the tenant still doesn't leave after you've won your eviction proceeding, the sheriff may have to be called to forcibly remove the tenant.

Some states also differ on these laws. For example, some states serve a five-day notice instead of a three-day notice. In order to learn your state's laws, consult with an attorney in your area. Keep in mind that even if two states have the same laws, one state's court may be more lenient or strict with the tenant than another state's court may be.

Loophole #24

The notice requirements for leaseholds have evolved over time. But remember their original historical purpose–to allow landlords a loophole to get their property back. While some states have become very tenant friendly, in the end the landlord will always retain possession.

But of even greater consequence than notice is...

Chapter Eighteen

Landlord Liability

The need for landlords to legally protect their assets stems from the heavy responsibilities the laws impose on landlords in managing their properties. Consider the following case.

Case #17
Karen, Guy, Bruce and Davy

Karen lived in Viewmont, which in the last five years had been discovered. Now it was a regular occurrence for artists and authors, families and empty nesters from large cities and suburbs to move into the scenic little mountain town. In response Karen decided to turn her quaint two-bedroom brick house near the town square into a rental property. Stretching her assets, she then bought a larger house in a new development on the outskirts of town. Karen felt that both properties should continue to appreciate in value as Viewmont's population swelled.

Karen was the only psychologist within a hundred mile radius and had well managed her small practice. She had conservatively husbanded her savings with frugal spending, and was not burdened by the costs of raising a family. Prudent in her affairs, she quickly grasped the business of a first-time landlord, and screened prospective tenants until she settled on a couple of artists: Guy and Bruce, who came with impeccable references.

They proved a good choice. They paid the rent on time, kept the house clean and tastefully decorated, and showed a talent for gardening. The only problem was the walkway to the front porch. It was uneven and cracked due to tree roots underneath. Guy had tripped on one of the large cracks and had asked Karen to fix it. Guy suggested that at the very least, better lighting on the walkway was needed so the cracks would be highlighted on dark evenings. Karen said she would consider the requests but nothing was ever done.

Three months later Viewmont was hit with a series of fierce winter storms. Even the old-timers couldn't recall such heavy snowfall. The mercury plunged. The drifts piled up and froze over, turning the city's streets into empty corridors of ice for several days.

Karen drove her truck over to the rental house as soon as she could. The pipes were in good order and the furnace was working well. She left her tenants a snow shovel and a bag of deicing pellets she had purchased at a home-supply store.

As the residents of Viewmont dug out of the blizzard, another storm rolled in. Davy, an acquaintance of Guy and Bruce's, visited late one evening. The uneven walkway was frozen and, as usual, was not well lit. Davy slipped and fell hard—fracturing his elbow and smacking his head so hard he suffered a bad concussion. He racked up tens of thousands of dollars in medical bills and could not return to his waiter's job for several months.

After visiting a personal-injury attorney, Davy sued not only Guy and Bruce, but Karen, too. Through his attorney, Davy claimed that Karen, through the exercise of ordinary care, should have ensured that there was adequate lighting at the house and the walkway was properly maintained.

Karen, through her attorney, said that her tenants were responsible for such maintenance. Neither side would budge, so the case went to trial, at which a jury sided with Davy. The fact that Karen had known the walkway was not well lit and could be dangerous—even bringing a shovel and a deicer to her tenants—was determinative. She had failed to ensure it was safe and clear. The jury applied the law as it exists in most states.

If the landlord is aware of a dangerous condition on her or his leased premises and does not take steps to remedy such a condition, the landlord can be liable for injuries resulting to others.

Karen's insurance company asserted that she had wrongfully allowed a dangerous condition to exist on the property. The company, as certain lesser insurance companies will do, declined coverage of the claim. Karen had not taken the steps to protect her assets. She lost a great deal of them at trial.

The Duty of Care

Over time, the legal concept of duty of care has evolved in concert with the objectives of another concept: Public policy. Public policy is the overall vision guiding jurists and lawmakers to achieve a social good. In the case of Karen's walkway, that social good is the prevention of unnecessary and avoidable injuries to innocents such as Davy, who was just walking to his friends' front door.

Case law and legislation by lawmakers across the country have established the public policy that landlords exercise reasonable care in managing their properties to prevent foreseeable injuries to others. Consequently, this duty of care is owed by landlords to all people — whether they live on the premises, are visiting as guests or even trespassing. That last category pushed the concept of duty of care into a gray area in respects to trespassers who are on a property with intent to commit a felony, such as theft. Resulting public outcry after several court decisions held that property owners owed a duty of care to those injured while illegally on a property led to laws in many states negating landlord liability to criminals. Had Davy, for example, been a burglar skulking up the walkway at night unexpected by the tenants, with the intent of breaking into Karen's house, she would be free of liability in most states.

Aside from that exception, a landlord who is cognizant—or should have been cognizant—of a perilous situation on his or her property will be held responsible for injuries incurred on that property. A point the courts will consider in deeming liability is the cost and availability of insurance to cover the risk. If a landlord fails to carry an easily purchased and reasonably priced insurance policy, it can cost the landlord even more. (Whether your insurance company will cover the claim is a separate issue.)

The best overall strategy for a landlord is threefold: To understand and meet the requirements of duty of care, to carry enough insurance to cover unforeseen claims and to have further protection with the proper legal entity.

The Duty to Inspect

Inherent in the duty of care to prevent injuries is that a landlord has a duty to inspect the property for unsafe conditions. A reasonable inspection is required every time the landlord renews, extends or first enters into a rental agreement. Negligence in inspecting the premises at such times leaves the landlord vulnerable later on to being charged with foreknowledge of an unsafe condition that the landlord should have found during the inspection.

Case #18
Eddie, Judy and the Bar

Eddie and Judy were very hard workers, and had turned a small, mom-and-pop convenience store into a little chain of E&J Markets on the central coast. Having grown confident in business, they sought out new opportunities, and decided to buy a failing restaurant atop a ravine overlooking the bay. The lot itself, of which the restaurant occupied a third of the acreage, was valuable. The view of the water, especially at sunset, was spectacular. But their time was quickly stretched too thin, so Eddie and Judy leased the restaurant to Vic, who was hot on the idea of building up the bar end of the business, filling the Bayside Grille by booking entertainment and instituting happy hours and other specials.

Vic renovated the bar, adding new outside doors and extending the dance floor. The crowds did come. They ate, they drank, and they danced to the bands. Then tragedy struck. One late-night reveler left and never made it to the parking lot. Instead, he somehow happened around back behind the building—and ended up tumbling down the ravine, incurring a spinal injury.

Eddie and Judy were stunned to be named in the lawsuit. It seemed like a cruel joke. They were just the landlords—not operators of the restaurant-bar. They had received no notice from Vic that patrons were straying behind the property in the area of the ravine drop-off.

The jury, however, had a different perspective. The plaintiff's attorney successfully argued to the panel of 12 average citizens that the landlords had allowed a dangerous condition to exist.

The duty to inspect premises to ensure they are safe from dangerous conditions applies when:

- The lease is renewed, extended, or initially entered into; or

- The landlord is granted the periodic right to inspect, or approve of construction.

The court decided that if Eddie and Judy, the landlords, had performed a periodic inspection as granted in their lease with Vic, they would have recognized that someone turning the wrong way out of the bar's doors and—instead of proceeding into the lighted parking lot—wandering behind the building (ignoring the dumpster and the muddy, unpaved ground), could approach the edge of the ravine and topple down the slope.

Never mind the "Private Property" sign that was posted behind the restaurant. Never mind that the previous owner had never mentioned any instance of a customer going behind the restaurant. The landlord has a duty to the public to execute reasonable care in inspecting the property. This meant that Eddie and Judy should have inspected the restaurant-bar after Vic's renovations.

The Duty to Disclose a Dangerous Condition

The lengthy list of a landlord's duties may include an affirmative requirement to warn tenants of current problems. Laws vary by state, but certain decisions in one state (often, it seems, California) that seem outrageous at the time end up being adopted into the mainstream.

Case #19
Ricky and the Revelers

Ricky owned a four-unit apartment complex across town from his house. Times were tough and the town's vacancy rate for tenants rose, so Ricky relaxed his policy of a minimum six-month lease and went to month-to-month to fill up his investment property, which now had two empty units. A recently divorced mother and her teenage daughter moved into one of these units. No red flags went up in Ricky's mind, because the mother was gainfully employed, passed the credit check and prepaid the first and last month's rent plus the damage deposit.

It wasn't until three months had passed that the other tenants began complaining about music blaring late at night from the mother and daughter's apartment. Ricky left several unanswered telephone calls at the unit, and even stopped by and knocked during the day, but no one came to the door. He mailed a notice to the mother warning her about the loud music and pointing out that the landlord-tenant contract forbade such behavior.

A week later, Ricky discovered spray-painted graffiti taggings on the retaining wall of the parking lot. He knocked on the door of Velma, a retired nurse and longtime tenant, who told Ricky that rowdy adolescents frequented the new tenants' apartment late at night. In fact, since nothing had been done about the pounding music, Velma was ready to file a police report. Why, Ricky asked, wasn't the teenage girl's mother controlling her daughter and her friends? Velma replied that she believed that the mother had gotten a new sales job with a pharmaceutical company and was often out of town.

Ricky filed a police report about the graffiti vandalism. Then he consulted his lawyer and began eviction procedures. He sent a 30-day notice to terminate the mother's lease. He felt bad, but decided that an empty apartment was better in the long run than a bad tenant.

Ricky's luck seemed to be looking up when, the following week, he succeeded in renting the empty fourth unit to a new tenant: Priscilla. She was a quiet, serious-faced schoolteacher, new in town, and agreed to put down extra money on her damage deposit since she owned a housecat.

Priscilla wasn't so lucky. Two weekends later, a drunken driver plowed into her car just after midnight as she was pulling into the parking lot after seeing a movie. Priscilla, who was wearing her seat belt, suffered whiplash and a broken nose. Her Honda Civic was nearly totaled. The other driver, who was pulling out quickly without the headlights on, was a minor who had become intoxicated at the problem apartment.

Ricky was named in Priscilla's lawsuit. The court ruled in her favor, finding that the landlord—who was well aware of criminal behavior at his apartment complex—owed a duty to his tenants to either provide extra security while problems persisted or warn his new tenant of the danger. The judge held that Ricky's failure to perform either of these duties created a risk that Priscilla or other tenants might suffer harm. She was awarded damages.

This is the law in California and several other states. As it may become the law in other states over time you need to plan and act accordingly.

Implied Warranty of Habitability

In addition to the duty to act reasonably in inspecting and maintaining a property, a landlord is legally bound to rent property fit for human occupancy. This seems obvious, but it took a great deal of time before the nation's courts reached such a requirement.

Do you recall the discussion of British feudal heritage in Chapter 17? It won't shock you to learn that in the days of yore, some greedy landowners, smug with their great power, were pleased to offer whatever foul, nasty little hovel they liked to the unwashed, unlanded masses. Such peasantry and riffraff should feel fortunate to even have a roof over their wretched heads, was the attitude of these landlords. No matter if the roof leaked with every rain, the walls were drafty, the water wasn't potable and raw sewage ran outside the door.

This attitude, protected by law, prevailed in Britain, America and other Commonwealth countries for centuries. Landlords could lease whatever filthy rat's nest they cared to and if the tenant didn't like it, he could move on to the next dank hole. The courts consistently backed the landlord's position that if the rental contract did not specify livable conditions, the landlord was not obligated to provide them.

Not surprisingly, few landlords cared to provide decently habitable lodging, given the expense of doing so. And tenants, bereft of options, typically had to settle for a pigsty, since there would be nothing but fouler pigsties down the pike. Ultimately, though, society paid a price for the dearth of clean living conditions. As societies shifted from agricultural to industrial and cities grew exponentially, street after street of squalor incubated diseases such as typhoid, cholera and the plague—creating a public-health nightmare. Still, landlords sustained a take-it-or-leave-it mentality.

What began to turn the tide was the democratic system itself. Upwardly mobile citizens who'd grown up in sordid rental situations entered the judicial system. The judiciary was no longer the sole province of the privileged. Judges whose childhood memories were scarred by unheated homes with no running water and inadequate toilet facilities had little compassion for stingy landlords. Still, an obstacle to requiring habitability standards was contract law—which held sway in common-law courts. A landlord-tenant contract could include whatever the parties agreed to. If the provision of sanitary conditions wasn't in writing, too bad.

But a second factor came powerfully into play. Massive outbreaks of cholera, typhoid, hepatitis and other diseases were ravaging cities. The public good was imperiled, and judges found a way to circumvent the constraints of contract law by deciding that habitability was *implied* in every rental contract.

Public policy had won out over contract law. A warranty of habitability existed from the start. And this implied warranty made perfect sense: Why would a tenant want to live in a place unfit for humans?

The ramifications for you, the landlord, is that you must maintain and manage your residential property to ensure its habitability. In the end—it is a sound public responsibility. And by the way, it is a responsibility you cannot delegate to a property manager. Although the property manager is hired to notify you about problems and needs of the property, the buck stops with you in the eyes of the law. In fact, you are ultimately responsible for your property manager's actions, as well.

In light of all this, it is clear that landlords bear far-reaching liability for their investment or rental real estate. As a landlord, your greatest risk will stem from dangerous conditions you allow on your property. The list of these conditions includes, but isn't limited to:

- Poorly maintained locks, doors, gates, lights, walkways and safety measures

- Broken fixtures

- Unfinished repairs

- Continuous criminal activity

- Dangerous animals

The failure to remedy a dangerous condition will result in potential landlord liability. Your first concern should be to never let such a condition arise. Tend to your property conscientiously, keeping it well maintained and in good repair. Give your tenants a clean, decent, safe place to live.

Loophole #25

Development of the implied warranty of habitability did landlords a favor. If everyone has to keep their property up, everyone's property values benefit.

Of course, life is unpredictable, and problems can pop up straight out of the blue. No matter how unexpected, fluky or downright bizarre the happenstance may be, responsibility for any resulting damage will fall squarely on you. You're the landlord. You're responsible. It's that plain. And that important. So you must take the intelligent steps of protecting yourself.

The two primary ways of protecting yourself are insurance and entity usage. These will be discussed in the coming chapters.

Chapter Nineteen

Insurance

Case #20
Greg and Benjamin

Greg and Benjamin were old friends from college who recently began investing in real estate. They bought two buildings next-door to each other on Monroe Street in an old area of the city that had recently been renovated into a bustling neighborhood of boutique shops, galleries and jazz cafes. The old brick buildings had been turned into apartments that were in high demand because of their newly cool location.

Though they both knew they had made a great investment, their management philosophies could not have differed more. Greg could be described as a bit of a risk-taker. He owned real estate rentals in another section of town and had never had a single problem. Therefore, he did not want to pay the expense of insurance that he didn't need. He decided to pay for only the minimum liability insurance and held the property in his own name because he didn't want to pay the initial and continuing fees of a limited liability entity.

Benjamin, however, was much more cautious than Greg. He always remembered his grandmother's advice about insurance. She used to say that insurance was like an umbrella on a cloudy day: If you carried one it definitely would not rain that day. But if you didn't have your umbrella with you, it surely would pour. He took this advice to heart and took every step possible to make sure he protected himself and his property.

Benjamin purchased a comprehensive commercial insurance package from his broker, which included liability insurance covering any injuries to third parties on the property. Since he would be hiring people to do repairs and maintenance, he made sure he covered any injuries to them by purchasing a workmen's compensation policy. Another feature of his insurance coverage included any additional construction costs required to bring the building up to code. He also was covered for loss of rent should more construction or another interruption take place. Additionally, he bought an umbrella override policy that offered another $2 million in extra protection. After consulting with his attorney, he decided to hold the property in a limited liability entity instead of in his own name so he could never be held personally liable in the event of a lawsuit. While Greg poked fun at his cautious ways, Benjamin believed his peace of mind was worth the extra expense.

It took an unexpected accident for them to realize the true value of proper coverage. One winter afternoon, after an unusually bad snowstorm followed by a week of rain, floods plagued the city. With the location of the two apartment buildings at the bottom of a hill, the damage to the Monroe Street buildings was particularly severe.

To Greg and Benjamin's relief, no one had been injured in the flood. However, the flood had damaged the personal property of almost every tenant in both buildings. One of Greg's tenants, Sandra, who lived on the ground floor and worked from home, had all of her files and business equipment completely destroyed. She would not be able to work for months.

After all the tenants had been relocated and things had started to settle down, Greg and Benjamin had to take a close look at rebuilding costs. It was at this point that the consequences of their different management priorities became very clear. The city notified Greg and Benjamin that if they chose to rebuild, the new buildings would have to be built to code, including handicap access and flood abatement regulations. Because the buildings were positioned at the bottom of a hill, these additions were not going to be cheap.

However, because of Benjamin's comprehensive coverage that included increased construction costs, the additions were covered by his insurance. Benjamin also received a monthly payment from the insurance company to pay his mortgage and other expenses while he was not receiving rent. His insurance was able to handle all of the claims filed by his tenants for their property damage.

Greg's situation, however, was causing him quite the headache. His insurance would only cover exactly what was lost—the older building. Any costs to construct the required improvements would have to be paid with Greg's own money. The insurance company did not cover lost rent, like Benjamin's did, and the mortgage payments were still due. In addition, Greg's tenant, Sandra, would not be able to work for quite some time because of her business losses, and Greg's low liability level was not enough to cover her claim. Because he held the apartment building in his own name, he could expect that Sandra's attorneys would seek recovery from Greg's personal assets. All of these extra expenses had to be paid out of Greg's own money. Greg was forced into bankruptcy and had to sell the land on Monroe Street.

Benjamin was able to purchase Greg's land from him—a move that aided them both. The plans for a new apartment building with eight units were approved. Benjamin made sure the new building was properly insured and was held in a limited liability entity. Even though Benjamin knew the probability of another freak accident occurring was slim, he also knew how reassuring it was to be fully covered.

Insurance Broker

The insurance broker is an essential part of the team you assemble when you purchase your real estate property. You must look for an experienced professional who strives to find personalized options for your business or investment. What you don't want is someone who is just interested in selling you the most expensive policy and collecting premiums.

A broker with years of experience can offer coverage pertaining to certain laws and requirements that clients are probably unaware of. For example, in Napa, California, all new single-family homes are required to have interior fire-retarding sprinkler systems installed. With this requirement in place, a policy providing only replacement coverage would be inadequate. A broker in that area would be familiar with such a requirement and would advise his clients to consider coverage for an increased cost of construction in the event of damage. This way, if the home is ever damaged and needs to be rebuilt, the required installation of the sprinkler system will be covered by the insurance.

Brokers can also advise clients on other types of coverage that are commonly overlooked. One example is the non-owned and hired auto coverage. If you have an employee that is making a delivery or deposit for your business in their own car and gets into an accident, you could be held liable if attorneys find out that the employee was on an errand for your business. The non-owned and hired auto policy would cover your defense costs and claims in this type of suit.

If you own a business and have just one employee, your broker may also suggest that you consider employment practices liability, which would cover any claims of wrongful termination, discriminatory actions, or sexual harassment filed against you. Whether these claims are legitimate or not, it still offers peace of mind should a lawsuit be filed. If you have an employee that handles large amounts of money for you, consider insurance that covers employee dishonestly, including embezzlement or theft.

Finding an insurance broker you trust can help you ensure you will be fully covered. The benefit of having a broker's advice is that your insurance coverage can be custom tailored to your needs.

Loophole #26

Remember that insurance companies have their own array of loopholes allowing them to escape the coverage of certain claims presented to them. Some of their loopholes are found (although not easily) in exclusions in fine print this big at the end of a long contract. Be sure to have your insurance broker cover these exclusions with you.

The insurance industry, in the face of record claims, is now in the process of reconsidering coverage on certain properties. If a number of water damage, storm damage, burglary or other claims have been filed against one property, insurance companies are now refusing to insure the property. Coverage is not based on the owner, who may have a spotless record, but on the property's history. As a potential buyer of the property, you need to know if it can be insured. Your bank will most likely not give you a loan if it can't.

The property's profile is found on an insurance industry database known as the Comprehensive Loss Underwriting Exchange, or CLUE. Since only the current property owner can order a CLUE report (online at www.choicetrust.com), buyers may want to require sellers to provide them with a clean and insurable CLUE report. A negative report may force owners to pay much higher premiums with a nonstandard carrier, such as Lloyds of London.

And remember, with insurance companies finding reasons not to insure you and even more reasons not to make good on claims, you need to protect yourself as best you can.

While insurance is the first line of defense, the correct use of entities is the second line of defense. And given the track record of the insurance industry in using their own loopholes to deny coverage, the use of entities as a second line of defense is a necessity. A legal entity is a legal structure chartered by your state government. They come in very handy for real estate ownership.

But before we discuss entities we must first discuss the issue of taking title. Because if you don't take title the right way, you will have no asset protection...

Chapter Twenty

Taking Title

Title to real estate sounds grand. As you think of titles let your mind wander back again to medieval England–when titles such as Duke and Viscount and Earl meant you were part of the British nobility and peerage system. And not coincidentally, if you had such a title you also owned real estate. In fact, entrance into the peerage ranks required the ownership of real estate. To have a noble title you needed a real estate title. In the Middle Ages this would have been a castle with loopholes. Back then, defending your title could be a matter of life or death.

As our legal and economic systems evolved, real estate title—the means by which you owned your valuable rights to land—remained ever so important and crucial. Because title conveyed so much power (and with power came corruption and fraud), a system attempting to accurately record the chain of title developed. Over time you had to defend your title with the proper paperwork. The 'checking system' that evolved means that there are two steps for the transfer of title.

The first step is the granting of a deed whereby the grantor (the owner) transfers the property to the grantee (the new owner). But that alone is not enough. As a check, a public repository of records affecting land ownership came into being. With these records an investigation of the sequence of deeds to establish an accurate chain of title is performed. (In the future block chain technology may perform this service.) If the grantor actually has clear title according to the public records to transfer the property, a policy of title insurance–insuring against the risk of other claimants to the title–may be issued and the property transferred. (Please note that property can be transferred without title insurance but that most banks won't take the risk in making a loan without it.)

A noticeable break in the chain of title means that the buyer—even though they believe they are the rightful owner—can be subject to the possible claims of others contesting the title. It can also mean that the property is now very difficult to sell, because future potential purchasers don't want any doubts about clear title.

Accordingly, title insurance is important. Before insuring you against the risk of future claimants, a title company is going to check the public records to see if there are any troubling gaps in the chain of title. If such gaps exist they won't issue a title insurance policy. If they won't issue a policy you won't buy the property. It is that simple. Follow their lead. They are in the business of insuring against risk. If they won't insure your transaction because there is too much risk that means you should probably walk away from the deal too. Unless you want the expense of a Quiet Title Action, discussed ahead.

Transferring Title

The specter of title insurance affects the way you will transfer title to property. There are two ways to transfer title:

1. Grant Deed. This deed (sometimes called a 'Warranty Deed') implies or warrants that:

    a. The Grantor (the person granting the property) has not transferred the property before, and that absolute ownership ('free and clear' title) is conveyed.

    b. Unless the Grantee (the person receiving the property) agrees otherwise, the property is free from any liens or encumbrances against it.

    c. Any after-acquired title (ownership that goes to a Grantor later) is also conveyed to the Grantee.

2. Quit Claim Deed. This much weaker deed only:

    a. Transfers whatever present right, title or interest the transferor may have. (If the transferor doesn't have any rights, neither do you.)

    b. No warranties are made as to any liens or encumbrances. (So if there are undisclosed mortgages against the property it's not the transferor's problem—as it is in a grant deed. Instead, it is now your problem.)

    c. No after acquired title is transferred.

While often advocated by promoters as the easiest means for transfer, the quit claim deed is actually not your best choice. There are two examples to illustrate this. First, know that in many bank involved REO (real estate owned) transactions the REO lender selling a foreclosed property will only use a Quit Claim deed.

Why is this?

It is because the lender has no idea what happened on the property prior to foreclosure. During the boom documents were not properly kept or transferred, the banking industry's MERS electronic recording system failed to keep up with it all and many documents were just plain lost. This is no way to maintain a good chain of title on the nation's real estate. The English noblemen of centuries past would have been bloody outraged by our recent muddle. It was so bad in 2009 that a large national title company announced it would no longer issue title policies to two large national banks. These lenders' records were just not trustworthy, and the title company was not going to take that kind of risk. Know that for years to come there are going to be title issues arising from the real estate collapse in 2008.

It is for this reason that sellers (mainly banks) of foreclosure properties are using quit claim deeds. They don't know what happened and they aren't about to warrant or guarantee that they have a clean title to convey to you. The quit claim deed they use instead says, "We don't know what we've got but whatever we've got we're giving to you. Good luck." (I might be too charitable on the good luck part.)

What is offensive is the lengths that some of these lenders will go to to get you to bite on a quit claim deed. They will tell you that it grants you full rights to the property. (It doesn't, because neither you nor the bank really knows what those rights are.)

To further get themselves off the hook after taking your money for the property these banks will bury the fact that they don't warrant good title in an Addendum at the end of a sixty page contract. They want you to waive any rights you may have in the matter. They may or may not know that the title is so defective that the property will be severely devalued. But they want you to release them from any future problems and sign off that everything is okay. There have been reported cases where the Addendum is intentionally withheld and only provided to you at the closing. (You know, at that last meeting at the title office where you are expected to sign 47 documents without reading them.)

Now, if you or I used such trickery to commit a fraud we would go to jail. But when you are too big to fail and contribute vast sums of money to the political establishment it is probably, as before, a slap on the wrist and a fine. It is indeed incredible what they get away with. Accordingly, please be very careful and have your own attorney review such transactions.

The second reason a quit claim deed is not preferred is because the quit claim deed severs an express or implied warranty of title. (Remember, you are just granting whatever you may own which may be something, or nothing.) As such, the title insurance doesn't follow. While this may not seem like a big deal, let's consider an example.

You buy a property in your name. Part of your closing costs includes a policy of title insurance. Several years later you want to transfer title to an LLC for asset protection. Your friend says a quit claim deed (which they mispronounce as a 'quick' claim deed) is the easiest and quickest way to go. You file the quit claim deed and now the property is titled in the name of your LLC. Later, you learn that the boundaries weren't properly surveyed. You seek recourse from the title company since they insured the boundaries were correct. But you now learn that by quit claiming the property into your LLC you have unwittingly cancelled your title insurance policy. The boundary issue is no longer insured.

The way to avoid this problem is to use a grant deed or a warranty deed. A title insurance policy isn't extinguished in such a transfer. (But know that not all title companies are consistent on this, so check ahead.) As well, a grant deed is just as easy to prepare as is a quit claim deed. But in either case, remember that easy isn't always best. If you are not an expert at title transfers, I would have a lawyer or a title company handle them.

Charged with Notice

The existence of the public land records serves not only as a checking system but also to provide notice to all prospective purchasers. Failure to take this notice can cause all sorts of problems.

Tax liens, whereby taxes are past due on the property, remain on the property whether the purchaser had actual knowledge of their existence or not. You, as a buyer, are charged with constructive notice of what is on the county land records. They are public and on display for you to see. If you ignore the chance to do so it's not the county's fault. If you go ahead and buy the tax-liened property you now owe the previous taxes assessed against the property. The same holds true for judgment liens, statutory liens and other encumbrances. The time to deal with these issues is before you buy the property, not after. Use your leverage as a buyer to have the liens paid off by the seller through escrow, or, if the seller won't budge on it, to walk away from the deal.

Beware of any seller or advisor who discourages you from reviewing the public land records or from buying title insurance. The real estate broker who counsels that title insurance is a waste of money is the broker who is sure to be sued for negligence and breach of fiduciary duty. Engage in your own due diligence review—check the title report for what, if any, encumbrances exist against the property. We shall discuss title reports further in Chapter 30.

Proper Recording

Because buyers are charged with notice it is important that they actually receive such notice. Deeds and the like need to be recorded in the right place for the public to see. Mistakes are sometimes made in a county recorder's office. It is your responsibility to make sure everything is recorded in the right place so notice can be accurately provided to future buyers.

In an interesting Minnesota case, the legal description on a mortgage document had the number '13' mistaken for the letter 'B.' (You can just imagine the harried assistant reading their boss's too close together '13' as a 'B'!) When the document was recorded it didn't track with the chain of title for the specific parcel and so no notice was imparted. As such, a bankruptcy trustee was able to avoid the mortgage. (In re Vondall, 364 B.R 820, 2010).

Imagine yourself in this case. You have sold one of your properties, taking 10% down and a 90% note. You prepare the mortgage and deed of trust documents but because of a typo the documents aren't recorded in the right place. Later, a prospective buyer does not have notice of your first deed of trust. It isn't on the public record. They buy the property as bona fide (or good faith) purchasers. They can get the property free from your first deed of trust, which is now void. Yikes!

The lesson is to make sure that your recordings are done properly. Mistakes do happen. Double check the public records to make sure your deeds and liens are recorded in the right place and in a way that gives notice to all later parties.

Lis Pendens

If in your title review you come across the term 'lis pendens' be very wary. A lis pendens notice recorded against the property means that the property is involved in litigation. The lis pendens puts everyone, including you, on notice that there is a pending lawsuit related to ownership of the property. If you see the term lis pendens you probably should walk away from the whole matter.

In an Oklahoma case some new buyers inexplicably ignored a lis pendens notice and went ahead and closed on a condo property. A court later found that the person who filed the lis pendens was entitled to the property. In a second action, the court found that the new buyer's interest in the condo was void. They were out their money and out their property. (Bank of Commerce, 256 P.3d 1053, 2011.) Again, the lis pendens notice is a matter of public record. You are charged with reviewing and understanding the public record. Closing on a property involved in litigation as to its ownership is one of the biggest mistakes you can make in real estate. And, as the Oklahoma case highlights, it does happen. And when it does, later buyers will lose what they paid for.

Quiet Title

Frequently, litigation over the ownership of real estate will come in the form of a Quiet Title Action. This is an equitable proceeding where the Court weighs the equities of the parties and the situation. As such, there is no black letter law or set precedent on how a judge should rule. Instead, the Court will try and decide what is fair and reasonable given the circumstances. Anyone, whether in or out of possession of the real estate, can bring such an action. The purpose of the Quiet Title Action is to resolve all the various claims once and for all. Rather than have people fight over ownership for generations this action 'quiets the title,' putting to rest all the issues and allowing the parties to move on.

The court will review the muniment of title, which are the legal documents and other written evidence indicating ownership of an asset. In 'muniment' we have another interesting ancient word. It is derived from the Latin word 'munimentum,' meaning a defensive fortification. Another version of the root word is munitions, or materials used in war, especially weapons and ammunition. (Yet another variation.)

Are you noticing a trend in these long ago words now involving real estate? They relate to the defense of your property. Real estate has always carried great intrinsic and emotional value. Throughout history, it has always been an asset to be vigorously defended and protected.

And now, with the modern day rabble of invaders at the castle wall coming in the form of plaintiff's lawyers and government agencies, you must still defend and protect as best you can. This is why we will discuss asset protection strategies several chapters ahead.

But first, let's further consider the muniment of title. It is the written evidence used to defend your title. Muniments are the deeds, wills, court judgments and other documents showing the validity of your title.

Please note that we will also be discussing the issue of land trusts ahead. Many land trust promoters argue that your name should never appear on a deed anywhere. That privacy is the be all and end all of real estate holdings. But does this secretive strategy help build up your muniment of title? Does this "no fingerprints" artifice lead to problems and fraud and a loss of title for a lack of evidence? (Please consider these penetrating questions as the skillful foreshadowing of a future chapter.)

In today's world there are two significant steps for shoring up your muniment of title:

1. Excellent spelling. The Grantee's name (the person receiving the property) must be spelled letter perfect. This will keep the muniment of title accurate and consistent.

2. In Existence. The limited liability company, limited partnership or other entity receiving the conveyance must have been formed prior to the date of the grant. If your entity is not yet organized the deed is defective. Your deed should not defy the laws of metaphysics. A grantee must exist.

Loophole #27

You want all the ammunition you can get to defend your muniment of title. Correct spellings, proper recording and title insurance will all be important in this effort.

Now that we have covered taking title concepts, let's review how not to take title...

Chapter Twenty-One

Joint Tenancies/Tenancies in Common
How Not to Hold Real Estate

There is a misunderstood myth among the public that real estate protection is easily achieved through jointly owned or trustee-administered property. As with many misunderstood myths, the opposite is actually true. There is no asset protection at all when holding real estate as a joint tenant, tenant in common, or in a land trust. Indeed, in some cases you are even exposing yourself to a greater range of problems.

Case #21
Calvin and Mariah

Calvin and Mariah were star-crossed lovers whose story would have made a great country and western ballad. It had all the elements: Jail, betrayal, pickups and misunderstood myths.

Calvin had met Mariah at Gilley's near Houston, when it was the center of the mechanized bull-riding universe. Calvin could ride that bull for eons and Mariah just had to get to know him. Leaving in Calvin's Ford F-150 pickup truck, they took a ride to his duplex to get further acquainted. Calvin and Mariah hit it off and were soon spending a great deal of time together at his duplex.

Calvin was an alpaca farmer and was raising eight alpacas out back of the duplex so that America could wear fine wool sweaters. The alpaca promoters had said he would be rich in eighteen months. He was at month sixteen.

Mariah was quite interested in his future. So much so that she wanted to be a part of it. She began persuading him through the withholding of rewards that she should be more involved in his big future.

Calvin had heard through his friend Ronnie that if you held your property jointly with someone else, a creditor couldn't get at your property. Calvin always had creditors looking for his money.

He could never qualify for a home loan so he had scraped together enough money through various scofflaw schemes to own the duplex free and clear. But then he didn't have enough money to pay for the necessary property insurance and maintenance items the place needed. Calvin hadn't told Mariah that there were some credit issues, but she didn't need to know. Instead, he could get her off his back at the same time he was keeping the creditors at bay by putting her name on the duplex.

Calvin went to a stationery store to pick up a jointly owned property form. The high schooler with glazed eyes behind the counter asked if he wanted a "tenants in common" or "joint tenant" form. Calvin asked what worked best. The clerk laughed a little too loud and said the joint one, and so that was the one Calvin bought.

With the form all signed and recorded Calvin informed Mariah that she was now a joint tenant in the duplex. She was very happy. Just as they were about to celebrate they heard a blood-curdling scream from out back. Rushing to the scene they found Willie, the tenant in the duplex, with blood all over his hands. Willie screamed that the alpacas had attacked him and that Calvin was liable for keeping dangerous animals on the premises. Calvin laughed and said that he and Mariah were both liable. Mariah raised an eyebrow at this but Calvin continued to assert that because the property was held in a joint tenancy, Willie couldn't collect anything on any claim he could concoct. He told Willie to go wash his hands and quit bellyaching over a little nip on the hand.

Willie washed his hands and went to the personal injury lawyer on the cover of the phone book. Bo Jones was ecstatic to see that Willie had lost half of his pinkie finger and part of his ring finger. He promptly sued Calvin and Mariah as joint tenants of the duplex. The lawyer alleged that because the two of them had an equal undivided interest in the property as joint tenants, they were equally and personally responsible for the dangerous animals. Because Calvin had no insurance coverage, upon prevailing in front of a jury of their peers, Bo Jones was able to attach the jointly held interest, partition the property, and sell the duplex to satisfy the judgment Willie had against Calvin and Mariah. To compound their problems, shortly after Willie had been bitten, the county's animal control division took the alpacas and destroyed them, calling them a public nuisance, one month before Mariah expected their fortune to be made.

Mariah was not happy at this turn of events. She threatened to leave Calvin. But Calvin persuaded her to stay. He would do better the next time. To do so, he visited his friend Ronnie in jail. Calvin angrily told Ronnie how the jointly owned property format he said to use offered no asset protection at all. The darned attorney went right through the joint tenancy and snagged the duplex.

Ronnie laughed at him and told him he had used the wrong form. The joint tenancy was totally improper, Ronnie explained, because it allowed Mariah to own all of the property if Calvin died. It was called right of survivorship and it meant that she, as the surviving joint tenant after Calvin's demise, got to keep everything. Ronnie asked if Calvin wanted any of his seven kids from the first three marriages to get anything. Calvin did, and so Ronnie said that next time he had to use the tenants in common form. By having Mariah's name on it, his assets would be protected and Mariah would be satisfied. Calvin grumbled that there probably would never be a next time, since he had just lost everything.

Headed home, Calvin was stopped at a light listening to Tammy Wynette and lost in thought when a huge black Ford F-350 pickup rear-ended him at forty five miles per hour. The driver hadn't even braked before impact and Calvin's F-150 was totaled. Calvin suffered severe whiplash and was in great pain.

After months of intensive chiropractic and massage therapy, Calvin collected from the driver's insurance company. He and Mariah then bought another duplex and, as Ronnie had counseled, took title as tenants in common.

Mariah wanted Calvin to be more successful this time. Eight alpacas weren't going to get her to South Padre Island. Calvin had to make more money, plain and simple.

Calvin told Mariah of his plan to brew what he called Golden Mash. They could start out small, build a market for it, and then make some real money. The real money part was of interest to Mariah, so they began using the upstairs bathroom in the duplex as their distillery.

Soon their Golden Mash was finding a market in the local area among the young, hip and very young. The still in the bathroom became crowded with equipment and tubing. Gallon bottles filled with mash were stacked to the ceiling. The weight of all of this was eventually too much for the small room. The bathtub crashed through the ceiling into the apartment below, severely hurting Jimmie, the downstairs tenant.

As he was being loaded into the ambulance, Jimmie yelled at Calvin that he was liable for leasing out unsafe premises. Calvin laughed and said that he and Mariah were both liable but that because the property was held as tenants in common, no one was going to collect nothing.

Attorney Bo Jones was ecstatic to see that Jimmie was so badly injured. He promptly sued Calvin and Mariah as tenants in common in the duplex. Each owned a divided one-half interest in the property but they were collectively and personally responsible for Jimmie's injuries. Because Calvin had little insurance coverage, upon prevailing in front of a jury of their peers, Bo Jones was able to attach their divided tenancy in common interests and sell the duplex to satisfy the judgment Jimmie had against Calvin and Mariah. As well, the county authorities learned of the unlicensed distillery and slapped them with a fine and an order to never again engage in such an activity.

Mariah was not a happy person. She scolded Calvin for ever listening to jailbird Ronnie and his obviously incorrect ideas about jointly owned property. Ronnie had been incarcerated for practicing law without a license. Bo Jones had taken two duplexes away from them with ease, like a hot knife through lard. If they ever owned property again Maria was going to a seminar to learn how to do it right.

A few days later Mariah was driving their new Ford F-150 pickup when she thought she saw a child chasing a ball into the street. Just to be safe she slammed on her brakes, causing a big Dodge Ram quad cab that was following too closely to slam into her. The Dodge totaled the pickup, and Mariah suffered extreme whiplash injury.

After months of highly intensive chiropractic and massage therapy, Mariah collected from the driver's insurance company. She and Calvin then bought another duplex. This time, having attended a free seminar given by a frail and excitable paralegal who sold expensive bundled form packages, she had the title to the duplex held in the name of a land trust. The paralegal said the land trust offered privacy and asset protection and, given their history, that was obviously what she and Calvin needed. For privacy protection the paralegal offered to serve as the trustee for $150 a year. For his money, the paralegal promised never to tell anyone anything. With his name on the deed as trustee, no one would really know who owned the duplex. That was good, thought Mariah, since every time their names were on the deed an attorney, and the same one at that, took the property away.

With their new duplex set up, Mariah informed Calvin that he needed to be more successful. This was their third duplex and she felt that she should be in a triplex by now. Mariah didn't want to do alpacas or mash or anything that took a lot of time. She wanted to try distributing a home remedy for depression. Her brother was doing it in Miami and making a huge amount of money from ordinary people who just wanted to feel good.

Soon, their home remedy for depression was finding a market in the local area among the young, hip, and very young. They were making a great deal of money and the duplex became known as the home remedy house.

The local prosecutor did not like home remedy houses. They were unlicensed and offered too great an opportunity for people to feel good. It had to be shut down. Finally the sixth officer who went in was able to get out with the proper evidence against the home remedy for depression masterminds. The prosecutor obtained a warrant for the arrest of Calvin and Mariah. At a hearing, Calvin was asked if he owned the home remedy house. Thinking that the duplex was owned by the land trust and the $150 per year trustee, he said no. The prosecutor then called in the frail and excitable paralegal, who was frightened to the point of almost uncontrollable twitching. Without hesitation the paralegal testified that Calvin and Mariah were the beneficial owners of the home remedy house.

As the criminal case was nearing trial, Bo Jones, now on behalf of Calvin and Mariah, made an interesting legal discovery. It turned out that there were no laws on the books outlawing the sale of home remedies for depression. Congress and all of the states were quickly implementing such prohibitions but for now Calvin and Mariah hadn't broken any laws because there weren't any on the books to break.

The prosecutor had to let Mariah go. But he kept Calvin. A settlement was reached whereby Calvin got to join his friend Ronnie for six months. Calvin had committed perjury when he said he didn't own the duplex. To say he didn't own the duplex was a lie and he knew—or at least should have known—he was committing perjury.

As the case illustrates, there is no asset protection to be gained from holding real estate as jointly owned or land-trust-administered property. Still, because over three quarters of real estate owned by married couples in the United States is held in joint ownership, it is important to understand the concepts and consequences.

Tenancies in Common

One of the most common forms of shared property ownership is the tenancy in common. Tenants in common each own a separate fractional share of the property, which a tenant in common may freely sell, encumber, bequeath by will or trust, or otherwise transfer. Unlike a joint tenancy, a tenant in common's sale of their share of the property will not change the nature of the tenancy. The purchaser or heir of an interest in a tenancy in common receives the same rights and privileges as the former tenant in common.

Each tenant in common has the right to benefit from the property. This includes the rights to use the property, exclude third parties from it, and receive a portion of any income produced from it. Legal remedies are available to tenants in common to enforce their fractional rights to the property. These include remedies that allow the property to be physically divided, divided by sale, or for tenants to demand an accounting and payment corresponding to their interest in the property.

So if you are tenants in common with Joe, and Joe gets sued by Bill and loses, you may have Bill as your new co-owner. You probably won't like Bill since he sued your friend. And Bill probably doesn't like you either. This is why Bill likely next brings a partition suit in court to sell the property and split the proceeds. A new co-owner suing to sell the property is not asset protection.

Tenancy in common does have its place in one unique situation. Say that Mary and Amy buy a 4 plex together. It is their first investment and they will want to invest in larger properties in the future using 1031 exchanges. But after the 4 plex investment they will go their own separate ways. Mary wants to invest in single family homes and Amy wants to invest in 8 plexes. If they held title in one LLC and they did a 1031 exchange, they would have to own the next property together through the same LLC. But they want to go their separate ways after the 4 plex deal. So, with the help of a good attorney, they structure the 4 plex investment as follows:

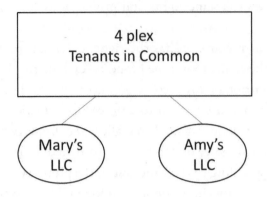

Title to the 4 plex is held as tenants in common with each tenant being a separate LLC, one for Mary and one for Amy.

From an asset protection standpoint, if someone sues over a claim against the property (more about this ahead) they can only reach the two LLCs, not everything that Mary and Amy own (unlike the case of Calvin and Mariah who were tenants in common as individuals).

From a 1031 exchange standpoint, when the 4 plex is sold the monies will flow towards each LLC, which can then do its own 1031 exchange. As we learned in Chapter 10, an intermediary will handle all the money for each LLC. But by using this structure Mary and Amy can part ways after their 4 plex investment and go on to do their own deals.

The structure we've just discussed lends itself to one other common scenario: Asset Protection Phobia.

As an attorney, I have seen many situations in which an older family member shall not, cannot and darn well will not ever consider using any form of asset protection. They've never been sued. They never will be sued. They hate the thought of paying lawyers, accountants and the state the extra monies for an entity. And, as they will say to me, "Don't you ever bring up this asset protection malarkey again, Sonny." And that's fine. I am not offended.

But I am able to offer a solution to the other family members who clearly see the various risks associated with owning real estate. Again, as with our 4 plex example, the structure is as follows:

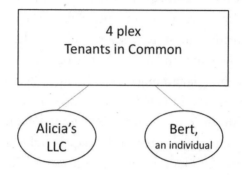

Bert, the coot, continues to hold his tenant in common interest in his own name. If someone sues over the property his personal assets are at risk. Alicia holds her tenant in common interest in an LLC. If someone sues over the property they can get what is inside the LLC (which is usually just the tenant in common interest) but cannot get beyond the LLC to Alicia's personal assets.

To finish this structure you need to take one more step. You need to prepare a grant deed transferring title from Bert and Alicia as tenants in common to Bert and Alicia's LLC as tenants in common. Title must now reflect that Alicia's LLC (and not Alicia individually as before) is the tenant in common. And remember, you won't use a quit claim deed for this or you'll lose your title insurance coverage. That would really raise Bert's ire, and no one wants that.

Loophole #28

While tenancies in common provide no asset protection, you can hold your tenant in common interest in a protective entity and still gain protection.

Joint Tenancies

Joint Tenancies were once, and still are in some states, a prominent form of shared property ownership. When two or more persons clearly agree in writing to hold real estate in equal and undivided shares, a joint tenancy may be created. Most states prefer tenancies in common, so any agreement attempting to create a joint tenancy should clearly state that a joint tenancy with survivorship, and not a tenancy in common, is being created. Joint tenancies are popular among married couples because joint tenancies uniquely provide for an undivided interest and survivorship.

During the life of joint tenants, each joint tenant owns the entire property. However, each joint tenant has equal rights to use and occupy all of the property. Unlike a tenant in common's divided and separate property interest, a joint tenant's interest is undivided. A joint tenant cannot sell his or her interest in the tenancy without severing the joint tenancy and creating a tenancy in common. In severing the joint tenancy, a joint tenant removes the unique features of undivided interest and survivorship.

While the conversion of the undivided interest to a divided interest in the severing of a joint tenancy has little practical effect, the removal of the feature of survivorship is detrimental to other joint tenants. Survivorship provides joint tenants' rights that differ from those enjoyed by tenants in common. A tenant in common may bequeath their interest through a will or trust or their interest may be transferred to an heir by operation of law. Joint tenants cannot bequeath their joint tenancy interest. Upon the death of a joint tenant, the surviving tenant(s) automatically own the entire property by operation of law. The property interest held by the deceased joint tenant simply ceases to exist, leaving the surviving joint tenant(s) with the entire interest in the property. This automatic transfer feature is called a right of survivorship. If a joint tenancy is severed, the surviving joint tenant(s) is (are) denied the right of survivorship.

The right of survivorship is the reason why married couples often use joint tenancies. If a married couple uses a tenancy in common and each spouse does not provide for the transfer of their tenancy interest in a will or trust, default rules of inheritance will apply through what is known as intestate succession. Intestate succession does not always provide the result the joint tenants would have wanted.

Furthermore, the deceased spouse's property interest must go through probate if it is handled under intestate succession or through the administration of a will. By holding property as joint tenants with right of survivorship, commonly abbreviated as JTWROS, married couples know how each spouse's property interest will be treated upon the other's death. If one spouse unexpectedly passes away, the real estate automatically will transfer to the survivor by operation of law. This may allow the surviving spouse to use or sell the property without waiting for the property interest to go through probate.

An example helps to explain the difference between a joint tenancy and a tenancy in common. David and Michelle own a speedboat together. If they own it as joint tenants, they have an undivided interest and a right of survivorship for the whole boat. David doesn't own the engine and Michelle doesn't own the steering wheel. Instead, together they own the whole boat, bow to stern, equally in an undivided fashion. The boat is an indivisible unit of property. Upon the death of either David or Michelle, the survivor will automatically own the entire boat. On the other hand, if they own the boat equally as tenants in common, David and Michelle own specific and divided interest in the boat and, again like a corporation, they can sell their half-interest to whomever they want without affecting each other's interests. While they still don't own the engine or the steering wheel separately, as tenants in common, they own and are able to sell a set percentage interest in the boat. Upon the death of either David or Michelle, the deceased's tenancy in common interest may be distributed pursuant to a will, trust or intestate succession.

There is one instance where suggesting the use of a joint tenancy for holding title may reveal you to be a complete idiot. And since no one likes being put into such a situation you may want to read this.

When you find a good real estate deal and bring friends, family and others in to invest in it, you are syndicating real estate. That is, you are creating a real estate investment deal, which subjects you to the securities laws. (For more on this topic see Chapter 14 of *Start Your Own Corporation*.)

One of the key elements of such a deal is how you will take title to the property. If you suggest taking title as joint tenants with right of survivorship what incentives and/or problems are you creating? The incentive, of course, is that the last person standing gets to keep the entire property. Maybe it's just me, but I am not keen on incentivizing people to benefit from my death. I've already got that risk with my wife by owning life insurance. (No, there's not a problem there, I'm just kidding. But I really don't need any further incentives on the deck.) And the problem for you in putting together the deal is that there are probably other people like me out there. So please don't offer to syndicate a joint tenancy real estate deal. You may be turning off the good investors and incentivizing the wrong ones. As well, there are many investors who want to be able to gift their interest to their family which is problematic using a joint tenancy.

Tenancies by the Entirety

A tenancy by the entirety is a unique form of shared property ownership that can exist only between married persons. Tenancies by the entirety are increasingly rare, but are used by spouses in some states in the same manner as joint tenancies. Like joint tenancies, tenancies by the entirety create undivided interest and provide a right of survivorship. However, unlike joint tenancies, tenancies by the entirety could not traditionally be severed by the unilateral act of one tenant.

Tenancies by the entirety, like all property interests, hark back to medieval English law and custom. Tenancies by the entirety were originally based on sexist (or was it chivalrous?) notions of property ownership. A married man and woman were treated as a unification of two people. Their property was treated as being owned by the unity or the "entirety" of the two, and not as being owned by two separate individuals. Under the modern joint tenancy, a husband can sever the tenancy and remove his wife's right of survivorship by selling his interest in the property.

Under the traditional tenancy by the entirety a husband could not sever the tenancy, but could only sell his right to use the property during his lifetime and his right of survivorship. This retained a right of survivorship for his wife, thus protecting her financial interests as a widow.

Modern treatment of tenancies by the entirety varies among the states. Contemporary notions of sexual equality remove the paternalistic basis for tenancies by the entirety. However, some states have retained this because they believe that tenancies by the entirety serve an additional function. Because this traditionally prevented a husband from conveying his wife's right of survivorship, they also prevented creditors from seizing the couple's property based on the financial obligations of one spouse. This may allow couples in certain states to use tenancies by the entirety to protect their assets; however, a United States Supreme Court decision indicates that tenancies by the entirety will not protect against federal taxes. See *U.S. v. Craft*, 122 S Ct. 1414 (2002). Because states treat tenancies by the entirety differently, and because they may not provide complete asset protection, you should consult with your local advisor before proceeding with transactions involving this.

Protection and Title

As we saw in our last case, jointly held property—be it in a joint tenancy or as tenants in common—does not limit your liability as an owner of real estate.

With a tenancy in common, a creditor can obtain a court order to sell the property to satisfy a judgment. In Calvin and Mariah's case, the property was sold to pay for a claim against the property owners. But what if one of the co-tenants has a claim against him or her for a problem that is totally unrelated to the property? The property interest may still be sold. As such, you may be an innocent co-tenant and find yourself owning the property with an entirely new person, who may not be to your liking and may not share your view of how to manage and benefit from the property.

If you must use a tenancy in common, do all that you can to be sure that your co-tenants are free from current or future financial problems.

While property held as a joint tenant cannot be seized as easily as that of a tenant in common, there is still no asset protection involved. Creditors of a joint tenant can obtain a court order to partition the property, thus converting the ownership to that of tenants in common, and then sell the property to satisfy their claim.

Loophole #29

The law is passive and allows you to make your own decisions as to holding title. But if you really want to defend your castle it is key to know the differences between the right and wrong ways to do it.

Because there is so much misinformation about land trusts we have included a full chapter on them...

Chapter Twenty-Two

Land Trusts

There is a great deal of buzz about using land trusts to hold real estate. Amid all the chatter it is imperative to note: Land trusts offer zero asset protection.

Accordingly, please be very cautious of the promoters who would talk you into a land trust as an asset protection device. We shall discuss the concept of a beneficiary ahead, but for now, know that if you as an individual are the beneficiary of a land trust, you are personally responsible for whatever occurs on the property. That is not asset protection, and you have just paid for a trust document that doesn't do what you needed. For true asset protection, the beneficiary of a land trust should be an LLC or LP. In that case, why not set up an LLC or LP to begin with? You'll save money on an unnecessary land trust that way. Consider the following:

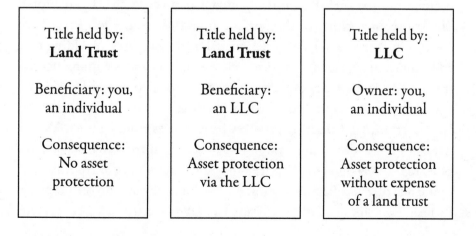

Title held by: **Land Trust**	Title held by: **Land Trust**	Title held by: **LLC**
Beneficiary: you, an individual	Beneficiary: an LLC	Owner: you, an individual
Consequence: No asset protection	Consequence: Asset protection via the LLC	Consequence: Asset protection without expense of a land trust

As you can gather, it is our position that in many cases a land trust is superfluous since an LLC or LP is required for the necessary asset protection anyway. However, because so many people are curious about land trusts, we shall discuss them here.

It is first important to note that, unlike LLCs and LPs, each state is different when it comes to recognizing land trusts. Tennessee and Louisiana have yet to officially accept them. In a number of states they only exist due to case law, which means a later court decision could out of the blue affect their use. So make sure you are aware of your state's position regarding land trusts before you set one up.

A trust is an arrangement in which one person (the trustee) agrees to hold the title to the property of another person (the beneficiary) for their benefit. This type of trust is somewhat unique because the trustee holds both legal title, meaning they are listed as the owner in official records, and equitable title, meaning they are entitled to the property. In most trusts, the trustee holds legal title only, with the beneficiary holding equitable title. In fact, in these other trusts, if one person holds both legal and equitable title, it is considered a merger and the trust dissolves.

Although land trust trustees hold both types of title to the property, they aren't required to do much more than sign the mortgage and other official documents when needed. The beneficiary has no legal interest because the trustee holds the title. However, the beneficiary's equitable interest in the property is considered personal property. (And remember, personal property held by you as an individual can be reached by creditors.) The trustee is entitled to the possession and use of the property. They are also in charge of all the duties related to the property, including rent collection and the payment of taxes. However, some states require that the trustee have more duties in order for the trust to be recognized.

Land trusts originated in Illinois. Promoters will claim that an Illinois-styled land trust will protect beneficiaries from liability. That is not true even under Illinois law. In Just Pants v. Bank of Ravenswood (483 N.E. 2s331, 335-336 (Ill. App. 1985)) the Illinois Court of Appeals held that land trust beneficiaries are responsible for negligence on the property. In People v. Chicago Title and Trust Co. (389 N.E. 2d540, 542-43, 546

(Ill. 1979)) the Illinois Supreme Court held that the beneficiaries and not the trustees of land trust properties were personally liable for unpaid real estate taxes. In the land of Lincoln and land trusts, beneficiaries are not protected. And this is true across the fruited plains.

So why hold property in a land trust? The proffered main advantage associated with land trusts is privacy. Your personal name supposedly does not appear on the trust or on any documents. Of course, you still would have to reveal your beneficial interest if asked in court or under oath.

Let's review a case on privacy and land trusts.

Case #22
Eli, Harry and Gertrude

Eli was a silver haired, well-dressed promoter who sold land trusts. He aggressively sold his incredible real estate holding land trusts to investors large and small for all the benefits they offered. Eli did not want to hear from others that while some of the benefits were real, others were concocted and without any basis in fact. Eli was certain of their benefits as he sold them and that was that.

One of the big benefits Eli sold was privacy. By holding title to your real estate in a land trust you could have complete anonymity. Eli had no use for muniments of title. Instead, privacy was paramount. For $500 per year, Eli would serve as the trustee of the trust. His name would appear on title as trustee and your name, as owner (or as beneficiary as an owner was termed in a land trust) would not appear anywhere. Eli would chart it as follows:

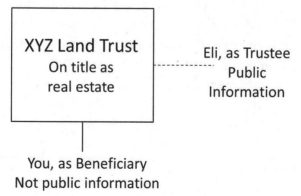

Eli's many clients really liked this option. They wanted privacy from all the predators that exist in our society. They wanted their assets to be protected from such claims. They didn't want their names found anywhere on the public land records so people could sue. Eli assured them that their names would never be seen again, and Eli glibly told his clients that this structure would protect them. They didn't need to spend money on LLCs and extra tax returns, Eli told them. This was just a scam by attorneys and CPAs to generate more fees. Eli explained he was there to protect them and save them from expensive costs.

Eli also told his clients that they could defer taxes indefinitely with a land trust structure. Because the beneficial interest in a land trust was not real estate but rather personal property, Eli explained that the interests could be transferred from one party to the next without paying taxes. Taxes, Eli explained, were only due once the property itself was sold.*

Harry and Gertrude attended one of Eli's seminars on land trusts. They greatly enjoyed what Eli called his "educational seminar" but which everyone understood was a sales presentation. Eli was an excellent and persuasive speaker, and Harry and Gertrude, along with everyone else in audience, were energized to sign up for Eli's services, which on that night only he had discounted just for their benefit if they signed up right away.

Harry and Gertrude, who didn't know each other before and had only met that night, agreed that this was a bargain they couldn't pass up. They both allowed Eli to structure a land trust strategy for them. Years went by, until once again the interests of Harry and Gertrude intersected on the same day.

Harry's main real estate asset was a 12 unit apartment building. A tenant had fallen down the stairs and severely injured himself. A plaintiff's attorney was now suing the land trust for the damages. This is known as Attack #1, or an inside attack.

---

* *Does this sound right to you?*

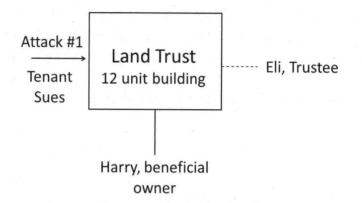

In Attack #1, the tenant can reach the asset involved. (The tenant leased from the land trust and the accident occurred on the land trust's property so the tenant gets to sue the land trust and perhaps get what the land trust owns, which is the 12 unit building).

When Eli, as trustee of the land trust, received service of the tenant's lawsuit, he called Harry to inform him of it.

Harry was confused. He asked Eli how he could get sued? Eli had said Harry had privacy and asset protection with his land trust. Harry thought that meant he couldn't get sued.

Eli had to explain to Harry that when a tenant sued over a problem at the property they could sue the land trust. Harry again was confused. Hadn't Eli told him that with Harry's name off the public record he could never be sued? Eli grew a bit agitated and said he had never really said that, to which Harry replied, "Yes you did!"

Eli went with a different approach. Since Harry had been sued over the building he needed to notify his insurance agent of the claim. "They will cover it," Eli said with assurance. Harry was flummoxed now. Because Eli had previously told him that with a land trust he had asset protection and could never be sued, he didn't carry insurance on the property. Harry thought he paid Eli $500 a year so he wouldn't have to pay $1500 a year for insurance. Eli again asserted that he didn't really ever say that. Harry again responded, "Yes you did!"

Eli grew short. He told Harry that since he had been sued he needed an attorney to represent him. Harry said he already had an attorney. He had been sued in a car wreck accident and had lost and they were coming after his assets.

This is known as Attack #2, or the outside attack.

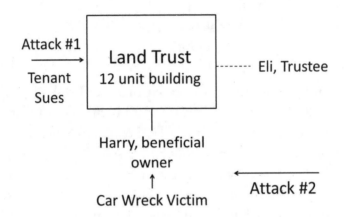

Unlike Attack #1, Attack #2 has nothing to do with the real estate. The person in the car wreck gets a judgment against you and wants to get at your assets. Different entities offer different degrees of protection (as we'll see).

When Eli learned that Harry had been sued in an outside attack he asked if Harry had disclosed his ownership of the 12 unit building. "Of course not," Harry replied. "You said I didn't have to."

Eli back pedaled further and said that if Harry was under oath he really had to tell the truth about his ownership of the land trust.

Harry yelled that was not what Eli had represented at his sales seminar and slammed down the phone. He immediately went to his attorney's office to learn the bad news—but the truth—about land trusts. His attorney explained that:

1. Land trusts offer no asset protection.
2. Land trusts are not a substitute for insurance.

Chapter Twenty-Two

3. In Attack #1, the tenant can get everything.
4. In Attack #2, the car wreck victim can get everything.

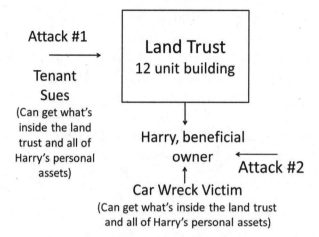

Attack #1

Tenant
Sues
(Can get what's
inside the land
trust and all of
Harry's personal
assets)

Land Trust
12 unit building

Harry, beneficial
owner

Attack #2

Car Wreck Victim
(Can get what's inside the land trust
and all of Harry's personal assets)

5. Privacy doesn't help you in Attack #1. The tenant's suit is against the property. Whether your name is on the public record or not doesn't matter.
6. Privacy doesn't help you in Attack #2. The car wreck victim has a judgment against you personally. When asked what assets you own you have to tell the truth and say you own the 12 plex (or go to jail for perjury later).
7. Whether your name is on the public record or not doesn't matter in either Attack #1 or Attack #2.

Harry lost everything. His attorney later sued Eli for misrepresentation and fraud. And with all the hundreds of people who had attended Eli's seminars, there were plenty of witnesses to testify as to what Eli actually said.

But before that lawsuit was served, and just after Eli got off the line with Harry, another lawsuit arrived. With the first being their attending the same sales seminar, this was now the second time Harry and Gertrude would intersect with Eli on the same day.

Gertrude had passed away years before. She had no relatives in Jameson County to look after things. The public administrator for the county settled her estate. As one would suspect, with hundreds of cases per year and very few employees to handle the case load, there was not a high degree of attention paid to each file.

But during her days, Gertrude had owned several apartment buildings in Jameson County. As Gertrude had grown older she had also grown very afraid of being sued by a tenant or a predator. She was fearful for her privacy. At that first seminar, everything Eli said resonated with Gertrude. And during Eli's consultation with Gertrude he heightened her fears even further.

But Eli had a solution. The predators could learn what Gertrude had through her tax returns. So Eli suggested the following structure:

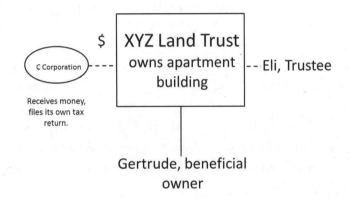

In this scenario Eli took care of all the apartment buildings' bookkeeping and payments for a fee. The remaining monies from the apartment buildings were not distributed to Gertrude where a predator could reach them or see the income on her tax return. Instead, the monies went to a C corporation. Because the C corporation paid its own taxes on its own separate tax return, one couldn't see that Gertrude had any money. Eli was the signer on the account for her further privacy. The money could accumulate in the C corporation and be Gertrude's private piggy bank. She could distribute the money to herself whenever she wanted. But Eli cautioned that to keep as low a profile as possible, it was best to just leave the money in the C corporation.

Gertrude liked the structure Eli set up. She didn't need the money flowing onto her personal tax return. She didn't need much money at all. Social Security covered her monthly expenses. She had no family to spend the money on. She was fine with letting the money sit in a protected account.

And so it went for several years until Gertrude passed on. The public administrator settling Gertrude's estate never knew about the apartment buildings or the cash rich C corporation. They weren't in her name anywhere. Eli never volunteered the information. Eventually, Gertrude's estate was closed without anyone knowing about the apartment buildings or the C corporation piggy bank. Except Eli.

After several more quiet years, Eli transferred the beneficial ownership in the land trust from Gertrude's name to his own name. As he had educated his students, the transfer was not public. No one would ever know that Gertrude's beneficial interests were now owned by Eli. Since he was a signer on the C corporation account, he withdrew the money, paid any taxes due to the IRS on behalf of the C corporation account, and shut down the C corporation. No one would ever know.

Until the lawsuit arrived.

Jason was Gertrude's third cousin once removed and her closest living relative. Jason remembered hearing that Aunt Gertrude owned several apartment buildings in Jameson County. He had been overseas for several years and was never contacted by anyone about her passing. Jason wondered what happened to his Aunt's estate.

Jason travelled to the Jameson County Recorder's Office. Contrary to what Eli taught in his class (and what Eli mistakenly believed) it was very easy to check the Grantor Index for property transfers. The records clearly showed that Gertrude had transferred her apartment buildings to the XYZ Land Trust. With the help of a private investigator (and a later look at Eli's tax returns) it was very easy to show that Eli had fraudulently taken over Gertrude's interest in the apartment buildings.

Jason and the private investigator easily used the Grantor and Grantee index (which are public records available for all to see, mind you) to learn that Eli, acting as trustee, had defrauded several estates in this way out of millions of dollars of real estate. His fraudulent scheme was to scare people about privacy so he could privately take their assets. But the public records pointed right back to him. As also discussed in Chapter 6 of *Start Your Own Corporation*, there are many fallacies regarding land trust privacy.

Amid all this fraud there was one transaction that really stood out as privacy akin to lunacy. Eli had encouraged his clients to buy real estate directly in the name of a land trust with Eli as both the trustee and beneficiary. When the land trust was on title Eli would secretly assign the beneficial interest to his client, the real buyer. This assignment document would never be recorded, so that the County's Grantor Index could never be used. In such cases, the Grantor would be the original seller of the property, not the original owner as in Gertrude's case, where she transferred the property from her name (the Grantor) into the Land Trust. By this artifice no one would ever know the beneficial buyer's identity. But this secrecy failed as a muniment of title. There was no record anywhere of the true buyer. Especially when Eli along the way lost the assignment document. Not only was it never recorded with the County but when Eli misplaced the document and over the years forgot the true buyer's identity there was no way to prove anything. When there is no muniment of title proving ownership, who receives title to the property? The state. It wasn't right for Eli to keep it. There was no way to prove anyone else owned it. In that case, it escheats (or reverts) to the government.

Loophole #30
Are you better served by privacy or a muniment of title?

When the IRS learned about all of Eli's nefarious dealings they sought to tax and penalize everyone involved. Contrary to Eli's teachings, the transfer of the beneficial interest from Gertrude to Eli was a taxable event for which taxes were due. And when Eli was forced to transfer the beneficial interest back to Jason that too was technically a taxable event.*

---

*How could it not be? Wouldn't everyone be using land trusts to transfer items of value if it was a legal way to avoid taxes? But, of course, the point here is that it is not legal unless the taxes are paid.

When the state's attorney general opened a criminal case against Eli they worked with the IRS to make certain that the appropriate taxes were paid, but that the innocents, like Jason, were exempted. The IRS then took the next logical step of looking into every single land trust Eli had ever been associated with. There were hundreds of people who had taken Eli's advice to make tax free transfers. These unthinking clients now, out of the blue, not only owed taxes but crushing penalties and interest.

It is important to know that taking advice from the wrong kind of person is not a defense in these cases. The IRS holds you strictly accountable to follow the law, no matter what some smooth operator told you to the contrary.

Jason received all of Gertrude's assets back, as did the other estates Eli had defrauded. Others, who had followed Eli's bad tax advice, did not fare so well. As mentioned, one unknown buyer had their property revert to the state government. In total, a number of lives were ruined.

Please know that land trusts neither offer asset protection nor many of the other benefits associated with them. And please, again, beware of who you take your advice from. Some will lead you down into the dark hole of privacy to a place where bad things can and do happen.

Loophole #31

There are no protective loopholes associated with land trusts. They offer zero asset protection. As to the privacy of castle ownership: Everyone in the village knows or can find out who owns the castle. But without a muniment of title, the king will get the castle back.

Now that we have reviewed how not to hold real estate let's explore how to do it right...

Chapter Twenty-Three

How to Hold Real Estate

As we have seen (and as you already know) there is risk in owning real estate. In doing so you are dealing with tenants, vendors and even strangers who interact daily with your ownership of the property. And one of them can become injured (or can at least appear injured) and sue. While insurance is the first line of defense not every claim will be covered. Insurance companies have an economic incentive not to pay out on every single claim and may find reasons in their own loopholes not to cover you. As well, you are operating in the most litigious society on earth. There is a litigation lottery mentality at work in our country. If you own assets there are predators out there willing to play the angles within the legal and medical system to take them from you.

But as we have also seen, there are tremendous tax benefits to owning real estate. The government wants us to own real estate. We just need a good way to protect it. And that's why you are reading this book, and this next chapter.

Case # 23
Marco

Marco had been an electrician for over thirty years. He ran his business as a sole proprietor from a building he had always rented. He ran his business his way, and never gave in to the pressures of others. He was a creature of habit who avoided change at all costs.

Marco's son, a successful businessman, constantly advised his father that he should be holding his electrical contracting company as a corporation, not as a sole proprietor in his own name. He was worried that his father was vulnerable. However, Marco didn't believe in paying the extra costs involved in owning a corporation when he didn't see the need for it. He had owned his business for thirty years in his name without a single problem. So, he shrugged off his son's suggestions.

Then, Marco's landlord, Dante, informed him that he was moving to live closer to his family in Peru. He didn't want to have to deal with the maintenance of the building from overseas, so he had decided to sell it. Dante wanted to give Marco the first opportunity to buy the property.

Buying the building was the last thing Marco wanted to deal with. He was quite content renting the building from Dante. Dante sensed Marco's hesitation and explained to him that if he didn't buy it, Dante would be forced to sell it to someone else that could possibly raise Marco's rent or even evict him if there was a new vision for the property.

So Marco finally decided that buying the building would be in his best interests. Before closing, Marco met with Dante and the loan officer. The loan officer asked him how he'd like to hold the title to the property. Marco was confused by this question—if the property was his, why wouldn't he hold it in his name?

Dante tried to explain that there are several options available for holding title to property. He suggested that it would be smart for a small business owner to own his property as a limited liability company or even in a limited partnership. Dante said these entities could offer Marco protection in the future.

Not surprisingly, Marco would have nothing to do with forming an entity to hold his real estate. He believed that these were useless services designed by greedy professionals to steal money from hard-working business owners. Against the advice of both Dante and the loan officer, Marco insisted that the loan be made directly to him, in his name only, and that his name appear solely on the title.

Then the inevitable nightmare occurred. A fire broke out in a million-dollar home after Marco did some electric work there, causing a great deal of wreckage. People were injured rushing out of the burning house. The losses were very large. The family sued him for negligence. Marco's woeful insurance policy could never cover the full amount of damage. A lawsuit was filed and Marco's assets were left completely exposed.

Because he owned everything in his name and did business as a sole proprietor, attorneys were able to reach his business and the building he owned. If he had listened to the advice of those around him and owned his business as a corporation and the real estate as an LLC, he would have had much greater protection.

By refusing to even listen to the advice of the knowledgeable people around him, Marco lost everything. This is the first lesson from Marco's story. Listen to the advice others offer to you. This doesn't mean you have to follow it—just be open to it. Robert Kiyosaki learned from his rich dad that investing and business are team sports. This is why it is so crucial to surround yourself with experts that you trust.

Loophole #32

There are professionals who know where the loopholes are to be found. You need to hear them out.

The other lesson to be learned from Marco's experience is that you should consider holding your real estate in an entity for protection purposes. A properly formed and maintained entity can discourage an attack. Holding real estate in your own name invites attacks.

So, how are you best protected when owning real estate? The answer comes down to six words: Limited Liability Companies and Limited Partnerships. They are the entities of choice for protecting your real estate holdings.

Why?

Because limited liability companies (LLC's) and limited partnerships (LPs) provide the greatest asset protection possible. Unlike a corporation, where a creditor can attack your shares and control the company[1], in

---

[1] *Except in Nevada, where the charging order applies to corporate shares.*

many states a creditor cannot assert voting control over your LLC or LP interests. They can't force you to sell the property. They can't vote in new management. Instead, they only obtain what is known as a charging order, which is a lien on distributions. This means the creditor has first dibs on any distributions from the entity. But because you remain in control, what if you decide not to make any distributions? The creditor gets nothing.

We will review how the charging order works after making one foundational point. It is not attractive for creditors to obtain a charging order when the result is that no distributions are received. In fact, knowing that your assets are held in LLCs and LPs may be enough to prevent a lawsuit from being brought in the first place. Lawyers know that lawsuits involve two battles: 1) winning in court and then 2) collecting. If they sense it will be difficult to collect against an asset they, in most cases, will rely on the insurance monies to satisfy their clients' claims and not go after any of your assets held in LLCs. That is why it is good to have both an insurance policy and asset protection entities.

The insurance policy is the first line of defense. It is the pot of red meat for the attorneys to go after. Most attorneys in these types of cases are on a contingency fee, meaning that only get paid when money is collected. The attorney will advance all the costs of the case and put in their time at no cost to the injured party. When a payment is received, either by a pre-trial settlement or a victory in court, they get a percentage of the payment (usually 33% to 45%). So on a $100,000 insurance payout the attorney gets, for example, $35,000. This is not a bad payday. But if the contingency attorney loses the case, they get nothing. This means they have to be careful about which cases to take, which is good for the rest of us. As well, these attorneys have to wisely allocate their time and resources. If the $100,000 settlement doesn't fully cover their clients' damages will the attorney look to the defendant's other assets? It depends. If they are easy to reach (as in a sole proprietorship or an individually titled situation) perhaps they will. But if those assets are held in properly structured asset protection entities, perhaps they won't. Remember, these lawyers are still mostly on a contingency fee. They don't get paid until they collect. Do they want to go after an LLC, get a charging order and wait for distributions to be paid? Probably not. It is not a good use of their time. There are too many other cases with new pots of insurance money to go after. This discussion is not meant to denigrate attorneys. It is rather to explain why rational, economic animals (as most attorneys are) will probably not pursue claims against properly structured plans. They are on a contingency and it is not worth their time. Knowing that, we plan accordingly.

The charging order protection is the key to protecting your assets from attack. It is important for you to know how it works, and in which cases it doesn't work.

We discussed Attack #1, the inside attack, and Attack #2, the outside attack, in a land trust setting in our last chapter. It is time to see how these two attacks play out with an LLC structure. (We will visit limited partnerships again but for now will focus on LLCs. The charging order procedure applies to both LLCs and LPs.) Our structure, which involves owning a 4 plex in the strong asset protection state of Wyoming, is as follows:

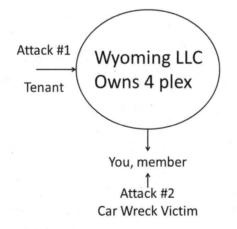

In Attack #1, a tenant falls at the property and sues the LLC (which holds the title to the 4 plex on the public record). If the LLC owner has insurance for such claims (which is always suggested) then perhaps a settlement is reached. If the insurance doesn't fully cover the claim or not enough of the claim then the attorney may decide to proceed against the LLC. In Attack #1, a claimant can get what is inside the LLC, the equity in the 4 plex. Suppose there is a first deed of trust in favor of the Lender against the 4 plex in the amount of $200,000 and the fair market value of the property is $300,000. How much equity do you have in the property? That's right, $100,000. (The fair market value of $300,000 subtracted from the $200,000 first deed to the lender leaves $100,000 in equity.) The attorney can't go after the full $300,000 value of the property because the bank has a prior claim. It has first dibs. They loaned the money and recorded the first deed of trust securing that loan before the tenant's accident ever occurred.

But, the tenant and their attorney can go after the $100,000 in equity in the property. And you say to yourself: That's not asset protection!

I disagree.

Look at our next chart:

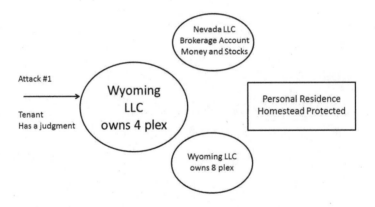

All the tenant can get is what is inside the 4 plex LLC. That LLC is the one he rented from. He has no claim against the 8 plex LLC or the other assets. And so you do have asset protection in that the tenant's claim is only against the one entity. He cannot get beyond that 4 plex entity to the other assets.

Compare this to our scenario with the land trust in the last chapter. In Harry's case, with the land trust offering no asset protection and no other protective entities, the tenant could reach everything Harry owned.

Will the attorney go after the equity in the LLC? Maybe yes and maybe no. Remember, the attorney is most likely still on a contingency fee basis. To force a sale of the property, deal with the bank and probably end up with a discounted sale price involves a lot of work. Assume that after commissions and fees and fire sale pricing the $100,000 in equity is brought down to $30,000. Is the contingency fee attorney going to all that trouble to make one third of that, or $10,000? Not likely. There are too many other surer cases to pursue.

But what if the equity in the house was the full market value price of $300,000? In other words, there was no loan against the property and it was owned free and clear. That is a much more inviting target for the attorney. The tenant and the attorney have a judgment against the LLC. To satisfy it they get a court order to sell the property. At a swift fire sale price they get $210,000 and the attorney pockets $70,000. That makes some sense for the attorney. Or what if the tenant and the attorney take over the property themselves. It becomes their rental unit on a 2/3 – 1/3 basis. That also makes sense for both of them.

As we are seeing here, debt is a form of asset protection. In the first example, where only $100,000 in equity was available, the target is lessened due to the debt of $200,000 against the property. But in Attack #1, with a claim against the LLC and the LLC holding a free and clear property worth $300,000, you have a more inviting asset to target. And this is why we have a strategy to encumber and protect your equity in properties subject to Attack #1 in Chapter 26 ahead.

Please know that a charging order doesn't apply in Attack #1. The Attack #1 claim is an attack against the LLC itself, so we don't even get to the charging order. (Fear not, we will.) As well, the Attack #1 claim plays out the same in every U.S. state. Whether you have a weak California LLC or a strong Wyoming LLC doesn't matter. The inside attack is against the entity itself. The claimant can get what's inside the LLC no matter what the state of formation. But again, they can't get what's outside the LLC, a beneficial measure of asset protection that's true even in California.

Okay fine, you say. So where does this special charging order come into play? The charging order protects you in an Attack #2 claim, the outside attack. Again, assume you were in a car wreck. The accident had nothing to do with your 4 plex. But because your insurance didn't properly or fully cover you, the judgment creditor (the car wreck victim who won a judgment against you) wants to get at your assets.

As we said, there are two legal battles to be fought. The first one has already been won. The car wreck victim went to court and the judge and/ or jury awarded a verdict of $300,000. Assume for right now that the insurance didn't cover the claim. The only way for the judgment creditor to collect is to get at your 4 plex.

Now the second battle begins. Assume we have a Wyoming LLC owning a Wyoming 4 plex. To get at the asset the judgement creditor must go back into court for a second time to try and get the 4 plex. The exclusive remedy in Wyoming (and Nevada) is the charging order. The court in Wyoming will review the judgment creditor's paperwork to make sure they have a valid claim. Satisfied that it is, the court then issues the charging order. That charging order 'charges' or allows the judgment creditor to stand in your place and receive distributions from the LLC. It doesn't allow the judgment creditor to force a sale of the 4 plex or control how it is operated. Instead, the charging order just allows for the receipt of distributions as follows:

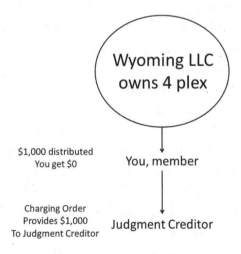

If money is distributed from the LLC it skips past you to the judgment creditor. What if no distributions are made? Then the judgment creditor gets nothing.

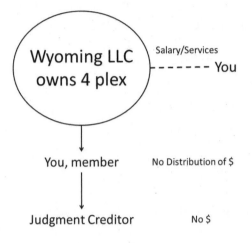

What if you get paid for services to the LLC? That is not a distribution for which the charging order applies. So you can take a salary and let the judgment creditor try to figure this out and then try to garnish your wages.

Loophole #33

The charging order is a key asset protection device. By slipping distributions, if any, through the castle loophole, you avoid having to give up the whole castle.

Remember our contingency fee attorney in all of this? The one who has done all the work and doesn't want to sit around waiting to be paid. Does this person like dealing with a charging order and the member's ability to direct monies away from distributions?

Of course not. The attorney wants no part of this colossal hassle. And so maybe they settle for any insurance monies. And if there is no insurance money to go after maybe they don't even bring the case in the first place. Sure, they can win the first battle easily. But if you can't win the second battle of collecting why even bother? There are too many other, more profitable cases to pursue.

The attorney's attitude changes a bit if we are in a weak LLC state like Georgia, California, New York and others. In certain weak states the courts allow judicial foreclosure:

Loophole #34

In weak LLC states you don't have protective loopholes. Instead, you have courts that order you to give up the entire castle.

Knowing this, there is a way for the Wyoming charging order to apply. We have the Georgia LLC owned by the Wyoming LLC.

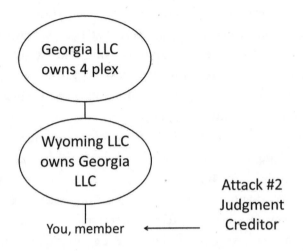

In this way the attacking judgment creditor may have to go to Wyoming (even if they live in Georgia) and hire an attorney to go to court and get a charging order. Remember, this is not an Attack #1 claim involving the Georgia 4 plex. In that case, the Georgia court would have jurisdiction. In Attack #2, because the Georgia LLC holding the valuable real estate is owned by a Wyoming LLC, the judgment creditor may have to pursue you in Wyoming. And that's what you want. The threat of the distance and trouble of fighting the case in Wyoming only to get a charging order allowing for distributions which may never come. You can understand why a contingency fee attorney may not like this bargain. Please know that some courts hold that they have the power to issue, for example, a Georgia charging order against a Wyoming LLC owned by a Georgia resident. In that case it is important to know how your state handles charging orders. It is a fluid area of the law. But not every attorney and client understands the wrinkle. Argue they must travel to Wyoming.

Loophole #35
Using a Wyoming or Nevada LLC to own your in-state property LLC is an excellent asset protection strategy. Let the invaders believe they have to travel afar to a place where you are still lord of your castle.

There are several more issues to discuss here. But first, be cautious of asset protection promoters who claim that their expensive system is so complicated that your regular advisors won't understand it. And because they won't get it the promoters will advise you that you shouldn't even bother asking your existing advisors about it. If anyone makes this type of pitch to you, get up and leave. They are a scam artist.

Secondly, beware of corporate and legal form promoters who guarantee 100% bulletproof asset protection. Yes, you will be better protected by using LLCs and LPs. But no one in a good conscience can offer a 100% guarantee. We do not live in a static society. Laws change and future court decisions may minimize current protections. LLCs are newer entities and we don't yet have a lot of court cases defining their features. You will do the best you can in our current framework but there are no absolute guarantees. Please be very clear that someone who offers a 100% asset protection guarantee is 100% of the time trying to separate you from your money.

An example of how the law can change happened recently in Florida. The Federal Trade Commission ("FTC") with the full power of the federal government behind it, sued a credit card scamster named Olmstead and won the case, obtaining a judgment against Olmstead. With the first battle out of the way, the FTC next sought to collect. But then Olmstead argued his assets were in an LLC as follows:

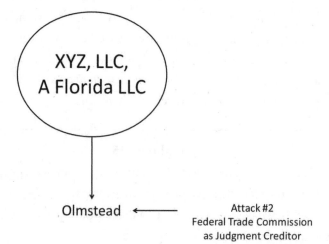

Under Florida law all the FTC was entitled to get was a charging order. And with a charging order the owner could decide not to make distributions and wave his middle finger at the Feds. Believe it or not, the Feds don't like to be treated that way. It actually pisses them off. And with a large number of attorneys and resources at their disposal, the FTC fought back. The case went all the way to the Florida Supreme Court (another government agency) and by zigging and zagging the court came up with its decision: The charging order did not apply to single member LLCs.

Because the LLC was only owned by Mr. Olmstead it was a single member LLC. If Mr. Olmstead had owned it with someone else it would have been a multi member LLC and the Florida Supreme Court would have had a tougher time with the case. They would have had to find that no one was entitled to charging order protection. That wouldn't have been good. But they were able to reach the end result they wanted—letting the FTC get at Mr. Olmstead's ill-gotten gains—by finding that single member LLCs weren't entitled to charging order protection.

This case shocked a lot of people. All of a sudden those with single member Florida LLCs had a lot less protection. And people outside of Florida worried if it can happen in that state it can happen in mine. As we said, the laws of asset protection are not static. They do change.

Which is why many people were pleased with how the states of Nevada and Wyoming responded after the Florida case. They changed their laws so that the charging order procedure was the one and only exclusive remedy a creditor had–even for single member LLCs. This was a very positive development in the world of asset protection, and is why Nevada and Wyoming are the favored states for LLC formation. More recently, Delaware, South Dakota, and Alaska have also protected single member LLCs.

It should be noted that a recent case in Nevada held that a single member LLC offered no protection in a bankruptcy setting. (This is also true in Colorado and other states.) The bankruptcy court held that the bankruptcy trustee could step into the shoes of the LLC's single member for the benefit of the bankruptcy estate. This is why many people consider multiple member LLC's to be a better way to proceed.

Along with asset protection, we need to consider state taxation. In that arena, California is the state to plan for. California has an extra tax on LLCs. If you have gross receipts (not profits but just revenues) of $250,000 a year or more in your LLC you pay an extra tax to the state of California. At a minimum, the tax is $800 but with millions in gross receipts you will find yourself paying thousands of extra dollars for the privilege of using an LLC in California. So on larger properties you will use a limited partnership, which are not assessed California's extra gross receipts tax. (At least not yet.)

Of course, the issue with the LPs is that it requires a general partner to manage it. And a general partner is personally responsible for everything that happens in a limited partnership. So if you list yourself as an individual you haven't really protected yourself. You're still personally responsible.

The key to using an LP is to make sure that the general partner is another corporation or LLC. In this way you encapsulate the unlimited liability of the general partner into a limited liability entity. Thus, for California and all other states your LP structure will look like this:

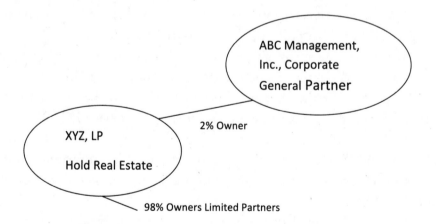

The beauty of the limited partnership structure is that with as little as 2% ownership, the general partner can exert complete control over the affairs of the limited partnership. This is an excellent way to handle properties with family members or investors involved. As limited partners they can be prevented from asserting demands or control over the investment. If your kids are a challenge and they want you to sell the 4 plex so that they can hit the road with the band you, as general partner, can say no. As general partner you are in control. The kids can own 50% or 70% or 90% of the limited partnership interests and as long as you are the general partner that 4 plex will not be sold. Absent fraud, the general partner reigns supreme.

The problem with properly structuring a limited partnership is that it requires the formation and maintenance of not one but two entities. To do it right you need not only a limited partnership but a corporation or LLC to serve as the general partner. (Remember, if you serve as the general partner in your individual capacity you are personally responsible for everything.)

In an expensive state like California, where the annual entity fee is $800 per year, the costs can add up. But there are two points to remember.

First, the extra $800 may pale in comparison to the many thousands of dollars in extra California state taxes to be paid on an active LLC.

Second, you can use your corporation (or LLC) to be the general partner of more than one LP. In other words you only need to pay the formation fee and annual $800 fee (in California) once, not every time you form a new LP. An example is as follows:

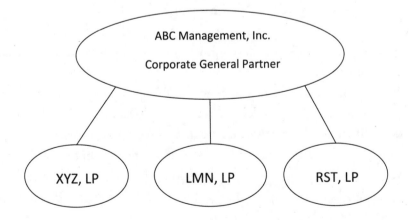

In this illustration, ABC Management, Inc. is the corporate general partner for three separate limited partnerships. This structure will work in any state. And if you read our companion books, *Start Your Own Corporation* and *Run Your Own Corporation*, along with Tom Wheelwright's *Tax-Free Wealth*, you will learn about the tax advantages and write offs you can achieve with a management corporation.

Loophole #36

An individual General Partner is not protected in a limited partnership's structure. You will need two entities (one to serve as the General Partner) for full protection.

As an alternative, some people are now using a Limited Liability Limited Partnership (an LLLP or Triple LP). In this limited partnership you don't need a second entity to be a general partner because, theoretically, everyone is protected by the LLLP. The problem is that these entities are too new. The state of California, for example, does not extend asset protection to the general partner within the LLLP. Until the law is fleshed out you are better off using LLCs or LPs.

Of course, we still need to plan some more for California. It is important to keep up with what is happening in the State of California because, as frequently happens, what starts there spills out over the rest of the country. But in this new development one has to hope and pray that these ideas stay put.

The state of California has implemented very broad rules (and costs) for business owners and holders of real estate located both within and outside California. These new rules are disturbing and draconian.

And because California's rules are ever changing (but consistently involve an expansion of the concept of doing business in the state) we have a link to keep you up to date with the latest changes. Please visit www.corporatedirect.com/california.

But, as an example of their overreach, consider the following:

The state of California's tax department, the Franchise Tax Board (FTB), has dictated that the Florida LLC above, which only owns real estate in Florida, is doing business in California because it has a 1% member who lives in California. When the Florida LLC issues a K-1 tax return to the California resident, the FTB will use that information to send a demand letter to the Florida LLC to pay California $800 per year. The Florida LLC, with the 1% California member, by the FTB's overly broad standards is doing business in California. Pay us $800 a year.

The Florida LLC must then make its case to the FTB that the California resident is a passive investor and not involved in management of the LLC. They must show their specially drafted LLC Operating Agreement to prove that the California resident has no management authority.

At some point, syndicators of real estate, who don't want to pay attorneys extra money for specially drafted LLC documents only to have to later prove themselves to the overly aggressive FTB, are going to come up with the logical solution: No Californians allowed.

When you learn about California's position on collecting taxes (and I encourage you to read the full, up to date article on the web) you have to ask yourself:

Are we now governed by a bureaucracy seeking only to maximize their salaries and pensions? How long can this last?

Due to the additional complications of actually investing inside the state, there is one option many of our clients are now considering: Don't invest in California real estate. While many are comfortable with investing locally and can cover whatever fees the FTB throws at them, others are starting to see a very disturbing trend and are voting with their feet. They are buying real estate elsewhere.

This is especially true when one learns of California's drastic penalties for failing to qualify an out of state entity in California. These include:

- A penalty of $2,000, in addition to other failure to file penalties;

- The inability to bring a lawsuit in California;

- A penalty of $20 a day up to $10,000 for failing to file California tax returns; and

- The treatment of all members as general partners and thus imposing unlimited personal liability for all acts committed in California.

The last item is particularly galling. You have done the right thing in setting up an LLC. Because of a mistake or inadvertence or an unclear law, you fail to qualify in California. And the state of California's response is to strip you of any asset protection and allow you to be held personally liable for the claims of others.

Loophole #37
Alot of money has been made in California. But you have to think twice about how a state treats its private investors.

Now let's look at how some savvy investors do it...

Chapter Twenty-Four

Asset Protection Lessons

Case #24
Sammy

Sammy was an astute real estate investor. He had started out as a carpenter working for a company that both built homes and filled in their time with remodeling jobs. Sammy learned his craft and more. He was a people person and got to know some of the clients. He soon realized that the clients who spent $10,000 with the company to remodel a property were turning around and making $50,000 when they later sold the property.

Sammy liked being a carpenter/jack-of-all-trades, but even more so, he liked to make money. So he started by buying a run-down property at a discount that he could fix in his spare time. While he experienced a few setbacks and some learning pains, when the remodeling and painting was completed, Sammy had a $20,000 profit after the sale.

That was enough to launch Sammy into his new career. Since then, Sammy had been buying distressed properties, fixing them up and selling them. In the last six years, Sammy had also been fixing up duplexes and 4 plexes and keeping them for his own portfolio. To further his real estate options, in the last year Sammy had started building spec houses for sale and profit.

Sammy had assembled a good team of professionals. He had learned from his CPA and attorney that each of his three real estate activities –

remodeling for quick sales, holding and keeping, and building homes for speculation, or spec home sales – required a different legal strategy and a different means of taking title. His strategy was as follows:

1. Remodel for quick sales. This is the strategy Sammy had first started with and it continued to constitute a significant portion of his profits. Still, as more new investors were getting into "fixing and flipping," the sale prices for distressed real estate were increasing. Sammy knew what his margins were and wouldn't bid on dilapidated yet overpriced properties as others were doing. Nevertheless, there were plenty of good fixer-uppers in his area to acquire. Sammy maintained good relations with the local brokers, always paid a full commission and never tried to wrangle a broker out of a fee. As a result, Sammy always heard of the best deals first, and could take his pick of acceptable properties.

Because Sammy was flipping several properties a year, he was subject to ordinary income taxation. This meant he had to pay a 37% tax (the highest federal income tax rate as of this writing) on all his flips instead of only a 23.8% capital gain tax rate (at this writing).

It is important to understand why Sammy had to pay the higher tax rate. There are two reasons.

First, when Sammy flipped he rarely held onto a property for over one year. Instead, he would acquire, remodel, fix up, and sell, all within a period of months. The faster, the better. But by selling his fixer properties within one year, he did not qualify for the capital gains rate. To get the lower 23.8% rate, you must have held onto the asset for over one year.

On these properties, Sammy didn't want to wait a year. He wanted to turn them and cash out as quickly as possible. If there was a higher tax rate, so be it.

Of course, as mentioned, there was a second reason Sammy had to pay the higher tax rate. And that was because flipping properties was his business. It was how he earned his salary.

When you earn money through a trade or business, whatever this activity may be, that income is subject to ordinary income rates. When you are flipping two or more properties a year, or if all you do is fix up properties (even at the rate of just one per year), your income is subject to income tax withholding. This income can also be subject to payroll taxes of 15.3% on the first $137,700 of income and 2.9% Medicare withholding above $137,700 (as of this writing). If a single employee receives wages in excess of $200,000 per year an additional 0.9% for Medicare must be withheld. (The threshold is $250,000 for married taxpayers filing jointly.)

This brings us to the best way to take title for Sammy's (and for your) flipping activities.

While in a large majority of cases, you will want to take title to your real estate in an LLC, for flipping you will consider using an LLC taxed as an S corporation. The reason for this, as with so many other things in life, has to do with taxes.

In a business operating LLC, all monies flowing through the entity to the owner can be subject to payroll and Medicare taxes. The same is not true for a passive holding LLC. So we must distinguish between an LLC that passively holds real estate and one that conducts a trade or business, including a business operating as a real estate flipping LLC.

An LLC that passively holds real estate for investment purposes offers excellent asset protection. As well, all monies flow through the entity (that is, there is no tax at the entry level as in a C corporation) to the individual. Because the individual (Sammy, you, whoever) usually has another job, payroll taxes do not attach to this stream of income. Likewise, receiving rents from investment real estate is not classified as trade or business income to which payroll taxes apply.

The result is different with a business operating LLC. Sammy's business of turning fixer-uppers (or any other service business where the LLC members are active in the business) conducted through an LLC results in all monies flowing through being subject to payroll taxes.

As we all know, Social Security withholding does not lead to glory, or glorious returns. The system is broken and may never be repaired. (The Social Security Administration to their credit, or to scare up more taxes, is now alerting taxpayers that short falls are coming.) So if we can pay our fair share without going overboard, instead of paying every last dollar into the system, we will be better off in the long run. The principle here is that you can spend your own money more wisely than the government can. It is a timeless and enduring principle to be followed.

Instead of having all monies flowing through a business operating LLC be subject to payroll tax, consider using an LLC taxed as an S corporation. You could also use an S corporation formed in Nevada, which offers charging order protection for corporate shares. With S corporation taxation, you will pay yourself a reasonable salary and pay payroll taxes on that salary. But any profits over and above your salary can be flowed through the S corporation as dividends. You will pay ordinary income taxes on this income, but unlike the business operating LLC, you won't pay payroll taxes on it. Again, payroll taxes—even the 2.9% Medicare tax on salaries above $137,700—can really add up, especially when you consider it may go toward a benefit you'll never see. (Of course, you are going to talk to your own tax advisor about a scenario that is right for you. Your situation may be slightly different than we are discussing here. One size does not fit all.)

The next question becomes: What is a reasonable salary? Can you have a lucrative LLC taxed as an S corporation with $1 million in profits and pay only a $10,000 salary and flow through $990,000 in payroll tax-free profits?

The IRS is all over this one. You've got to remember that the IRS is made up of some pretty smart tax collectors who aren't that easily fooled. Their position on this issue comes down to the question of marketplace salaries. Could you hire someone skilled enough to manage a company that makes $1 million in profits per year and pay them a salary of $10,000? The answer, of course, is no. Neither you nor I would work to benefit someone else so greatly for such a pittance in return. The question then becomes what is an appropriate salary in such a case? Given the profits, a justifiable salary would be more in the range of $100,000 a year.

Work with your CPA to come up with an acceptable salary level. Comparison information for your industry and region can be found at www.salary.com. By paying yourself a reasonable salary and payroll taxes on that amount, you are then free to flow profits through your LLC taxed as an S corporation (or your Nevada-based S corporation) as dividends and avoid payroll taxes on those monies. By using the lower end of the acceptable salary range, you will avoid an IRS audit and not pay more than your fair share of expensive and nonproductive payroll taxes. (Again, be sure to work with your tax advisor on this, or a similar, strategy.)

As a result of the foregoing, Sammy conducted his remodel and fixer-upper business through an LLC taxed as an S corporation. Working with his CPA, he paid himself a reasonable salary and flowed his profits through the entity for payment on his individual tax return at ordinary income rates.

2. Hold and keep. As Sammy analyzed each new property, he would always ask himself whether it was one to flip or keep.

While he knew how to accelerate the return on his money by quickly flipping properties, he also knew that his long-term retirement needs would be in part satisfied by rental real estate income. Sammy's goal was to acquire one new apartment building per year. Typically, his ideal candidate was a duplex or 4 plex that needed some repair. In such cases he could buy below market and perform improvements over time at his convenience. When he didn't have a quick flip to work on, he could keep his crew busy on his hold and keep properties.

Sammy always held his hold and keep properties in an LLC. He valued the asset protection benefits of keeping his properties in separate entities, especially after suffering two lawsuits early in his career. The first lawsuit arose when he operated his construction business as a sole proprietor and held his first investment property, a duplex, in his individual name. A client had sued Sammy over some very careless work a subcontractor had performed. The plumber had gone out of business and left the state, leaving Sammy holding the bag. A judgment was rendered whereby Sammy's sole proprietorship was held liable for the significant damages. Since the sole proprietorship offered no asset protection whatsoever, all of Sammy's personal assets were fair game for collection. And because Sammy hadn't used a protective entity to hold title to his duplex, the property was completely exposed to the claims of the judgment creditor.

Loophole #38

Doing business as a sole proprietor and holding title to real estate in your individual name invites attack. With no castle walls, the invaders are free to take whatever you own.

As a result, Sammy lost all of his sole proprietorship assets, his trucks and equipment, as well as the duplex. All lost to satisfy the claims for damages he did not cause. It was a bitter experience Sammy vowed would never happen again.

Sammy immediately started operating his construction business for flipping properties through an LLC taxed as an S corporation. He began acquiring hold properties with a vengeance, putting them all into an LLC. Before long, he had three 4 plexes and one triplex in his one LLC.

Then the second lawsuit was filed.

A tenant had fallen at the triplex. Normally, an A-rated insurance company would have covered the claim. But Sammy's insurance company was C-rated and after paying huge brokerage commissions to attract the business, it had very little money left to actually cover any claims. The insurance company used their loophole escape hatches to argue that Sammy had intentionally maintained a dangerous condition on the property. They argued that such intentional conduct was exclusion to the policy, meaning they didn't have to cover the claim.

Sammy was furious with the company and the insurance agent who sold him the commission-rich and coverage-poor policy. The "dangerous" condition was a step that had just broken. It wasn't intentionally maintained that way. Sammy and his attorney considered bringing a bad faith lawsuit against the insurance company for failing to cover the tenant's claim. But that involved a great deal of time and money, and all of Sammy's extra time and money was now being spent defending the tenant's claim.

As the chart below indicates, the tenant prevailed against the LLC that owned the triplex.

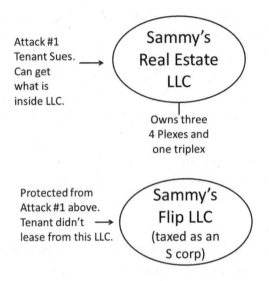

Attack #1
Tenant Sues. → **Sammy's Real Estate LLC**
Can get
what is
inside LLC.

Owns three
4 Plexes and
one triplex

Protected from
Attack #1 above. → **Sammy's Flip LLC** (taxed as an S corp)
Tenant didn't
lease from this LLC.

The good news was that Sammy's construction business and personal assets were not exposed to the claim. The bad news was that the judgment allowed the tenant to proceed against all of the first LLC's assets. Two of the 4 plexes were owned free and clear. The tenant's attorney was able to easily attach the 4 plexes and sell them to satisfy the claim.

Loophole #39

In Attack #1, a successful invader can get what is inside the castle. Consider having separate castles for separate properties.

It was after this experience that Sammy came to appreciate that one did not want to own too many properties in one LLC or LP. By holding four properties in one LLC, a tenant with a claim involving one of the properties can reach the equity in all four properties.

Sammy decided that in the future, only one property would be held in each LLC. Putting too many properties in one LLC created an attractive target for the professional litigants of the world. It was well worth the increased annual LLC filing fees for Sammy to segregate his real estate into individual LLCs. It was a form of insurance, in case his insurance company once again failed to protect him as promised.

Sammy knew that some states made it expensive to use individual entities for each parcel of real estate. He knew that California charged a minimum of $800 per year per entity for a weak asset protection law. Sammy knew that to better his legal position he needed to pay the extra, yet reasonable fees for entities formed in Nevada and Wyoming. For Sammy, after losing two 4 plexes to a tenant's claim, the increased protection was another form of insurance and well worth the extra cost.

And so Sammy used an LLC or LP to hold each of his hold and keep investment properties.

3. Spec home sales. Whether building one home for speculative sale purposes or building a subdivision full of identical tract homes, Sammy knew that a unique protection strategy was needed. This was because more and more lawyers across the country were bringing lawsuits alleging damage from mistakes during construction, known as construction defect litigation. Plaintiff's lawyers were filing lawsuits on behalf of homeowners alleging monetary damages due to settling, cracks, improper construction practices, and the like. These suits were especially prevalent in California and Nevada, where a ten year statute of limitations allowed suits to be brought a decade after a house was built. Lawyers were targeting subdivisions built nine and a half years earlier, and, as Sammy perceived it, were stirring the pot with homeowners to identify both real and imagined problems for which a contingency lawsuit could be brought.

Sammy and his lawyer realized that a new strategy had to be used to confront the construction defect litigation explosion.

Each time Sammy built a spec home (a home built on the speculation that someone who had nothing to do with the designing and planning will buy it "as is") he used a new entity. Again, because of its asset protection benefits and efficient flow-through taxation of income, Sammy used a separate LLC for each custom home he built. In California, because of the extra state taxes on LLCs, he would use an LP with a corporate general partner as his developer entity.

The key to Sammy's strategy was to keep each entity active after the house had been sold. This was to thwart the aggrieved homeowners and their lawyers who had ten years to bring a construction defect claim. By keeping the entity alive during the ten-year statute of limitations period, any claim would be brought against the LLC or LP, not personally against the owners. (If the owners had instead dissolved the entity without properly dealing with any future claims they could be held personally responsible for a later claim.) And nine-plus years later, after selling the spec house, what was in that surviving LLC or LP? That's right: Nothing. The entity that built and sold the house was not a very attractive target.

But isn't it expensive to keep an entity alive for ten years? What about all the filing fees and tax returns? As Sammy knew, it isn't a burden if done the right way.

As far as tax returns are concerned, once each house was sold a final tax return for the entity was prepared. The LLC or LP could stay alive but have no activity and thus not have to file an ongoing return. In terms of annual filing fees, some states are more expensive than others. For example, the annual LLC fee in Massachusetts is $500 per year. Including a $125 annual resident agent fee, the ten-year cost per entity is $6,250.

But what if your Massachusetts entity was originally formed in a low-cost state such as Wyoming? That was Sammy's money-saving strategy. The developer entity was formed in Wyoming and qualified to do business in Massachusetts. Qualifying in Massachusetts was required since the house was being constructed in Massachusetts. But once the house was sold, the entity no longer conducted any Massachusetts business. It was free to stop paying Massachusetts fees and only had to pay the minimal Wyoming fees of $50 per year. Assuming the same $125 annual resident agent fee, the cost of maintaining a Wyoming entity for 10 years was only $1,750 versus $6,250 for Massachusetts. By forming the entity in Wyoming, qualifying in Massachusetts for only as long as necessary and then keeping the entity alive in Wyoming until the ten-year statute of limitations ran out, Sammy was able to affordably protect himself and his other assets.

By using only one developer entity per one or two houses, a litigant nine or more years later was left to sue an empty shell, not an attractive or lucrative target. Of course, a litigant could always sue the builders and subcontractors involved on the job for all the alleged construction defects. But again, the incentive for the plaintiffs' lawyers is to bring as many homeowners into one contingency lawsuit as possible.

They prefer to represent a homeowner's association of 30 to 300 or more homeowners. The more aggregated claims, the more money to be made. That incentive is greatly diminished when the claim is to be brought against a developer entity that developed not an entire tract of homes, but just one or two spec homes.

And so Sammy kept each developer entity alive in Wyoming for ten years. Sammy's CPA prepaid the $1,750 ten-year holding cost to the law firm in Wyoming. For Sammy, the money was a cost of doing business passed onto the buyer and an affordable form of additional insurance. Once the statute of limitations had run out and any defect claims were time barred from being filed, Sammy had the choice of dissolving the entity or keeping it alive and using it only for the next spec home. After all, it had a ten-year history at that point and the formation fees had already been paid.

Sammy's three strategies for remodels, holdings, and spec home developments served him well and he prospered without any further devastating litigation.

Loophole #40

The laws of asset protection allow for flexibility and customization. Beware of any professional who insists that one size fits all.

Now let's consider protecting your prized real estate...

Chapter Twenty-Five

Protecting Your Home and Related Asset Protection Strategies

There are four ways to protect one of the most valuable assets you will ever own, your primary residence. One way you know, one we have discussed, and the second two may surprise you.

The way you know is through insurance. Everyone has homeowner's insurance, right? But let's consider this method. It is ironic that you can never ensure that insurance will insure you. As with Sammy's case, there are loophole exceptions buried deep in the four-point, magnifying glass required type that let insurance companies off the hook. Which leads us to ask: How did paying all those premiums benefit us?

As well, insurance companies are notoriously petulant. If they don't like your state and its rates they'll pick up their marbles and go home, as they do every decade or so in California. Or they'll raise the rates everywhere after a local disaster. California's Sonoma County Wildfires of 2017 sent rates skyrocketing throughout the West in 2018. As well, a great insurance rate today that contributes to an acceptable investment analysis and eventual property purchase may later turn to an inability to even acquire any insurance at all. They set the rates and then, because you accepted them, punish you by withdrawing from the state. Can we insure some order around here?

So while insurance is the first line of defense for any real estate holding—be it your home or an investment property—because it is never bulletproof we need to develop other secondary lines of defense.

For your primary residence another line of defense is one we discussed—the homestead exemption. Texas, Kansas, Oklahoma and Florida offer unlimited homestead protection. Massachusetts offers $500,000 in home equity protection, whereas Kentucky only offers $5,000. Each state has different rules and dollar limits. A summary is found at www.corporatedirect.com/asset-protection/.

The remaining two defense lines may surprise you. The first is debt.

Many people assume that debt does not provide asset protection because debt is money owed to someone else. This is true. But while you owe the money, remember that protected assets are in the eye of the attacker.

As an example, suppose you live in Nevada and own a $750,000 house with a $250,000 mortgage on it secured by a first deed of trust. You have $500,000 in equity and have just put a homestead on your house, which in Nevada offers $550,000 in homeowner protection.

How does an attacker see your situation? They don't care that you owe the bank $250,000 on your mortgage. All they care is that the bank has a secure and superior claim to the first $250,000, which means they can't get at it. Looking at the remaining $500,000 it is now protected by your Nevada homestead exemption. This means you as the homeowner have first dibs on that money. As such, with the first deed of trust and the homestead in place the attacker cannot get at any equity in the property. It is already spoken for to your benefit.

In this case, and in many like it, mortgage debt is to your advantage because it discourages and prevents an attacker from coming after you. You may also be better off taking the equity out of your house using debt so you can invest in more real estate or other income producing assets. In recent times, some people weren't so lucky with this strategy. Still, we will consider how it can work for you in the next chapter.

What about the situation where your primary residence has a great deal of unprotected equity above the mortgage and the homestead exemption? Say your mortgage is $50,000, your homestead exemption is $10,000 and the remaining equity on the mansion is $1.2 million? How do you protect so much equity?

The last line of defense is the single-member limited liability company. As you already know, a limited liability company (or LLC) is an excellent way to hold real estate. You can elect favorable flow-through taxation and, especially with LLCs formed in Nevada and Wyoming, achieve outstanding asset protection. To do it correctly, there should be a simple lease in place between the LLC and the occupiers of the home. Mom and dad will pay rent to the LLC, which in turn will pay the mortgage.

Until recently, however, personal residences were not held by LLCs. This was because the mortgage interest deduction could not be claimed through an LLC. Additionally, the $500,000 capital gains exclusion for married couples on the sale of a principal residence was not allowed through an LLC.

All this changed when the IRS issued regulations extending such tax benefits to personal residence holding LLCs as long as certain requirements were met. (Please note that while the capital gains exclusion and mortgage interest deductions can now be achieved through LLCs, homestead exemptions are still only for individuals, not for their primary residence holding LLCs.)

The two key requirements are that the LLC must be a single-member LLC and a disregarded entity for income tax purposes.

A single-member LLC can be an LLC with a catch. The single-member part refers to one member or one membership interest holder. This means that the LLC has just one owner. The catch is that the holder can be a husband and wife, together, for example, as joint tenants. Or the single member can be their living trust, in which both have an interest, and which makes sense for estate planning purposes. So a single member, if done right pursuant to the catch, can be two people.

The upshot is that because most primary residences are owned by husbands and wives together, the flexibility of a single-member LLC allows for that joint holding to continue with added asset protection.

Qualifying as a disregarded entity for income tax purposes is easy to do once you have a single-member LLC in place. You simply do not apply for an Employer Identification Number (EIN) and instruct your CPA to flow all the LLC tax items onto your personal tax return. (However, opening a bank account may be an issue since many banks insist on an EIN ever for single member LLCs.)

The single-member LLC is considered disregarded for tax purposes because there is only one member (or—remember—two people according to the catch.) And with only one member, the tax obligations flow through the LLC directly to the member.

Several questions frequently arise at this point.

First, what if a single-member LLC (for example, ABC, LLC) is owned by another LLC (XYZ, LLC), which is then owned by two members? (While this doesn't work in a personal residence scenario since the mortgage interest deductions must flow directly onto your personal return, this can work in an investment holdings scenario.) A chart illustrates the concept:

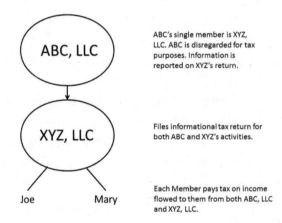

ABC's single member is XYZ, LLC. ABC is disregarded for tax purposes. Information is reported on XYZ's return.

Files informational tax return for both ABC and XYZ's activities.

Each Member pays tax on income flowed to them from both ABC, LLC and XYZ, LLC.

How do tax returns get filed? In the example above, ABC, LLC is a disregarded entity and the tax obligations flow to XYZ, LLC. Because XYZ, LLC has two members it is not a disregarded entity and must file a return. Which is fine. This strategy is used when a series of single-member LLCs are owned by one multiple member-holding LLC as follows:

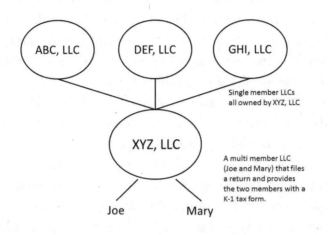

Because the three single member LLCs flow their tax obligations to XYZ, LLC there is only one tax return. The use of disregarded entities can really cut down on the need to prepare a myriad of tax returns. What if ABC, LLC holds an Arizona property? Since you must file a return in Arizona, ABC, LLC files a state return there. The obligation to file a federal return flows to XYZ, LLC. Because it is a Wyoming entity and no state returns need to be filed in Wyoming, XYZ, LLC just files a federal return. Again, the number of tax returns is minimized.

The second question relates to asset protection. If the LLC is a disregarded entity, don't you then lose all the limited liability protection?

The answer is no. The fact that for tax purposes the IRS considers it a disregarded entity doesn't mean that for legal purposes the asset protection is compromised. The LLC, if properly formed and maintained, provides limited liability protection to its members, whether disregarded by the IRS for tax filings or not.

Loophole #41

A tax loophole is different than a legal loophole. Just because you receive a tax benefit doesn't mean you automatically lose a legal protection.

That said, as we have mentioned, single member LLC's are not afforded complete asset protection in Florida, California and Colorado. And on this issue you may have to consult with your advisor to weigh the alternatives. If protection is more important than taxation you may want to use a multiple member LLC in those states.

Back to our personal residence. A bankruptcy court in California has ruled that an LLC may not protect your personal residence in a bankruptcy. This should not surprise anyone. Bankruptcy trustees have extraordinary powers and denying LLC protection in a personal bankruptcy is one of those powers. But this should not dissuade you from using an LLC to protect against all other creditors. If you go bankrupt so be it. It may be the right strategy for you. However, short of bankruptcy, an LLC remains a good, protective choice for holding title to your personal residence.

Loophole #42

We have several ways to protect your personal residence. Work with your advisor to consider and utilize 1) insurance, 2) homestead exemptions, 3) debt, and 4) LLCs.

Now let's look at some other creative ways to protect...

Chapter Twenty-Six

Protecting Your Equity

As we have learned in Attack #1, the inside attack, a creditor can get what is inside the LLC. And we have learned that if there is no equity inside the LLC there is not much worth pursuing, making the LLC a lesser target.

Debt is a form of asset protection. The more debt, the less equity, the lesser chance of litigation.

But what if you like owning your property free and clear? You like not having to pay on a mortgage and instead keeping that cash flow for yourself. What can you do then?

Have you ever heard of the term 'equity stripping?' It is sometimes called equity transfer.

With equity stripping you protect your equity by encumbering the property yourself. Debt is asset protection. Why not create the debt yourself?

Of course, we have to be cautious here. You can't put the debt on after you've been sued. That would be a fraudulent conveyance, meaning improperly putting your assets out of the reach of creditors. (Any time you hear of a term with the word 'fraud' in it, know that it is not a good thing.)

As well, you must always tell the truth. If you are called into court and asked about how much debt there is against a certain property you will answer honestly. If a line of credit for $200,000 is secured by a first deed of trust against your property and the credit line has only been tapped in the amount of $1,000 you will answer that the amount of debt is $1,000. We don't want this strategy to get you in trouble for perjury.

Instead, it is to keep you out of court altogether.

Let's look at several ways this can be done.

Spousal Transfers

The first—and, perhaps, most common—method of this type of asset protection is through a spousal transfer. This is simply done by transferring your interest in your property to a spouse via a deed. In states where the assets of a spouse cannot be seized as a result of the debts of the other spouse, this is a quick and inexpensive way to protect assets from creditors.

There are several drawbacks to this method, however, that make it the least practical method of equity transfer:

- Because of its common usage, attorneys will look for this method first. The idea behind asset protection is to make it harder for the creditor to get at your assets, not easier.

- Courts are likelier to rule that such a transfer is a fraudulent conveyance.

- If a divorce occurs, you may lose some or all of that which was transferred to your spouse, depending on the laws in your state.

Be sure to work with an attorney on this and any of the other strategies herein.

Use your Property as Collateral

The second method of equity transfer involves the pledging of your home or other real estate assets as security of collateral for a money loan, which is then placed into use elsewhere (perhaps in the purchase of another asset), optimally out of the reach of creditors.

Let's say that you live in California, own a home worth $500,000, and you have fully paid it off. With a homestead exemption of only $75,000 and your state's unfriendly stand towards the California LLC, the bulk of the equity in your house is left unprotected. Knowing this you go to your bank and obtain a cash loan for $400,000, using your house as the security for this loan. With a fair market value of $500,000 and a loan of $400,000 you now have $100,000 in equity. Of the remaining $100,000 in equity, $75,000 can be protected using a California homestead, leaving only $25,000 of equity exposed. The $400,000 that you've stripped from the home can then be placed into other protected assets. As an example, you could place the $400,000 into a Nevada-based annuity account owned by a Nevada LLC. Under Nevada law, this structure cannot be touched by creditors. Your home is encumbered and the proceeds from it are protected.

Since the bank has recorded the security interest in the home, they have priority over any later creditors who would attack the home. The creditor would have to pay off the loan first before getting their shot at any equity. In the scenario above, going after just $25,000 may not be worth it.

If your transfer action has been properly executed, creditors will not have the incentive to chase after assets with little or zero equity. As with the use of LLCs, this strategy can give you the leverage to negotiate a favorable settlement.

As with any method of asset protection, there are other advantages and disadvantages to consider in selecting this method of equity transfer.

Advantages	Disadvantages
When using your home's equity, you may become eligible for a home mortgage deduction on your federal income tax return.	You must make your loan payments to the bank. You cannot prevent the bank from foreclosing on your home if you don't pay the loan back.
If you have no notice of pending claims, judgments, or liens against you or the property, it is less likely to be considered a fraudulent conveyance.	You can end up losing money if the assets acquired with the loan do not derive more income than you pay towards the mortgage and other costs.

There are some other things to keep in mind when engaging in this sort of equity transfer, which will be discussed a little further on.

Secured Line of Credit

A third method of equity transfer involves obtaining a secured line of credit—instead of a money loan—against the asset. This works under the same principle as the money loan; you are free to take the money or not take the money as you see fit. And even if you do not take the money, the institution that issued the line of credit is listed as the primary secured creditor against the asset. So, like the money loan, if the creditor chooses to attack the asset, they must pay the bank any money that is drawn from that line of credit.

We will consider the strategy of setting up your own line of credit using a Wyoming LLC in our case ahead. Business owners and professionals can use the secured line of credit to protect assets that cannot always be titled in another name, such as equipment or accounts receivable. These assets can be used to secure the line of credit, which can then be drawn against if and when legal action is perceived. And since business owners frequently pledge their equipment or other assets in order to secure credit for business reasons, it is difficult to establish that a fraudulent conveyance occurred in such a transaction.

Cross-Collateralization

If you own multiple entities, it may be possible to use one entity to provide the loan to the other entity. This technique, known as "cross-collateralization," is the fourth common method of equity transfer.

Let's say you hold a free and clear commercial strip mall in a New York LLC, which is then owned by a Nevada LLC for better asset protection. The Nevada entity protects against Attack #2, the outside attack. But you are still worried about Attack #1, the inside attack, where a tenant sues.

They could reach your free and clear strip center. You also have a Wyoming LLC which holds your brokerage account and a large amount of cash.

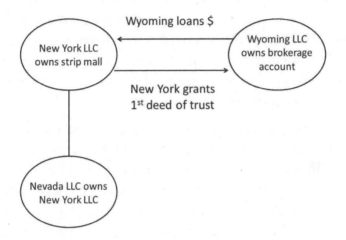

Wyoming loans money to New York in exchange for a first deed of trust. The commercial strip mall now is fully encumbered. A tenant (and their attorney) later considering a lawsuit will see an entity that does not show a lot of equity. The money has actually been loaned by Wyoming and New York is making loan payments back to Wyoming. The loan was made before the lawsuit was being considered. The risk of a fraudulent conveyance issue is low. And the risk that a tenant and their attorney will go after assets beyond the insurance coverage is also low. (We will go through this strategy once again in the case ahead.)

Things to Look Out for When Moving Equity

There are several things to keep in mind, however, when you consider whether this is the right strategy for you:

- Consider what you do with the money. Transferring your equity will only work if you move the money into an entity that is protected. Simply leaving it in a bank account in your individual name, for example, offers you no protection, defeating the purpose of the transfer.

- Equity transfer may not be the best strategy in all situations. If you live in a state with a high or unlimited homestead exemption (i.e. Texas or Florida), you are better off accruing as much equity as possible (up to the maximum) in your home, because the law will protect it. Moving the equity out of your home or other protected asset (such as a Nevada annuity account) may actually leave the equity value less protected than if you had done nothing, which also defeats the purpose of the transfer.

- Watch your personal credit score. When dealing with financial institutions you may want to renew the loan every so often in order to move equity that accrues as you repay the loan. However, repeated loans may negatively impact your FICO score and hamper the ability to secure credit for other things. Also, having high amounts of debt may end up having the same negative impact on your personal credit rating.

Also, keep in mind that moving your equity may work best when as much of the equity is removed as possible. It is possible, given the right conditions, to remove all of the equity from your home or investment real estate and move it to another protected entity. Then again, this may not be the best idea for several reasons:

- As mentioned, your homestead exemption may already protect your personal residence. Unless you feel that all of your equity is better served elsewhere, it does no harm to leave in the portion of the equity that is exempted by your state's homestead exemption. The money is already protected by law.

- Though mortgage lenders and banks will give loans for 100 percent or more of your home's equity, the costs associated with such a loan may not make it a viable proposition. Consider what you plan to do with the money, and how much income you feel you can derive from that money, before you consider such a loan.

- Leaving some equity in the home acts as a buffer against a fluctuating real estate market. If the value of your $500,000 home suddenly drops to $300,000, and you have overleveraged your equity, you may end up either having to sell your home at a loss, or you may end up staying in a house that you can't afford to sell.

Most importantly, like any other protection mechanism, it is better to put the plans for equity transfers in place well in advance of any anticipated troubles. If not done properly, any judge has the prerogative to rule that such a transfer was made fraudulently, meaning that a creditor can ignore the transfer and attack the asset.

Case #25
Bradley, Roger and Sandra

Bradley owned a 4 plex free and clear. He was very proud of the fact that he had paid off the note and now received $3,000 a month in positive cash flow. Without a mortgage to pay, the property was a nice income generator. Bradley liked going to his area's real estate club meetings. He always gained a few nuggets of information. But at the latest meeting he learned that his friend Roger had lost his free and clear triplex to a vengeful tenant. The tenant was the maniacal type of person who could not only believe their own pathological lies, but convince others of their 'truth.'

The tenant sued Roger personally and his LLC that owned the triplex. The tenant asserted that Roger had made an unwanted and horrible sexual advance at the property. The tenant convinced a jury of this aggression. When polled after the case, the jurors said that because Roger owned rental real estate, he was rich. Because the tenant wasn't rich they decided Roger should pay. (Please know that these types of jury verdicts are popping up around the country as our politicians now play the poor against the rich.)

Roger's insurance company did not cover claims of sexual harassment in their general property insurance policy. And because this was an inside attack (Attack #1 brought by the tenant against the LLC) the tenant was able to reach inside the LLC with the jury verdict.

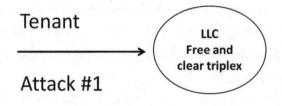

Because the triplex was owned free and clear, the tenant, with their judgment, was able to seize it. The tenant was now the landlord, lived in one unit free, and collected rents on the other two units.

Roger, who the jury had mistakenly and improperly seen as rich, was now, in fact, destitute.

This case sent a chill through the real estate club and the local investment community. Bradley and others wanted to know how they could protect the equity in their properties.

A woman then stood up at the real estate club meeting. Her name was Sandra and she explained that the equity in your property could be protected through equity stripping. There was a buzz in the meeting. "What was equity stripping?" people wondered.

Sandra went to the white board and drew the following:

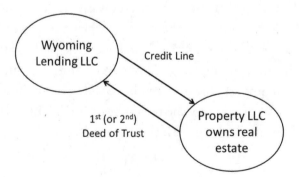

Sandra explained that equity stripping involved setting up a second LLC to lend to the first property-holding LLC. The lending LLC extended a line of credit to the property LLC. This line of credit could be for an actual loan of monies or for an extension of credit to be made in the future. In exchange for the line of credit, the property LLC gave the lending LLC a first (or second—depending on priority) deed of trust.

The club wanted clarification and so Sandra went to the white board again and drew this example:

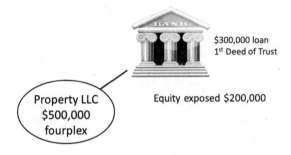

In this example Sandra explained that a later claimant could not get all the equity as they did in Roger's case. That was because a bank has a first and secured claim against the first $300,000 in the property. Debt is a form of asset protection. But in an Attack #1 claim brought against the LLC, a claimant could get the remaining equity in the property – in this case the remaining $200,000 in equity. As a practical matter she explained the claimant would get the remainder of whatever the property sold for above $300,000, the bank's secured interest. So if the $500,000 property sold at auction for $425,000 the bank would receive its $300,000 first and the claimant would receive the remaining $125,000.

Sandra then drew another chart:

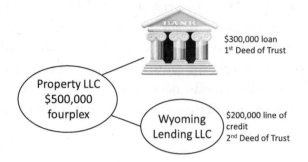

In this example, the property 'appears' to be fully encumbered. The bank clearly has a first of $300,000. The Wyoming lending LLC has a 2nd deed of trust securing a $200,000 line of credit. If the line of credit has been exercised to its full extent, there is no equity exposed.

Then Sandra was asked, "What if only $5,000 of the $200,000 line of credit was utilized?" In that case, she responded, then $195,000 in equity was exposed, or the amount not utilized on the line of credit. But the important point, she noted, was that was information a potential litigant would not know.

A future claimant, like the tenant in Roger's case had done, can call up a preliminary title report to see if there are any liens against the property. If there aren't any, as in Roger's case, a potential litigant is more likely to sue.

By encumbering the property with lines of credit (which may or may not be tapped) secured by deeds of trust, a potential claimant only sees that the property does not have any equity exposed. The property 'appears' to be fully encumbered.

A potential litigant is not entitled to know whether the lines of credit have been fully tapped until after a lawsuit has been brought. In some courts and cases they aren't entitled to know until after they have won the lawsuit. And that was the key, Sandra noted. A lawsuit was less likely to be brought if the property appeared to be fully encumbered.

The club understood. After Roger's case, Bradley and others would be setting up Wyoming LLCs to offer lines of credit to their property holding LLCs. Those lines of credit would be secured by deeds of trust that would shield the equity from prying strangers.

Sandra offered several points of caution. First was that your Wyoming lending LLC could only loan to your own properties. If you loaned to others you could be considered engaged in the banking business without proper licensure. The second point was that if the case did go to court you had to tell the truth about your credit lines. Either they were tapped or they weren't. Either you have equity exposed or it was partially or fully encumbered. She stated that some attorneys found this strategy too aggressive and wouldn't help their clients implement it.

Sandra then noted that one of her clients did tap the line of credit after he had been sued to access money for attorney's fees to fight the lawsuit. In that way, the equity in the property was reduced, and the property owner had funds to fight it out in court.

As Roger's case illustrates, a tenant, vendor or other litigant directly suing the LLC holding real assets can reach the equity of the real estate inside the LLC. By stripping out the equity using lines of credit, you can reduce the likelihood of litigation by reducing the perceived value of the property.

But this strategy can only take you so far. Once you get into court the dynamics change. Remember, you are under oath and have to tell the truth.

The next few pages deal with some of the more technical issues surrounding equity stripping.

The term "equity stripping" has two different connotations: (1) the term can refer to several different types of predatory lending practices, such as foreclosure rescue scams, where the equity in a home is stripped out of the home; or (2) the term can refer to an asset protection plan, as we have discussed here, where the equity of an asset is encumbered, or stripped, to frustrate collection efforts by unsecured creditors.

As of this writing there are 71 state and federal court cases after 1944 that use the term "equity stripping." Of these cases 70 use the term "equity stripping" in the context of a predatory lending practice. Only one of these 71 cases uses the term "equity stripping" in the context of an asset protection plan. *See, Otero v. Vito*, 2009 U.S. Dist. LEXIS 86638 (M.D. Ga. Sept. 22, 2009).

In the Otero case, the plaintiff, Jay Otero ("Mr. Otero"), sought to show that the numerous defendants (the "Vito Entities") were "sham entities" acting as the nominees and/or alter egos of the defendant therein, Dr. George R. Vito ("Dr. Vito"). The undisputed evidence did in fact show that the Vito Entities were alter egos of Dr. Vito, used to defeat justice and evade contractual or tort responsibilities. In a lengthy decision, the Court concluded that Dr. Vito had conceded that he had conceived the various business entities in this case as a strategy to place his personal assets and income out of the reach of his creditors, including Mr. Otero; that he had consistently used these business entities as his alter ego and as an instrumentality for his own affairs; that he had attempted to continue to enjoy the use of his personal resources while shielding himself from responsibility for his liabilities; and that, given the complete unity of interest between Dr. Vito and the Vito entities, to adhere to the doctrines of corporate identity would promote injustice in this case. In a lengthy decision, the Court concluded that the evidence showing that the business entities were alter egos of Dr. Vito was also sufficient to show that the transfers of money, real property, and personal property from Dr. Vito to those entities were fraudulent under the Georgia Uniform Fraudulent Transfers Act.

In reaching its decision in *Otero,* the Court relied heavily upon Dr. Vito's own affidavit in which he explained that he had designed a layered system of corporations, limited liability companies, and trusts to operate his personal and business affairs, in a deliberate strategy to put his assets out of the reach of his creditors without losing control of those assets.

The Court also noted that Dr. Vito regularly presented seminars teaching other physicians how to keep their money "safe from lawsuits or creditors," and that Dr. Vito practiced what he taught:

"Most interestingly, perhaps, evidence presented by the Receiver during hearings related to Dr. Vito's civil contempt showed that Dr. Vito regularly presented seminars on behalf of Lucian Global, teaching other physicians how to keep their money 'safe from lawsuits or creditors.'...Among the strategies he discussed were: encumbering business receivables with debt to 'make the debt laden assets less attractive to creditors...; creating 'as many hurdles as possible for potential creditors to jump through,'...; and 'equity stripping,' that is, taking out loans against the value of real property and placing the proceeds into an annuity or insurance policy....

"The record of this case shows that Dr. Vito practiced what he taught, and did so effectively. He did indeed create as many hurdles as possible for creditors to jump through. By weaving a complex web of trusts, corporations, and limited liability companies, by channeling his income through numerous accounts in numerous names, by transferring his property to alter egos, by encumbering his property and income stream with various obligations, and by refusing to cooperate in the discovery of his assets, Dr. Vito fashioned a daunting challenge for his creditors. Overcoming that challenge has required more than two years of arduous, expensive litigation by a very determined Plaintiff, the appointment of a special master and a receiver, the incarceration of Dr. Vito, and considerable time and effort on the part of this Court and its staff. To this day, it cannot be said that the web is completely untangled or that the hurdles have all been removed. Enough is known, however, to warrant summary judgment in the case."

Beyond unique cases such as the Otero matter, bankruptcy courts will also review equity stripping transactions. Bankruptcy courts apply a five-factor test to determine if a lien is legitimate.

The five-factor test is as follows:

1. The adequacy of the capital contribution.
2. The ratio of shareholder loans to capital.
3. The amount or degree of shareholder control.
4. The availability of similar loans from outside lenders.
5. Certain other relevant questions, such as:
   a. Whether the ultimate financial failure was caused by under-capitalization.

    b. Whether the note included payment provisions and a fixed maturity date.

    c. Whether a note or other debt document was executed.

    d. Whether advances were used to acquire capital assets.

    e. How debt was treated in the business records.

In applying this five-factor test, no one factor will result in the determination that a loan in question is actually a contribution to capital. The ultimate issue is whether the transaction had the substance and character of an equity contribution or of a loan. Thus, the courts look at the totality of the circumstances.

It should be noted that the typical equity-stripping scheme will fail most, if not all, of the five-factor test enunciated by the United States Bankruptcy Court as previously mentioned. For example, it will fail Factor 3 because the real estate operation and finance LLC are controlled by the same owners; it will fail Factor 4 above because no outside lender would make a loan to the real estate operation on the loose terms imposed by the finance LLC; and it will fail Factor 5 above because the note has no real fixed maturity date and the advances were not used to acquire real assets.

In summing up the legalistic side of it, while equity stripping can be done as a legitimate technique, it must have some real commercial substance to hold up in court.

But as a practical matter the point here is not to be in court. The point is to use equity stripping to make you less of a target so the case never goes to court. As long as you do the equity stripping before there is a problem and then not lie in court (if it ever gets there) about the true nature of the loans you will be fine. Know that equity stripping can serve as a perceived road block to later claimants and should be considered as part of your asset protection planning.

Loophole #43

Equity stripping makes the castle less attractive. Let the attackers look for another castle somewhere else—like in France.

Chapter Twenty-Seven

Seven Steps for Success

As a conclusion to this Part Four on Legal Strategies we will offer a checklist for how to proceed once you are ready to get a property in escrow. For more information on the actual creating and maintaining of your entity please see my books *Start Your Own Corporation* and *Run Your Own Corporation*. But for now, let's get you protected.

1. **Getting in Escrow.** On the offer to purchase the property, list the name of your entity as the buyer if it is formed. If it isn't yet formed list your name and the right to assign the contract to an assignee (your new LLC or LP). So the offer would be from "Your Name and/or assigns."

2. **Form your Entity.** If you are going to be in escrow for a period of time (30 to 45 days) in order to get your due diligence inspections done you will have time in most states to get your entity formed. Also know that Nevada has an expedite service whereby LLCs and LPs can be formed in a matter of hours. Wyoming's service is usually very swift, as well. Remember, your entity must be in existence at the time of transfer.

3. **Financing Issues.** Some lenders do not want you to take title in the name of your LLC or LP. (We will just refer to LLCs from here forward.) Some will offer very technical arguments for why they don't allow it, others will tell you straight out they think you are trying to hide assets.

The way around this is to take title in your individual name and then transfer the title from you into the new LLC. More and more lenders are okay with this solution. The banks I work with certainly are.

Know that in such a transfer the lender's position hasn't changed. They still have your personal guarantee and a first deed of trust against the property. There is still a 'continuity of obligation,' a technical term you can use with them. But I personally wouldn't ask the lender if such a transfer is okay. Have you heard the old saying, "Is it better to ask for permission or forgiveness?" It applies here. Pay the mortgage from an LLC checking account. Virtually all lenders are not going to call a performing note. Have a title company or attorney prepare a grant deed (remember our discussion in Chapter 20) and transfer title to your LLC.

4. **Transfer Taxes.** If you immediately transfer from your name to the LLC beware of transfer taxes. Many states make an exception and don't charge a fee when you are transferring from yourself (your individual name) to yourself (your new LLC). Others, like Nevada, don't charge when the property goes from you to the LLC but do charge, as in a refinancing scenario, when you transfer from the LLC back to yourself. The key state to be careful in is Pennsylvania. They charge a 2% transfer tax no matter what. So say you have a $1 million property with $900,000 in financing on it and you want to transfer into your LLC. A 2% tax on a $1 million property is $20,000. Ouch!

5. **Insurance.** As we've said, insurance is the first line of defense. When you insure the property make sure the insured is the LLC. (There have been cases where the title has been transferred from an individual to an LLC, the insurance company wasn't notified and, using their contract loopholes, claims were denied because they didn't insure the LLC.) If the insurance company says an LLC is a business and higher fees apply (which is nonsense since they are insuring the same property and the same risk) ask them to list the LLC as an additional insured. So the policy is in your name and the LLC is also

listed as an additional insured. Send a C.Y.A. letter to your insurance agent notifying them that the LLC is on title to the property.

6. **Banking.** You will open up a bank account in the name of the LLC. You will take a copy of your state filed articles of organization into the bank along with your EIN (tax id) number. If you are a single member disregarded entity you can try to use your Social Security Number instead of the EIN. However, in our experience most banks want an EIN to open an account. If you are a foreign national investing in the U.S. the procedures are a bit different and too far afield for this section. Consider calling our office for an explanation. (Please know that it is not a problem and can be done.) The bank may ask for a copy of your operating agreement. Have it with you in case they do. Your checking account will list the name of the LLC (including the designation "LLC") right on the check. You want the world to know you are doing business as "XYZ, LLC" and not as an individual. Have your tenants make out their rent checks to "XYZ, LLC."

7. **Succeed.** Do all your business in the name of the LLC. Contracts, vendor work and the like are all done not for you personally but for the LLC itself. Always pay the annual LLC filing fees and prepare an annual tax return for the LLC. You want ongoing protection and to get that you have to follow all the rules. For more information on following the formalities see *Run Your Own Corporation*. Consider segregating properties into separate LLCs. We don't want to create a target rich LLC. When you sell the property it is sold by the LLC, which receives the money and then distributes it to you. Enjoy the process and succeed with protection.

Loophole #44

To maintain your protection you have to follow some very simple and ongoing rules. You've got to keep the castle in compliance.

Part Five:
Selection Strategies

With your familiarity of the tax and legal advantages utilized by successful real estate investors, it's time to select the right property for you to invest in.

As soon as you make the decision to start investing, you will be subjected to everyone's opinion about where they think you should invest. You will surely hear about the greatest, hottest real estate markets of the moment. This year it's Phoenix and Dallas. Next year it's Tucson and Houston. However, you should not be overly swayed by any hype about the market of the day. Instead, know that there will always be real estate deals available in every market. In other words, if you don't live near one of the anointed hot spots, don't forgo investing altogether–you can find a deal no matter where you are.

Put your energy into thoroughly analyzing the property, conducting the necessary due diligence, and performing the investigative review. By using the following tips and secrets about these processes, you can make any real estate deal a great opportunity.

As we have just learned, there are powerful tax and legal advantages associated with real estate investing. Incorporate your knowledge of these key loopholes as you select your investments. And consider the counsel in this next section as you move forward.

Chapter Twenty-Eight

Property Analysis

Although you are understandably enthusiastic about your real estate investment, you cannot jump in without first doing some preparatory work. The most important step to take before you even start running numbers is to come up with a plan.

In this plan, you first must clarify the specific purpose your real estate will serve. Are you buying this property in order to develop and resell it, or are you hoping to capitalize on the cash flow it will bring in? Becoming clear on exactly what you want will help you narrow your search.

Investing for Cash Flow

Be aware that investing for cash flow is much different than investing as a real estate speculator. Cash flow investing is a slow process. While you won't get rich quickly, the investment will most certainly pay off eventually. If this is your goal, you must focus specifically on creating cash flow by following these steps:

1. Specify the type of property you'd like. Are you picturing a single-family home or multi-family units? How much money do you have to invest? How much of a loan can you qualify for?

2. Stake out locations. It is recommended that your first investment be located near you. You will hear plenty of promoters say that with the internet and communication access that investing locally really is an

outmoded concept. But it is clearly the case that: a) the promoters want your money and b) you will be more familiar with trends in your own area and it will be easier to work with a local real estate agent. You may want to consider looking for properties in working-class neighborhoods – they usually require less money down than high-end properties, meaning more return for your money.

3. Once you've picked out a few specific neighborhoods, assess the area. Walk around and ask around to determine the state of the neighborhood. Neighborhoods are always changing—it is your job to figure out if the area is improving or declining. If someone tells you the neighborhood is "stable," you just might reasonably interpret that to mean it is declining. What do you see when you look around? Are the houses well maintained and is there obvious pride of ownership? Or do you see numerous "For Sale" signs? Use your real estate agent as a resource here. They can provide you with the comparative values of the properties over the years. Have the prices gone up or down?

4. Identify properties you may be interested in. Ask everyone you know whether they are aware of a property for sale. Don't think that your real estate agent is your only resource. The team you have assembled, including your broker, appraiser, accountant and attorney can be great sources of information. Keep in mind, however, that just because someone you trust recommends a property doesn't mean you don't have to do your investigative work.

5. Assess the state of the property. Once you have found a property in which you are interested, you must gather information on the surrounding properties to get an idea of the value. To do this, investigate comparable values, comparable rents, and the relative values of the properties in the neighborhood. Keep in mind that an ideal investment property generally is at the middle or lower end of value for the neighborhood. Evaluate the cosmetic state of your property. What does it look like? Are there things that could be easily fixed (i.e. not structural) with little effort or money that would make a big difference in the aesthetic appeal? Get feedback from your home inspector on this.

Also consider the numerous ways to increase your cash flow. Some ideas include:

- Update the look of the property. Sometimes inexpensive remodels such as new paint, flooring, or wallpaper, can make all the difference in the world. These simple and inexpensive changes are more likely to get noticed by the typical renter rather than more expensive and involved structural changes.

- Add a garage or carport. Most people would rather park their cars inside. If the cost of this improvement is reasonable, it just may be justified by the increased amount of income.

- Add a fence. If the other properties around yours have fencing, you might want to consider putting one in.

- Consider building a storage unit. Apartment renters always need more space to keep their belongings. If your property has some extra room, you could bring in extra income from renting these units to your tenants.

- Install laundry facilities. If your apartment building doesn't have laundry facilities, think of how quickly those quarters could add up. Consider adding washers and dryers for your tenants' use.

For more information on these strategies, see *The ABCs of Real Estate Investing* by Ken McElroy (RDA Press, 2012).

What if property values go down?

Keep in mind that in cash flow investing, your rent determines your income. If the property value goes down slightly but you are still able to charge the same amount of rent, you will see no change in your cash flow.

However, if your property depreciates so much that you are forced to charge less rent, you would see a decrease in income from the property. You would have a negative cash flow – but only for the period of time that the rents were down. However, as we have learned in recent years, rents may go down for a significant period of time. Can you withstand a prolonged downturn?

Although we have advised you that the geographic location should not be the sole basis for your decision, some geographic areas are predictably influenced by the economic conditions there. These are characteristics that you can capitalize on if you are aware of them.

For example, geography and the economy make a difference in certain areas of the northeastern United States. In some cities, you can purchase a duplex or two-family home for as low as $30,000. Property values are not increasing, and income levels are dropping. Many people are even moving away. However, properties still rent for $500 to $800 per unit. By plugging these numbers into the calculation chart, it is easy to see that buying property in this area can bring in decent returns.

Another entirely different example is shown by the property values throughout California. At one time certain areas were increasing by 20 percent or more per year, showing great appreciation potential. However, the rents could not keep up with this growth, so it was not easy to bring in positive cash flow on such properties. Recouping negative cash flows with annual appreciation gains worked until the merry go round stopped. Many investors were caught, and not only in California. This cycle continues.

Investing for Appreciation

Investing for appreciation can be a successful strategy, but it can also be a risky one. First time investors can make big mistakes if they are blinded by dollar signs and don't consider these crucial scenarios:

- How long would you be able to keep the property if you lost your current job? Since investing for appreciation usually means you will have little, if any, cash flow, how can you afford this property? How many such deals could you afford?

- What will happen if you can't sell the property as quickly as you had planned? For instance, if it takes you many years to sell the property in order to double your money, your actual return may be less than if you owned a property for cash flow.

After considering these warnings, realize that investing for appreciation will only be truly successful if the circumstances are right for both you and the property.

How to analyze properties held for appreciation

First, identify what type of market you are about to enter. A buyer's market has more sellers than buyers. This can be a great situation for buying property -- you can get good deals since there are a lot of properties to consider but not many buyers. The only catch is that if the market continues to decline after you buy, you could have waited and gotten an even better price.

In a seller's market, there are more people looking to buy than there are properties for sale. In this situation, it may be hard to find a good deal unless you look for properties that need some work. Real estate agents may not even bother with this type of property in a seller's market. They may be more interested in quick and easy sales. Therefore, you may have to deal with the seller directly.

Property Analysis Calculation

You can make an offer "subject to inspection and financing" on a property so you don't delay the process while you do research. However, at some point before closing, make sure you run the numbers through the following chart.

Step #1: Calculate how much cash down the property will require:

Down payment	_____
Closing costs	_____
+ Estimated fix-up costs	_____
+ Carrying time for fix-up (number of months times monthly payment)	_____
+ Carrying time for marketing (Number of months times total payment)	_____
= TOTAL	

Now you must determine if you have, or are able to get, this much money.

Step #2: Calculate cash-on-cash return:

Rent received   A. _____

Monthly payment, including taxes
and insurance   B. _____

Cash flow (A minus B)   C. _____

Your investment (from Step #1 above) D. _____

Amount from tenant/lessor   E. _____

The cash-on-cash % formula is: (12 x C) / (D-E)

Do these calculations before you finalize an offer. If your final calculation does not equal your established minimum return, don't carry through with the deal.

Once you identify a prospective property, enlist your real estate broker's help to find valuation trends for that area. Since the best indicator of future appreciation will be the past recessionary cycles, look to identify patterns in the appreciation. Does the property appear to be increasing in value with every cycle? If there seems to be an identifiable cycle, are you able to determine where the property is in the current cycle?

If the property and local appreciation fits your profile, then review the cash flow again. Consider how long you could hold the property if your funds dried up, as well as how long it would take to sell it if you needed to do so. In certain cases, the appreciation may be strong enough to overcome these concerns. But again, please be careful.

Property Development

Keep in mind that while investing in property for development purposes can make you very rich, it also can just as likely make you bankrupt. Buying a property to develop requires a different type of analysis than buying for cash flow or appreciation. Property development is considered a trade or business whereby profits are not taxed at a lower capital gains rate, but rather at higher ordinary income rates. If this is your first attempt at investing for property development, it would be a good idea to surround yourself with an experienced team to advise you. Remember that every property, and thus its legal considerations, will be different.

Loophole #45

Your offer to purchase "subject to inspection and financing" is an excellent loophole. If you don't like what you see after an inspection or what you can get in terms of funding (or for any other reason whatsoever) you can escape the deal.

Now let's understand the duties owed to you...

Chapter Twenty-Nine

Duties Owed by Real Estate Brokers and Agents

When looking to buy or sell real estate you will certainly consider using the services of a real estate broker or agent. The good ones know their markets, the properties in the market and the deals on properties. The good ones will be a big help to you.

A broker is generally a real estate professional with a greater level of experience than an agent. In many states, an agent must hang their real estate license with a broker, which is a means of having brokers supervise agents. That said, there is no reason not to work with an agent. Many are very good at what they do and some don't want the increased burdens of being a broker.

Real estate brokers and agents generally work on commission, meaning that they don't get paid until the property transaction closes. Being economic animals like all of us, their incentive is to close as many deals as possible. Again, closings equate money.

But in that rush to close, certain corners may be cut. So, in response to that dynamic, duties have been imposed on brokers and agents. These duties require them to work in their clients' best interests (as opposed to their own). Over the years these duties have become characterized as fiduciary duties, meaning they come with the highest level of trust.

There are six main duties owed by brokers and agents to you. (We shall just refer to brokers from here on.):

1. Fiduciary Duty of Due Care.

A real estate broker must use all of their skills, including using reasonable care and due diligence, to the best of their ability on behalf of their client.

2. Fiduciary Duty to Account.

A real estate broker must account for all funds entrusted to them and must not commingle client funds with their personal and/or business funds.

3. Fiduciary Duty of Loyalty.

A real estate broker owes undivided loyalty to their client. A real estate broker must act at all times in the best interests of their client and must put their client's interests above all others, including their own. Loyalty includes diligently using their real estate skills and knowledge to further their client's interests in the real estate transaction.

4. Fiduciary Duty of Obedience.

A real estate broker must obey all lawful orders that their client gives them, and must promptly follow all lawful instructions of their client. However, a real estate broker is under no fiduciary obligation to obey any unlawful order or instruction from their client.

5. Fiduciary Duty of Confidentiality.

A real estate broker must keep confidential any information given to them by their client, especially information that may be damaging to their client in negotiations. A real estate broker must safeguard the client's secrets, unless keeping the confidence would violate disclosure requirements about the property's condition.

A real estate broker cannot reveal confidential information about a client at any time during or after an agency relationship. Confidential information includes facts concerning a client's assets, liabilities, income, expenses, motivations to sell, purchase, or rent, and previous offers received or made that are not a matter of public record. However, confidential information does not include information authorized to be disclosed by the client, that is a matter of general knowledge or that is in the public record. Significantly, property condition is not considered to be confidential information. While a real estate broker must keep personal information about a former client confidential, a real estate broker is always required to disclose information about the physical condition of the property, regardless of how the broker obtained the information.

6. Fiduciary Duty of Full Disclosure.
A real estate broker must disclose all known, relevant facts about the property and the transaction to their client.

The specific duties owed by real estate licensees to you are defined by your state's law. Nevada's real estate licensee requirements are found in Appendix C. This statute is representative of other states' laws.

Know that as a real estate licensee you owe the utmost duty to your clients. And if you are buying and selling real estate, know that your brokers and agents owe you the highest level of trust and care.

Loophole #46

If you are 'wholesaling' properties by bringing buyers and sellers together you may technically be acting as a real estate agent. California requires you to have a real estate license for such activities. Each state has a different take on it. Check with your state's Department of Real Estate to understand if you need such a license to wholesale properties.

Getting your real estate license is not a big burden. You take a class (there are some excellent online ones available). You learn a lot of good information and you take a test.

If you are buying properties for yourself you will disclose to the seller that you are a real estate licensee and you will use that fact to get a discount (the 3% buyer's side commission or more) on your purchase.

All right, now it's time for due diligence...

Chapter Thirty

Legal Due Diligence

Buying any property is a big step—one that should not be taken without some in-depth research. This investigative process performed on a property in which you are interested in buying is called legal due diligence. Properties can have any number of problems or claims associated with them, from structural or electrical problems to environmental and hazardous waste issues. These are things you need to be aware of before you buy. It is always best to find out exactly what you are getting yourself into.

How to prepare the offer

If you are wondering how it is possible to perform a lengthy investigation without slowing the buying process, the answer is you must write an offer in which the due diligence is included as a contingency for purchase. This way, if your investigation turns up something you don't like, your contract loophole will allow you to back out of the deal, no questions asked, with all deposits refunded. These clauses in offers usually read like this:

> *"This offer is contingent upon buyer's inspection of the property and acceptance of its condition within 30 days from acceptance of the offer."*

You can choose a shorter time period in which to perform the inspection. Some states have a 10-15 day range for inspections. In any case, for a thirty-day period, if the seller accepts your offer on October 1, then you have until October 31 to inspect the property and decide whether you will accept the property as is, back out of the deal completely, or request that certain repairs be made.

Your offer can include flexibility, which means you can have several contingencies that may allow you to back out. These contingencies may include:

Financing Contingencies

A condition of your offer should be that you successfully obtain suitable financing and show proof of loan commitment within a certain time frame.

> *This Agreement is contingent upon Buyer obtaining the following type of financing: a _____ (eg. FHA, VA, Conventional, Rural Development, etc.)with an interest rate not to exceed _____% payable over a period of _____ (eg. 15, 30) years at a _____ rate (eg. Fixed).*

Appraisal

The property should have to appraise for at least what you agreed to pay for it. If it does not the Buyer can use this loophole to void the contract or the Seller may agree to reduce the price.

> *Within 7 calendar days of acceptance Buyer, at his option and expense, may have the property appraised by an appraiser licensed in the State of _____ . If the appraised value is less than the amount of the purchase price contained in this Agreement then this contact is voidable at Buyer's option and all earnest monies shall be returned; if Buyer chooses to void this Agreement in accordance with this paragraph then Buyer shall notify Seller in writing of such decision, and provide Seller with a copy of said appraisal, within 2 business days of receipt of the appraisal.*

Professional Inspection

You will want to have the property inspected. A general inspection contingency can cover a variety of concerns. For example, certain properties should have environmental tests, such as land that once housed a gas station. You may also want a home tested for radon, toxic mold, the water tested for purity, structural soundness, electrical, mechanical, plumbing, etc. However, the contingency language will have a time frame in which these inspections must take place so you will want to get on locating the proper inspectors immediately. It is important to understand that a general home inspection service will not cover many of the types of inspections you may want conducted on the property. Home inspection services are not conducted by structural engineers or persons with any level of expertise in plumbing, electrical or similar specialties, nor do many check for building code violations such as snow loading, earthquake protection or hidden defects. Inspection by a qualified, licensed structural engineer is advisable as is using a plumber or electrician or any other specialist for any specific areas of concern.

Buyer shall have the right to conduct any inspections, investigations, tests, surveys and other studies on the subject property at Buyer's expense. Buyer shall, within _____ business days of acceptance, complete these inspections and give Seller written notice of disapproved items.

If Buyer does not give Seller written notice of any items disapproved of within the time period specified, Buyer shall be deemed to be satisfied with the results of any such inspections.

If Buyer does give Seller notice of disapproved items within the time period specified then Buyer shall also provide Seller with copies of any pertinent inspection reports. Seller then has the option of correcting the deficiencies within _____ days of receipt of notice of disapproval or voiding the contract and returning all earnest money deposits to Buyer.

Personal Inspection

A personal inspection contingency will give you an easy out should you want to back out before its expiration. It should be worded subjectively, allowing you to get out of the contract simply because you decided you did not like the property after all.

> *Buyer shall have until _____, 20____ to personally inspect the subject property and give Seller any written objections regarding any aspect of the property that does not meet Buyer's subjective approval. If Buyer does not provide any written objections by this date, Buyer will be deemed to be satisfied with the personal inspection. If, on the other hand, Buyer gives written notice of disapproval by _____, 20____ (date above), this contract shall be voidable in writing at Buyer's option and all earnest money returned.*

General Due Diligence

A general due diligence paragraph is also a very good idea, especially if you plan on adding a guest house, or developing the property in any way. You will want the offer to contain a due diligence period so that you can obtain approval for your plans from the proper authorities.

> *Seller shall grant to Buyer a period of thirty (30) calendar days from the date of acceptance in which to conduct any due diligence investigations regarding the subject property, including governmental regulations regarding the division or development potential of the subject property. Buyer shall give Seller written notice within this same time period in the event that the Buyer should determine that any of the items of due diligence should prove to be unacceptable, at which time this contact shall be voidable at the Buyer's option and all earnest monies returned.*

Survey

It may be a good idea to have the land surveyed or the corners marked. Your approval of the corners can be a condition of the sale.

> *Seller(s) shall have the property surveyed and the property corners marked by a professional, licensed engineer in the State of _____ by _____, 20____ . Buyer(s) shall have until _____, 20____ to inspect the marked property corners. Buyer(s) shall give any disapproval in writing by _____, 20____ . If for any reason Buyer disapproves of the property corners then this contact shall be voidable at the Buyer's option and all earnest monies returned.*

Review of the Plat, Covenants, Conditions and Restrictions

Plats often have notes that contain restrictions not found in the covenants or deed. It is important that the plat and any other restrictions on the property be reviewed by an attorney and that any restriction be approved by the buyer.

> *Buyer shall have until _____ , 20____ to review the plat and any covenants, conditions or restrictions affecting the property and to give Seller any written objections. If Buyer does not provide any written objections by this date, Buyer will be deemed to be satisfied with the plat and all restrictions affecting the property. If, on the other hand, Buyer gives written notice of disapproval by _____ , 20____ (date above), this contract shall be voidable in writing at Buyer's option and all earnest money returned.*

1031 language

If you are purchasing the property through a 1031 exchange, it is important that your contract mention this as well as provide that the closing must occur within the bounds dictated by the exchange and that the Seller will cooperate with these needs.

Seller herein acknowledges that it is the intention of the Buyer to complete a Section 1031 Tax-deferred exchange. Seller agrees to cooperate with the Buyer in any manner necessary in order to complete said exchange at no additional cost or liability to Seller.

Review of Title Commitment

You will want your title commitment reviewed by an attorney (or a title company in some states) as the commitment will tell you if the Seller has marketable title as well as list items of record that affect the subject property.

Within _____ business days of acceptance Seller shall provide Buyer with a commitment of title insurance policy showing the condition of the title to said premises. Buyer shall have _____ business days from receipt of the commitment within which to object in writing to the condition of the title and any of the liens, encumbrances or exceptions set forth in the commitment. If Buyer does not so object Buyer shall be deemed to have accepted the condition of said title. If Buyer does make written objection within the above time frame then Seller can either clear any title defects or objections to any exceptions within _____ business days of written notice or this contract shall be voidable in writing at Buyer's option and all earnest money returned.

Approval of any Leases associated with the property

If you are purchasing rental property where any leases or tenancies are in place you will want the offer to be contingent upon your review of those agreements.

Within _____ days of acceptance Seller shall provide Buyer with any rent or lease agreements currently in effect along with an affidavit or letter stating whether or not such rent or lease agreements have been strictly adhered to by both the landlord and the tenant. If such agreements have not been strictly adhered to the letter shall list any defaults or waivers in detail.

Buyer has ____ days from Buyer's receipt of any such agreements and said letter to provide written notice to Seller that such agreements or their current status are not acceptable and thus void the contract and have all earnest money deposits returned in full.

Water Rights/Mineral Rights

If water rights or mineral rights are a concern, be sure to make the review of those rights a condition of the offer.

Seller shall deliver to Buyer within ____ days of execution of this Agreement copies of all documents relating to water or mineral rights. Buyer shall have ____ days from receipt of such documentation to object to the condition of said water or mineral rights and to declare this Agreement void and all earnest money returned.

Contingent on another closing

If you need to sell your present home prior to closing on the home that you are offering on, then it is important to make closing your own sale a condition of your offer. Otherwise, you may find yourself making two mortgage payments instead of one.

This offer is specifically contingent upon the Buyer closing on the following property: [insert legal description of property] within ____ months of the acceptance of this offer.

General Contingency

One attorney I know likes to put a general contingency in any offer – something to the effect of: "Within 30 days of acceptance, Buyer may back out of this contract for any reason with no further obligation and full return of his earnest money deposit." You can make a sales contract conditional on anything you would like. For example, you could make winning the lottery in July a condition of closing. But, remember, these contingencies are put into the offer and as such could be the basis for a rejection or a counter offer.

Each of the above loophole contingencies gives you one more chance to back out of the deal if you aren't completely satisfied with what you find. Buyers should not hesitate to use the acceptable financing clause. If you are not able to obtain financing that you feel comfortable with, you should be able to get out of the deal completely.

At the end of your inspection period, many good brokers will prepare a written statement for you to sign in which you, for example, accept the condition of the property, therefore removing that contingency on the offer. If you do not want to accept the property after your investigation, you don't sign the agreement.

Sometimes, if communication isn't as strong, it will be assumed that if the agreed upon date comes and goes without you contacting the broker or seller, that you have accepted the property's condition and are willing to proceed with the sale. If you are not planning on purchasing after your investigation, it is always best to send a written letter before the deadline to the seller or broker, or both, to notify them that the deal is off. If you do not do so, and they assume you are going to purchase when you are not, you may end up forfeiting the deposit you have already paid. However, this may still be better than being sued for the entire amount of the transaction.

In all cases, whether you want to buy or call the deal off, it is best to clearly communicate your intentions in writing to both the seller and the broker before the deadline so that no party involved makes an incorrect assumption.

Loophole #47

Use your contingencies as loophole escapes. If you don't like the property for whatever reason, you need to be able to get out of the deal.

Inspections – the Repair Addendum

Chances are any property you are considering purchasing has minor superficial issues you'd like to correct eventually. Home inspections should not focus on these little imperfections since every home has its fair share. Your pre-purchase inspection should be aimed at uncovering problems that aren't so minor—meaning issues with the foundation, roof, or heating, plumbing and electrical systems.

If problems are found in any of these components, you will want them to be addressed and resolved before you take possession of the property. You can request that these repairs be completed before closing by drafting a repair addendum, a summary of required repairs acknowledged by the buyer, Realtor and seller. Not only will this ensure that you won't have to face these expenses immediately after purchase, it reduces the risk that lawsuits will be filed disputing the condition of the property.

Any major problems found during the inspection will be summarized in the inspector's report. A detailed description of the problems will need to be transcribed into the repair addendum, thus communicating the findings to the seller. Always include a copy of the inspector's report so the seller can reference it. Then list, in the order you would like them completed, the repairs you would like the seller to address before re-inspection.

Include as much detail in the description of repairs as possible. First list the specific part of the system that needs to be repaired. Use language that communicates your expectations clearly. If you want a component completely replaced, be sure to use the word "replace" rather than "repair." Make a request that once the work has been completed, you will receive copies of receipts.

After work has been completed, another inspection of each of the items included in the repair addendum is required. This should be done well in advance of the final walk-through and closing just in case additional work is still required. If this is the case, another inspection report and repair addendum signed by the buyer must be presented to the seller.

Loophole #48

It is better to have repairs made before closing than to fight about them afterwards.

Title Insurance and the Preliminary Title Report

The title report holds all the specific information about a particular piece of property: The physical details, the type of ownership, and exactly what rights are granted to the owner of that property. Sometimes there are flaws in the title that can bring about challenges for the owner. As discussed, title insurance can offer protection from such difficulties.

Many of the flaws found in titles are very subtle. Because of this, many lenders require title insurance and will not loan money until they receive a clear and insured title report. Most title insurance protects against defects in, or liens or encumbrances on, the title to a piece of property. The insurance company will help in defending against challenges to your title to the property. However, insurance companies will only agree to insure against certain things. You must be aware of what coverage your company is providing. Again, they have their own loopholes.

The first step in obtaining title insurance is to receive a preliminary title report. This is the product of the title insurance company's review of public records that relate to the property in question. However, in most states, the preliminary title report cannot be relied upon as a representation of the status of title to the property. It will, however, inform you what exactly the insurance company is willing to insure you against.

When you receive the final title report from the insurance company, it will include all the risks the title company has refused to insure against. This is important to note because should there be a problem in the future, your insurance company will not involve itself regarding any of the matters it has chosen to exclude coverage on. Weigh the risk as you consider the purchase.

When you receive the title report, time spent carefully inspecting it will be well worth it. You should consider having your lawyer look it over as well. If you close a real estate deal and then realize your insurance does not cover problems that were disclosed in the preliminary report, there is no going back. At that point, you will not be able to rework the terms of the purchase agreement in order to protect yourself. It is important that you know exactly what the title contains and how much coverage your insurance company is providing before you close a deal.

How to review a title report

Reviewing the title report is one of the most important steps potential buyers should take to be sure they are making an informed decision. Check the entire report for inaccuracies or inconsistencies. Any that you find must be discussed with your attorney and the title insurance company. Some of these issues may require you to work with the seller to resolve the problem with the title.

In order to play an active role in your real estate transaction, review each of the following items in your title report for accuracy:

- *Addresses*: Specifically check the addresses of the party who will close the deal, prepare the contract, or close the loan. Also make sure the addresses of the seller, buyer's real estate agent, lender and attorney are correct as they will receive a copy.

- *Current Owner (Vested Owner):* Make sure the name of the seller of the property is accurate.

- *Description of the Property:* This must be the same description that appears on the real estate purchase agreement. If the description on the title report differs, the title company may not have performed a title search on the excluded property, thus leaving that part uninsured. You must make sure that all of the property you intend to purchase will be covered by the title insurance policy.

- *Plat Map:* This describes the lot size and may include street names and the nearest intersection. Be sure the plat map included in the title report matches the legal description of the property.

- *Interest or type of estate:* This will describe the type of interest in property you are buying from the seller. The most common type of property interest is the fee simple absolute. This and the other forms of interest are described in Chapter 16. If a type of ownership other than the fee simple absolute appears on the title, you must be knowledgeable of the type of interest you are acquiring and the limitations it involves.

- *Effective Date:* When the title insurance company prepares title reports, they generally get their information from a collection of public records called a title plant. The effective date will tell you the date through which the title plant is current, and therefore the facts known through that date.

- *Type of Policy Requested:* This will describe the details of your relationship with the insurance company. This should include the limit of the liability assumed by the insurance company, the premium to be paid, etc. Make sure that these details match those you discussed with your title insurance agent.

- *Report Number and Contact Person:* This information must be correct – this is whom you will contact if you have questions regarding the report. Use the report number to direct questions you have to the agent in charge of your file.

Once you have checked the above points for accuracy, now you must carefully inspect anything the insurance provider has chosen to not insure you against. This is where you will find any restrictions or limitations on the property. These can come in many forms and have different consequences for the buyer. The following are examples of what you might find.

- *Easements*: This is when another person or the public has certain rights to your land. Although easements may not necessarily have a negative effect on your real estate deal, you must first be aware if one exists and then you must consider what type of impact it will have. These are common types of easements:

1. A right of way: A third party's right to use a path or road located on your property.
2. A utility easement or right to place or keep something on the land. This also can include a third party's right to use and maintain a sewer pipe, telephone line, garage, or anything else on or across your property.
3. Right of entry: Allows a third party to enter your property for certain and clearly defined purposes.
4. A right to the support of land and buildings: This may be applicable if you purchase a lower-story unit in an apartment complex.
5. A right of light and air: Gives a third party a right that may limit your ability to use or build on your property if that use violates their rights.
6. Right to water: Gives a third party a right to use a waterway or divert water from a waterway located on or adjacent to your property.
7. A right to do some act that would otherwise amount to a nuisance.

- *Covenants, Conditions, and Restrictions*: These are usually referred to as CC&Rs. They can limit your ability to use or sell the property and are enforceable by the seller or third parties. These can include building limitations, limitations on use for business, and even aesthetic requirements for the building. Be sure you are aware of the consequences of a violation of such a restriction. Sometimes they can result in financial liability or may cause ownership to revert back to a prior owner or third party. Although CC&Rs don't necessarily have an adverse affect on your property (and may actually serve to increase property values), it is important to carefully study them. After all, they do affect your ability to use and sell the property.

- *Mortgage or Deed of Trust*: These reflect loans against the property. In some states, an existing mortgage or deed of trust can affect the title directly or can create the potential for a lien or foreclosure and sale of the property. You must determine if this will affect the nature of the property. In many cases, the mortgage will be paid off through escrow at closing. Make certain such directions are in the escrow instructions.

- *Notice of Default*: This indicates that there is an existing foreclosure proceeding against the property. If this is the case, you should not independently purchase the property. Instead, you may want to purchase it as part of the foreclosure proceeding. Always consult with your attorney before buying a foreclosure.

- *Parties in Possession*: This exception means that any rights or claims of parties that currently possess the property and are not recorded in the public records will not be covered by the insurance policy. To protect yourself from this, especially from the rights of someone who is wrongfully in possession of the property, have the property surveyed. This can determine whether any part of the property is currently in the possession of a third party.

- *Survey Exception*: This can include any rights or claims of parties in possession; easements or claims of easements not shown by public records; boundary line disputes; overlaps or encroachments; and any matters not of record that could be exposed by a survey and inspection. Simply by having the land surveyed and inspected, you can protect yourself against such an exception.

- *Mechanic's Liens*: These can be tricky because they may not appear on the record even if they exist. Mechanic's liens take effect when construction or improvement work starts, but aren't recorded until the work is finished but not paid for by the owner. This type of exception means that the insurance will not cover any lien or right to a lien for services, labor, or materials for any prior or subsequent development. However, some insurance companies may provide coverage if the seller guarantees against mechanic's liens, and if both buyer and seller have proper documentation in place.

- *State or Federal Tax Liens, Judgments, Bankruptcy*: Any taxes, assessments and judicial proceedings not shown as existing liens in public records will not be covered by the title insurance. It is a good idea to get a warranty from the seller that no such issues exist. (And remember, a Quit Claim Deed from the Seller offers no such warranty.) Notice of default is important. In bankruptcy proceedings, a title insurance company will usually hold insurance until a court order is filed that removes the property from the bankruptcy court's jurisdiction.

- *Lis Pendens*: As discussed, a lis pendens filing means that the property is involved in litigation. A title company certainly won't insure it. You most certainly should not buy into it either.

Loophole #49

Analyzing and understanding the title report early in the due diligence process can save a great deal of time and energy later in the acquisition process. Acceptance of the title report can also serve as another loophole contingency.

Environmental Concerns

Another very important contingency to include in your offer is one regarding the property's environmental condition. This is a crucial part of your due diligence. If you don't become familiar with your building's entire environmental history, you could end up liable for any previous problems that may exist. The following story is an example of what can go wrong if you don't investigate a property thoroughly.

Case #26
Allison and Antonio

Allison had always wanted to own her own restaurant. She was finally in a position financially that allowed her to start realizing her dream. She began looking for a unique space to house her gourmet restaurant and wine bar. Because she believed that a new building wouldn't have the character she desired, she started looking in an older section of town.

It was there that she fell in love with a charming brick building located right on the edge of the river. From the moment she saw the place, she knew its old charm would provide the perfect backdrop for her restaurant. To her surprise, the price was lower than she had imagined and the seller, Antonio, was motivated to sell because of a divorce.

Antonio was in such a hurry to sell that he offered Allison a discounted price if she could have her inspection performed within 15 days. Allison was initially uncomfortable with this short time frame, but she didn't want to lose the building, or the great price. She agreed to Antonio's stipulation and made her offer.

A quick inspection was performed. Allison was satisfied there were no structural problems. Although the inspection process was not as thorough as she would have hoped, Allison felt she could take care of any problems that might arise with the extra money she would be saving.

A few months later, as she was painting the bathroom for her restaurant's upcoming opening, she noticed a strange smell. She decided it probably was just because the building was so old, but made arrangements to have someone come in to check out the pipes.

What they found was worse than Allison could have ever imagined. The sewage tank was as old as the building itself. It had never been replaced or updated, and now it was leaking. Sewage was seeping into the ground below the restaurant and out into the river. Worse yet, the previous tenant had been a dry cleaning business. Instead of properly disposing of their hazardous solvents, they had simply poured them down the drain.

The rotting sewage tank had been breached and was now leaking into the river. Dozens of children who had spent the summer months swimming downstream from the restaurant became ill. When doctors discovered the pattern, the city began testing the water in the river. Sure enough, they found sewage in the water, and traced it back to Allison's building and its disintegrating tank.

Even though Allison had been unaware of damage, the town's residents were outraged. Allison paid to have the tank replaced, but then she faced lawsuits that the insurance company would not cover. She was forced to sell the building, with its new sewage tank, just to pay the settlements. By the time the nightmare was over, she had lost so much that she was never able to realize her dream of owning a restaurant.

How to protect yourself

Allison was held strictly liable because she was the responsible party. The fact that there was hazardous waste on her property was all that had to be proved. There is strict liability in such cases, meaning that ownership, rather than guilt or innocence, is the issue. If waste is found on property you own, you are liable. Federal law recognizes four classes of parties responsible for cleanup of hazardous waste:

1. The current owner and operator of the property.
2. The owner and operator of the property at the time the waste was deposited.
3. Those who generated the waste and sent it to the site.
4. Those who transported the waste to the site.

In our example, Allison is a liable party as she is the current owner. She could sue the dry cleaner, but he had died with no assets.

So what could she have done differently to protect herself? She should have had state-licensed engineers perform a Phase I environmental report, a survey of the potential environmental problems on the property. In a Phase I report, the engineers will either find no problems and record that in writing, or will find a problem and suggest a more detailed Phase II report.

If you are unable to get a clean Phase I report on a property, it is probably not something you want to get involved in anyway. Banks most likely won't loan money for a property that does not have a clean Phase I report.

The importance of having a clean Phase I report is that it can protect you if a problem should arise in the future. You have a good argument that because you had an engineer inspect the property and the property was found to be clean at that time, you had no notice of any problems. If Allison had had her property inspected by engineers, they either would have found the problem and she could have backed out of the deal – or she would have had a clean Phase I report that would have proven she was unaware of the problem and it had occurred after the inspection.

Keep in mind that you will also be held liable for any environmental hazard caused by your tenants. This means if one of your renters runs a methamphetamine lab out of your apartment building, you will be responsible for a toxic cleanup. This is just one important reason why you should know exactly who your tenants are and what they are doing.

Refer to Appendix B for a checklist of environmental documents you should review before you purchase any property. Also found in Appendix B are other checklists of items to be reviewed during your due diligence process. While these checklists provided are not comprehensive and are not intended to be the only resource you use to the exclusion of all others, they will provide a guideline to begin the review of your property. Checklists can be used to remind you and your broker to deal with items you may have overlooked. The more thorough of an investigation you conduct on your property, the more likely it is that you will be completely satisfied with your purchase.

Loophole #50

When buying your castle use the legal loopholes to your advantage to get in, or out, of the deal.

Now let's start selecting...

Chapter Thirty-One

Real-Life Selection Stories

An excellent way to learn is to gain insight from the mistakes and successes of others. So here are some of my experiences for your review.

Selecting Properties, Selecting Managers

My first foray into real estate investing began by accident. Although I was licensed as a California real estate broker for many years, I personally had never held property for investment purposes. I did own a small starter house in a pleasant Reno neighborhood, but soon after my marriage and the birth of our first child, we decided we would need something bigger. We realized that after all the broker's fees and transfer fees that we were going to lose money if we sold the house. So we decided to rent the place out.

Our first tenant was the type that always had a creative excuse for why he was late with his rent payments. This came as a shock because whenever I had rented places, I never turned in a late payment. My parents had instilled in me the value of timeliness, and here I was, landlord to someone who could not care less about being on time. As a lawyer, I had spent years listening to other people's problems and lack of follow-through on contracts. However, this situation was becoming personally annoying because I still had a mortgage to pay.

On top of it all, I realized I didn't have enough time to deal with any of it. I felt I would be better off hiring a management company to take care of the details while I spent my time working to earn my own money. I figured it would be worth the fee they charged to get rid of some of the hassle. After interviewing several companies, I chose one with a good reputation around town as well as a reasonable fee structure. The company charged ten percent of the gross rental revenues, but would take care the bills, arrange repairs, and line-up new, and hopefully responsible, tenants. When I calculated the value of the time I spent managing the place on my own, I was paying twice the amount the management company charged. Everything became so much simpler. In fact, the only contact I have with the company is a monthly statement.

However, for some reason, when it came time to purchase my next property, I had forgotten my lesson about the value of property managers. I figured that with the bigger property, I could manage it myself and hold on to all of the gross rents.

So the bookkeeper and I now had the duties of lining up vendors and handling repairs, paying bills and collecting rents, handling the bookkeeping, setting up new leases, and doing everything else involved with managing such a property.

Now instead of just one excuse every month I received many including:

"I am an artist. I don't pay rent."
"The bartender took all my money."
"The Raiders lost again."
"My wife met my girlfriend."

Again, for someone who lives with a fairly strict view of timeliness and fulfillment of obligations, these casual, half-baked excuses were maddening. More than once I asked the question: "Am I a landlord or a life skills counselor?"

The last straw, when my lesson was finally learned for good, was when a tenant called my law office and insisted that I be pulled out of a meeting. As I got on the phone, she demanded that I come down to the building right away. When I asked what the problem was she explained me that someone had left their laundry in the dryer, and since she didn't know whether the laundry was sanitary, she would not touch it. She wanted me to come remove the laundry from the dryer myself.

That afternoon, I began interviewing management companies.

How to select and use property management companies

The previous story was not included to advise that everyone use a property manager. Some people enjoy the one-on-one interaction and maintenance of a rental property and feel a sense of pride about doing it themselves. Certainly, some will save a great deal of money by managing their own real estate. But for others, for whom a management company will actually save money and headaches, there are some guidelines to follow when selecting a company.

The following are key elements to consider when selecting a management company:

- *Local Reputation and References:* Since the company you choose will be handling your money, it is important that they be trustworthy and well respected around town.

- *Vendor and Service Contracts:* Many management companies have strong relationships with vendors and service providers. This may result in lower costs for maintenance and upkeep than you would be able to find on your own.

- *Market Knowledge:* You want your management company to know what the local market will bear in terms of rents.

With the field narrowed by using the recommendations above, now you can do more in-depth investigation into their management contracts. Items to consider include:

- *Compensation for services:* Management companies usually charge a percentage of the gross rental receipts, ranging from 5 percent to 10 percent. If they receive a percentage, this gives them extra incentive to keep all the units full.

- *Duties and Responsibilities:* Make sure the contract clearly defines who is responsible for what. What do you, as an owner, want to be involved in and what do you want to leave to the managers exclusively?

- *The Term and Termination Clauses:* You will want the option to give thirty days' notice to the company and be able to move on if you are not satisfied with their management of your property.

- *Spending Issues:* This will define how much the managers can spend without consulting with the owner. For example, you will want to approve any large repairs and improvements.

- *Special Contract Issues:* Read the contract for any catches or small print. If a management company asks for a percentage of the brokerage commission if you decide to sell the building, either get the clause removed or use a different company.

- *Reports:* As the owner, you will want to receive regular reports detailing income, expenses and reserves.

After contracting with a management company, give them a few months to get settled. Then you will need to craft a system to analyze their performance. You can measure their success by the following:

- A lower vacancy rate
- Greater return to the owner
- Better collections
- Lower turnover
- Fewer complaints
- Better condition

If you take the time to choose the management company that works best for you and your property, it can benefit everyone involved.

Loophole #51

Management companies are not loopholes for owners. As an owner you are responsible for what happens on the property, whether you use a management company as your agent or not.

Tips from experienced real estate brokers

George and Gayle are real estate brokers who specialize in Lake Tahoe properties, and invest for themselves around the western United States. Over the years, they have developed their own set of guidelines they have found useful in helping their clients.

The first thing they believe every potential investor should clarify is the stage of real estate investing they are in as well as what they'd like to accomplish with their real estate. For example, George and Gayle advise their older clients to buy property that will bring them cash flow. However, they work with younger clients differently. If they are just starting out in real estate, they have time to reap the rewards of long-term appreciation. These clients are also more likely than older, more established ones to buy a place that needs lots of improvements or sweat equity.

Once you have decided where you and your investment goals fit in to this picture, here are some other pointers from George and Gayle:

- Talk to everyone you know about real estate. It is always a good topic for discussion and you can actually learn a lot and even find deals simply from talking to others.

- If you have a choice between investing in an older, established neighborhood, or a brand new suburban development, choose the older neighborhood. The homes there will have more character and charm that cannot be replicated. Homes in the suburbs are a dime a dozen.

- Even if you hear that Miami Beach is *the* place to invest, if you can't get there easily and regularly and you aren't familiar with the market, you will be more successful investing close to your home base.

- Hold onto a property that is appreciating—don't sell. If you can, refinance the property and use the loan proceeds to buy your next property.

- Be careful when considering condominium units. Don't buy if 70 percent or more are not owner-occupied. In these situations, there may be little pride of ownership in the area.

- Also remember that with condominiums, you will have to pay association fees. Consider whether this money would be better spent on a larger mortgage payment.

- Invest near colleges or universities. Although there inherently will be some damage done to the property with this group, you can be assured you won't have much trouble finding tenants.

- If you are trying to choose between a two-bedroom one-bathroom home and one with three bedrooms and two bathrooms, choose the latter. Two-bedroom, one-bathroom homes are always harder to sell.

- Look at every potential property like you were going to re-sell it. What type of improvements would you have to make? If you were to purchase it, would it be economical to make these improvements in order to sell it later?

- Also look at every property from the perspective of a tenant. Is it close to shopping, transportation, etc.? Would the type of tenants you want to rent to find the property suitable for their needs? If not, could you improve it so it would attract your ideal tenant? Also keep in mind that the lower the rent, the larger the pool of potential tenants you will attract.

- Get started in real estate investing as early as possible.

In addition to these guidelines that can be put to use anywhere, become knowledgeable about your city's own regulations regarding rent, such as the existence of rent control measures. When looking for a real estate broker, it can be helpful if the broker owns investment properties of his or her own. This way, they have an especially clear understanding of what is involved, and can even share some of the lessons they have learned in their own experiences.

George and Gayle like to share one of their personal experiences with their clients. Several years ago, they were considering buying a home in Truckee, California for $150,000. Although they knew it was a great deal, the property also needed $5,000 of plumbing work done on it. While they liked the location and look of the property, the couple was apprehensive about paying the plumbing expense right after the purchase. So instead, they bought a house in a nearby, albeit lesser, neighborhood for $125,000. Years later, their investment was a sound one—they recently sold the house for $250,000 and doubled their money. However, the house they passed up sold soon after their own—for $550,000. From this experience they learned to look at the bigger overall picture when investing. Had they not overanalyzed their purchase years ago, they would have made a phenomenal return, even after paying for that plumbing work. Learn to respect your own judgment and intuition about a property.

Loophole #52

Develop a good eye and instinct for what types of castles you will buy.

All right, now let's answer some questions you may still have.

Chapter Thirty-Two

Frequently Asked Questions

I n the home stretch, it is useful to answer the questions that frequently come up...

Should my corporation hold real estate?

No. For tax reasons we don't recommend that you ever hold real estate in the name of a C corporation. Your C corporation will still pay more in capital gains (even under the new tax law) when you try to sell that property than would a flow-through entity, such as an S corporation or an LLC. If your S corporation is holding the property and you are sued personally, a judgment creditor (except with a Nevada corporation) may be able to reach your shares in the S corporation and effectively take control of those shares and through them, control of the S corporation and its assets. If properly structured using Nevada and Wyoming LLCs and LPs you will have much better asset protection than with other entities. For these reasons we recommend that real estate be held in either an LLC or a limited partnership (LP). As well, transferring property out of an S corporation is a taxable event whereas it is not taxable in an LLC or an LP. When it comes time to refinance you will appreciate an LLC or LP.

Even if it doesn't own it, can I use my corporation to buy real estate?

Yes. One method is to have your corporation pay rent for an office building which is owned by a separate LLC that you own. The rent paid by the corporation is a tax deduction for the business and the income from the rent is offset by operating expenses as well as the phantom expense of depreciation. This strategy is discussed in Chapter 14.

What type of entity should I hold property in?

We recommend using either an LLC or an LP. Both offer flow-through income and taxation opportunities, and both offer excellent asset protection. In Wyoming and Nevada, for example, legislation prohibits creditors of an LLC or an LP from directly seizing assets of either type of entity, even if only owned by a single member. Instead, judgment creditors must secure their judgment against the LLC or limited partnership by way of the charging order procedure. Most attorneys and their clients don't like to wait around for distributions to be made.

What is a charging order?

A charging order is, in essence, a lien filed against the LLC or limited partnership's earnings. After winning a case and getting a judgment, the judgment creditor wants to get paid. He goes to court and gets a charging order, which 'charges' him with the right to receive distributions. When profit allocations are made by either entity to their members, a portion would be paid to the judgment creditor to pay down the judgment. Having a charging order placed against an LLC or a limited partnership does not convey voting rights, so creditors cannot take control of the entity and through that control, reach the assets. In addition, in a situation where the entity is profitable but management decides that the profit needs to be re-invested into the entity or to pay an owner for services rendered, no distributions of profit will be made at all, frustrating a creditor. Holding real property in either of these entities can be a great deterrent against nuisance litigation and claims.

Should I set up an LLC for each piece of property?

That is a judgment call on your part. Remember, the more properties you hold in a single entity, the more you risk your income being impacted in the event of a lawsuit. For example, if you hold five rental properties in a single LLC and that LLC is sued by the tenant in Property #1 on an inside attack (Attack #1) the tenant can reach the equity in all five properties. You may want to segregate these properties into separate LLCs. You may also want to use the equity stripping strategies discussed in Chapter 26.

Will a land trust give me the asset protection I need?

No. Land trusts offer zero asset protection. And while they are touted as offering excellent privacy there are holes in such claims. As we discussed in Chapter 22, be very cautious when using land trusts.

What are the benefits of holding property in a Trust as opposed to an LLC?

There are many types of trusts. A living trust is a common estate planning vehicle that offers probate avoidance but no asset protection. In such a case, the real estate is best titled in the name of the LLC with the member interests owned by the living trust. When one party passes, the LLC membership interests are transferred according to the terms of the trust but the property does not have to be retitled, since the LLC continues to own it.

Another trust is the spendthrift trust, an irrevocable vehicle set up by parents for their children. The assets of the trust may not be reached by later creditors, thus protecting immature and free-spending kids from themselves. Because an independent trustee administers the property until it is distributed, a greater measure of control is achieved. However, some trusts pay higher taxes than LLCs and may not be advisable for strong income properties.

Should I put my family home into an LLC?

You can do so. However, as discussed in Chapter 16, you should first consider using a homestead to protect your personal residence. If you are in a state with a low homestead value, such as California with $75,000 for singles ($100,000 for marrieds) in protection, then you may want to consider an LLC. (Know that you can't use a homestead with an LLC.) Other states, such as Texas and Florida, have unlimited homestead protection, which means an LLC is not necessary. For a list of homestead exemptions by state visit http://www.corporatedirect.com/homestead-exemptions/.

Can I write off repairs done to my own house?

You cannot deduct the repair costs for your personal residence. But, the costs of repairs or improvements for your home office are a deduction.

What can I do with my home office in the basement?

Consider renting that portion of your home to the business as a home office. There needs to be exclusive business purpose on that part of your home (in other words, that space is not merely a part of the dining room) and the space needs to be used in your business. It should be noted that you would only rent and not sell a part of the house to the business. Selling would involve complicated and burdensome title issues.

When a rental property is not rented, can I take that as a loss of income?

The expenses of operating the rental property including the advertising costs are still expenses. However, if you have an empty unit you cannot take a loss for "lost revenue." You do not pay tax on something you don't receive and thus can't take a loss on it either. So, you can't write off $800 for the month you didn't receive rent on your $800 unit.

Can I set up a management company to manage my own properties?

Yes. A separate LLC or corporation may be established to assume management duties. Please know that in some states you need a real estate license to manage other people's properties. So while you can manage your own real estate without a license, to then handle other properties will require licensure. A separate management company (which doesn't own any real estate) can be used to build business credit, pay medical expenses, contribute to retirement plans and maximize business deductions.

Can we use our vacation home as a corporate retreat for our corporation?

Your corporation (or LLC) can pay a fair market value of rent for the time used as a legitimate meeting place.

Should I have both insurance on my properties and a protective entity?

Yes, insurance is the first line of defense. But insurance companies use their own contract loopholes to deny coverage. So the second line of defense is a properly structured LLC or LP, which will offer charging order protection and flow through taxation.

What is the difference between a Grant or Warranty Deed and a Quit Claim Deed?

A Quit Claim deed transfers whatever rights the grantor may have at that present time. Title insurance does not follow with a Quit Claim deed. A Grant or Warranty Deed is a much stronger grant of rights and is the preferred format to use. For more information on this see Chapter 20.

lichigan but own property in Nevada, can I set up company?

ly. Nevada has no residency requirements for people or entities ant to use Nevada entities to operate their real estate businesses. ever, bear in mind that as a Michigan resident, and assuming you ld your property in a flow-through entity such as an LLC or limited partnership, the income flowing back to you in Michigan will likely be subject to Michigan state tax, even though it was earned in Nevada. This is the rule for most U.S. states.

Assuming my investment property is held in an LLC, can this be given to my spouse upon my death?

Yes. It can be done in many ways, from passing through in your will, being transferred pursuant to a living trust or by holding your LLC interests as joint tenants, with right of survivorship (JTROS). If you choose the JTROS or living trust route, upon your passing the investment property will automatically be transferred to your spouse or other named beneficiary, saving the problem of having your estate probated before title can be transferred. Know that the LLC is preferred over a joint tenancy or living trust as only the LLC also offers asset protection.

What types of repairs are deductible for a rental unit?

Expenses incurred to repair an item, like fixing a leaky faucet or repairing a handrail on a stairway, are deductible in the year paid. Expenses that are incurred to extend the life or improve the property must be capitalized and then depreciated. Examples of capitalizable items would be a complete new roof (as opposed to fixing a hole in the roof) or a room addition. Be sure to work with your CPA on these issues.

Are Section 1031 exchanges still done?

While the new tax law repealed personal property exchanges, Section 1031 Like Kind Exchanges are still very much done in the real estate world. They are an excellent way to defer tax on the sale of a piece of investment property for those investors wanting to move up to bigger and better properties. Please review Chapter 10 for more information on this key strategy.

What are the benefits of an LLC compared to an LP for holding real estate?

The LLC provides for limited liability for all owners (members) whereas an LP only has limited liability for the limited partner. The general partner of an LP has full liability, which is why you need to form an LLC or corporation for complete protection. As such, an LLC requires one entity filing whereas an LP requires two filings for full protection.

Can I write off the interest for more than one mortgage in a calendar year?

Absolutely! The IRS practices a "matching" program for Form 1098s which are prepared by mortgage companies and banks to report mortgage interest. Make sure that you report the same amount on your tax return that is shown on these forms. If there are changes to the amount reported, make that change on a different line item with an attached statement explaining the change.

Do I have to have a real estate license to be considered a Real Estate Professional?

No, you do not need to be a licensed real estate agent in order to be a Real Estate Professional. The test for Real Estate Professional status relates to the hours you work in the real estate capacity in relationship to the other work you do. If you work more hours in real estate activities, and a minimum of 750 hours per year, then you likely qualify as a Real Estate Professional. For more information see Chapter 9.

My wife and I are both retired. Are there any benefits if both of us become Real Estate Professionals?

As a Real Estate Professional taxpayer you can match real estate losses against other ordinary income. If you and your wife file a joint return, then only one of you need qualify as a Real Estate Professional in order to take advantage of this provision. While there is no tax advantage, you might find it is very rewarding to investigate and invest in real estate together.

Can I write real estate losses off from one piece of property against the income of another?

As long as both properties are similar, such as both rental properties in which you actively participate, then the loss against one can offset the income from another. If they are dissimilar, such as in the case of a motel operation (which is considered an active trade or business) and a piece of property held for future development, they cannot offset.

Where can I get a list of personal property items included in a rental property that can be depreciated at an accelerated rate?

Personal property items can be depreciated at 5 – 15 years as opposed to the longer 27.5 to 39 year depreciation required for real property. See Chapter 8 for more information on this, and a list of personal property items that can be depreciated more quickly.

What does depreciation recapture mean?

When you sell certain property, whether personal or real estate, that you have depreciated, and have received a benefit from that depreciation, the tax law may require you to report part of your income (equal to the depreciation you have taken and benefited from) as ordinary income taxed at a higher level than the capital gains tax rate. This is called the recapture of depreciation. Consult your tax advisor as to the possibility of depreciation recapture because it may make a big impact on your after-tax income. In certain circumstances, you may be able to "roll over" your gain on real estate through a 1031 exchange, which can defer your gain further into the future. See Chapter 10 on Tax-Free Exchanges.

At what point should I consider forming an LLC to hold my properties?

Preferably before acquiring the real estate, since you will want title to be held in the name of the LLC or LP. If you already own real estate you should consider promptly taking the steps to form an LLC or LP.

Where can I get more information?

For resources and checklists involving real estate transactions please see the Appendices.

Loophole #53

Your castle is protected by legal loopholes and benefitted by tax loopholes. Know them, use them and succeed with them.

And now in closing...

Conclusion

You now know that loopholes provide for the defense of your valuable real estate. These loopholes have structurally existed in castle walls since at least the 1300s, and have existed in the law since then as well.

You also now know that the muniments of title—the deeds and contracts and how you hold title—provides you with further ammunition for the defense of your real estate. Be respectful of these age old protections.

Defending one's title and realty has been a human priority for several millennia, and it will continue to be so for many generations to come.

Understanding the past prepares you for the present and the future. As you acquire real estate develop a sense of this historical context. Think of your castle and how to protect it.

With the groundwork we've provided, you now have the foundation you need to start investing in real estate. We have shared the tax, legal and selection strategies that successful investors use to choose, protect and maximize their real estate. You are ready to build your castle, to build your own portfolio of real estate that can help secure financial freedom for you and your family.

As a real estate investor, your learning never ends. You should always strive for more knowledge, especially since many laws that affect you are constantly changing.

Build a great team around you and continue to update your real estate knowledge and you will do well. Good luck in all of your investing.

Garrett Sutton

Appendix A:
Real Estate Resources

BOOKS

Start Your Own Corporation
By Garrett Sutton, Esq.

Run Your Own Corporation
By Garrett Sutton, Esq.

Tax-Free Wealth
By Tom Wheelwright, CPA

ABC's of Real Estate Investing
By Ken McElroy

How to Use Limited Liability Companies & Limited Partnerships
By Garrett Sutton, Esq.

Writing Winning Business Plans
By Garrett Sutton, Esq.

*Exchanging Up: How to Build a Real Estate Empire Without Paying Taxes...
Using 1031 Exchanges*
By Gary Gorman, 1031 Exchange Expert

ABCs of Getting Out of Debt
By Garrett Sutton, Esq.

GAMES

Rich Dad's CASHFLOW 101 Board Game and electronic game
Rich Dad's CASHFLOW 202 Board Game and electronic game

ON-LINE RESOURCES

corporatedirect.com
Corporate Direct

sutlaw.com
Sutton Law Center

mccompanies.com
MC Companies

wealthability.com
Wealthability

expert1031.com
The 1031 Exchange Experts

nmhc.org
National Multi Housing Council

realtor.org
National Association of REALTORS®

narpm.org
National Association of Residential Property Managers

american-apartment-owners-association.org
American Apartment Owners Association

richdad.com

Appendix B

Buyers Disclosure Checklist

Owner Information

- [ ] Name, address, phone number, business number
- [ ] Reason for selling
- [ ] Occupation
- [ ] If owner broker/agent

Loan information

- [ ] Name/address of lender
- [ ] Is current loan assumable? If yes, with or without qualification?
- [ ] Name title vested in
- [ ] Loan number
- [ ] Asking price
- [ ] Assessed value of property
- [ ] Interest rate
- [ ] Closing costs
- [ ] Original loan amount/dates
- [ ] Balance of original loan
- [ ] Is loan assumable
- [ ] If second can be discounted, if any
- [ ] If balloon payment/due
- [ ] If prepayment penalty
- [ ] Will seller help finance/pay points
- [ ] Yearly tax amount
- [ ] New loan amount
- [ ] Length of loan
- [ ] Monthly payment amount
- [ ] Insurance costs/requirements
- [ ] Home guarantee
- [ ] CC&R's/restrictions
- [ ] Move in date
- [ ] How long on market
- [ ] If previously listed/length of time

Fees

- [ ] Application
- [ ] Appraisal
- [ ] Loan fee
- [ ] Credit report
- [ ] Escrow fee
- [ ] Points

- ☐ Inspections/pest, structure
- ☐ Recording fee
- ☐ Title report/insurance
- ☐ Insurance

Property

- ☐ Legal description of property
- ☐ Zoning of property
- ☐ Proximity of schools
- ☐ Extent of landscaping
- ☐ Sprinkler system/type
- ☐ Inspection report/environmental concerns
- ☐ Square footage of lot
- ☐ Location of property
- ☐ Easy access to shopping
- ☐ Size of yards/front and back
- ☐ Fences/condition of

Building

- ☐ Age of structure
- ☐ Number of stories

- ☐ Type and condition of roof

- ☐ Number of rooms
- ☐ Square footage of structure
- ☐ Condition of wiring
- ☐ Gas or electric heating/condition of
- ☐ Alarm system/owned or leased/ if leased, will it remain in home after sale
- ☐ Kitchen amenities/condition of

- ☐ Utility costs/heating costs
- ☐ Condition of carpeting

- ☐ Number of bathrooms

- ☐ Inventory of what included/ draperies
- ☐ Garage/size/condition

- ☐ What kind of view

- ☐ Builder
- ☐ Condition and type of construction inside and outside
- ☐ Inspection report of structure/ termite, etc.
- ☐ Number of bedrooms
- ☐ Condition of plumbing
- ☐ Condition of foundation
- ☐ Air conditioning/condition of
- ☐ If fireplace/condition of/ has the chimney be cleaned recently

- ☐ Gas or electric appliances/water heater
- ☐ What kind of flooring
- ☐ Number of bedrooms/square footage
- ☐ Other rooms/ description/ condition of
- ☐ Number of windows/condition of

- ☐ Insulation up to code/storm windows, doors
- ☐ Any needed repairs

Seller Disclosure Checklist

- ☐ Home insurance
- ☐ Previous pest inspection reports
- ☐ Any additions to building made by current and past owners/were additions properly permitted
- ☐ Restrictions on property
- ☐ Easements on property
- ☐ Anyone having right of first refusal or option to buy
- ☐ Known future problems affecting property
- ☐ Property owned near this property

- ☐ Property in designated zone/ flood, hazard

- ☐ Previous inspection reports
- ☐ Year structure built
- ☐ Pending legal actions

- ☐ Liens against property/explain
- ☐ Is property leased/when expire
- ☐ Known conditions affecting property
- ☐ Pending expansion/real estate development of area
- ☐ Problems with stability of ground beneath property, settling, cracks in cement - describe

Roof

- ☐ Condition of roof
- ☐ How old is roof

- ☐ Any problems with roof/ leakage/ date

- ☐ Roof composition
- ☐ Any repair/ resurfacing of roof/ date

Heating/Electrical

- ☐ Date heating system installed

- ☐ Condition of heating system
- ☐ Manner of ventilation/describe
- ☐ Insulation up to code
- ☐ Available voltage
- ☐ Date of last inspection/service

- ☐ Kind of heating system/make, gas or electric
- ☐ Previous heating inspections/date
- ☐ Acceptable ventilation
- ☐ Condition of electrical equipment
- ☐ Known defects/describe

Water/Sewer

- ☐ Water supply source/city, septic tank

- ☐ Type of water pipes

- ☐ Condition of water supply
- ☐ Known prior plumbing leaks/rust problems
- ☐ Any Flooding/date, how repaired
- ☐ Drainage problems/describe
- ☐ Capacity of water heater

- ☐ Location of water heater

- ☐ What company did inspection
- ☐ Condition of landscape sprinklers/describe

- ☐ Any water pressure problems
- ☐ Known standing water areas

- ☐ Adequate drainage/roof, ground
- ☐ Condition/age of water heater
- ☐ Safety/pressure release valve on water heater
- ☐ Last date water heater inspected and/or serviced
- ☐ Safety device for water heater

Commercial Property Due Diligence Checklist

Objective

- ☐ Estate Building
- ☐ Tax shelter
- ☐ Other/description

- ☐ Equity return
- ☐ Spendable income/amount

Background search

- ☐ Better Business Bureau
- ☐ Lending institution

- ☐ Department of Commerce
- ☐ Utility companies

Owner information

- ☐ Name, address
- ☐ Bank reference
- ☐ Owner occupying property
- ☐ Attorney/legal status
- ☐ Amount of capital
- ☐ Date business was started

- ☐ Reason for selling
- ☐ Previously listed/price/time on market

- ☐ Business phone/residence phone
- ☐ Occupation tax bracket
- ☐ Tax accountant
- ☐ Broker or real estate agent
- ☐ Annual gross income
- ☐ Operating statements for years in business

- ☐ How long on market

Lease

- ☐ Lessee's name
- ☐ Time left on original lease/option to renew/rent increased
- ☐ Rent based on percentage/how computed
- ☐ Paid monthly/yearly
- ☐ Tax clause in lease
- ☐ Get copies of lease/agreements
- ☐ Type of lease/original or sublease
- ☐ Method of computing rent
- ☐ Rent based on square footage/building only or frontage included
- ☐ Option to buy/renew/first refusal
- ☐ Who performs maintenance/interior, exterior, landscaping
- ☐ Copies of contracts/management

Loan

- ☐ Type of loan/loan number
- ☐ Name title vested in
- ☐ Assessed value of property
- ☐ Assumable loan/transferable
- ☐ Will seller help finance
- ☐ Balance of original loan/date reported
- ☐ Any liens on property
- ☐ Prepayment penalty
- ☐ Interest rate
- ☐ Lender name and address
- ☐ Type of new loan/dates
- ☐ Can second be bought at discount/amount of discount
- ☐ Original amount loaned/date
- ☐ Balloon payment in the future
- ☐ Interest rate locked in/time
- ☐ Preliminary title report

Building

- ☐ Age of building
- ☐ Condition of basement/foundations
- ☐ How building constructed
- ☐ Square footage
- ☐ Architectural design
- ☐ Exterior finish and condition
- ☐ Adequately view from street or parking lot

Building Interior

- ☐ Number of floors in building
- ☐ Efficient design of space
- ☐ Number of windows
- ☐ Condition of space
- ☐ Ceiling height
- ☐ Condition of windows

☐ Adequate lighting
☐ Condition of floors
☐ Condition/age of wiring
☐ Condition/age of air conditioning
☐ Security patrol/burglar alarms installed
☐ Inventory included/description, estimate of value

☐ Toilet location and number
☐ Adequate wiring
☐ Condition/age of heating system
☐ Fire protection/overhead sprinklers, number and location
☐ Number and condition of locks

Service costs

☐ Services provided by shopping center
☐ Water/garbage
☐ Security
☐ Equipment cost/rental cost, depreciation
☐ Accounting/legal fees

☐ Heating/air conditioning

☐ Electric/gas
☐ Insurance
☐ Advertising costs

Property

☐ Legal description
☐ Restrictions
☐ Covenants/conditions/ restrictions
☐ Square footage of property lot
☐ Room to expand
☐ List of repairs needed
☐ Adequate parking
☐ Condition of parking lot

☐ Survey report
☐ Zoning restrictions
☐ Map of area showing property plot
☐ Storefront footage
☐ Inspection report of property
☐ Landscaped/condition of
☐ Adequate loading area

Location of Property

☐ Easy access to building

☐ Foot traffic in front of building
☐ Population within range of business

☐ Closeness to main roads/freeway/ bus line
☐ Area traffic patterns
☐ Estimated income/size of area families

- [ ] Condition of streets/ neighborhood
- [ ] Nearest closely related business

- [ ] Estimated area population growth
- [ ] Category of shopping center

Environmental Due Diligence Checklist

Documents to Review

- [ ] Lot description/square footage
- [ ] Primary Use description
- [ ] Regulations/requirements, local state, federal
- [ ] Complaints by citizens

- [ ] Contracts with disposal services, waste transport
- [ ] Insurance coverage/ claims for environmental loss with resolution
- [ ] Pending litigation
- [ ] Judgments, settlement agreements

- [ ] Building description
- [ ] Operating permits
- [ ] Maps, aerial photos, diagrams, technical reports
- [ ] Environmental assessments, Phase I and Phase II reports
- [ ] Reports on produced pollutants

- [ ] Description of noncompliance penalties

- [ ] Environmental violations

Environmental information with descriptions

- [ ] Standard Industrial Classification Number
- [ ] Manner disposed of
- [ ] Spillage of waste
- [ ] Underground tanks
- [ ] Records of spills/accidents

- [ ] Claims against company for shipping waste
- [ ] Water pollution history
- [ ] Last site check

- [ ] Hazardous waste on property

- [ ] Recycling done
- [ ] Stored materials
- [ ] Known leaks
- [ ] Known contamination to water or ground on this property

- [ ] Prior claims against owner

- [ ] All permits

Reports/permits/citations

- [ ] Ownership history/detail

- [ ] Hazardous Material Site Characterization

- ☐ Geotechnical
- ☐ Water quality
- ☐ Sanitation Department
- ☐ Air quality
- ☐ Department of Health Services
- ☐ Environmental Protection Agency

Setting

- ☐ Type of soil
- ☐ Soil stains
- ☐ Destination of surface water runoff
- ☐ Healthy vegetation
- ☐ Groundwater depth

On Site Facilities Used For/Description And Storage Of Chemicals Used

- ☐ Businesses of:

  Dry cleaning

  Plant nursery

  Gas station

  Paint/repair of automobiles

- ☐ Manufacture, store, etc.
  - Copiers
  - Glue/rubber products
  - Pesticides/fertilizer
  - Furniture/wood preservatives
  - Plastics/foams
  - Chemicals/explosives
  - Glass
  - Semiconductors/ Electrical devices
  - Detergent/soap
  - Paper products/pulp
  - Jewelry/metal plating or products
  - Petroleum products
  - Paint
  - Auto parts

A review of the previous information as it relates to your transaction will provide you with the background necessary to either walk away or purchase with confidence.

Appendix C:
Duties of a Real Estate Licensee

The law in the State of Nevada as to real estate duties, as set forth in the Nevada Revised Statutes ("NRS"), is as follows:

NRS 645.252, pertaining to "[d]uties of licensee acting as agent in real estate transaction," provides:

"A licensee who acts as an agent in a real estate transaction:

"1. Shall disclose to each party to the real estate transaction as soon as is practicable:

"(a) Any material and relevant facts, data or information which the licensee knows, or which by the exercise of reasonable care and diligence should have known, relating to the property which is the subject of the transaction.

"(b) Each source from which the licensee will receive compensation as a result of the transaction.

"(c) That the licensee is a principal to the transaction or has an interest in a principal to the transaction.

"(d) Except as otherwise provided in NRS 645.253, that the licensee is acting for more than one party to the transaction. If a licensee makes such a disclosure, he or she must obtain the written consent of each party to the transaction for whom the licensee is acting before he or she may continue to act in his or her capacity as an agent. The written consent must include:

"(1) A description of the real estate transaction.

"(2) A statement that the licensee is acting for two or more parties to the transaction who have adverse interests and that in acting for these parties, the licensee has a conflict of interest.

"(3) A statement that the licensee will not disclose any confidential information for 1 year after the revocation or termination of any brokerage agreement entered into with a party to the transaction, unless he or she is required to do so by a court of competent jurisdiction or is given written permission to do so by that party.

"(4) A statement that a party is not required to consent to the licensee acting on behalf of the party.

"(5) A statement that the party is giving consent without coercion and understands the terms of the consent given.

"(e) Any changes in the licensee's relationship to a party to the transaction.

"2. Shall exercise reasonable skill and care with respect to all parties to the real estate transaction.

"3. Shall provide the appropriate form prepared by the Division pursuant to NRS 645.193 to:

"(a) Each party for whom the licensee is acting as an agent in the real estate transaction; and

"(b) Each unrepresented party to the real estate transaction, if any.

"4. Unless otherwise agreed upon in writing, owes no duty to:

"(a) Independently verify the accuracy of a statement made by an inspector certified pursuant to chapter 645D of NRS or another appropriate licensed or certified expert.

"(b) Conduct an independent inspection of the financial condition of a party to the real estate transaction.

"(c) Conduct an investigation of the condition of the property which is the subject of the real estate transaction."

NRS 645.254, pertaining to "[a]dditional duties of licensee entering into brokerage agreement to represent client in real estate transaction," provides:

"A licensee who has entered into a brokerage agreement to represent a client in a real estate transaction:

"1. Shall exercise reasonable skill and care to carry out the terms of the brokerage agreement and to carry out his or her duties pursuant to the terms of the brokerage agreement;

"2. Shall not disclose confidential information relating to a client for 1 year after the revocation or termination of the brokerage agreement, unless he or she is required to do so pursuant to an order of a court of competent jurisdiction or is given written permission to do so by the client;

"3. Shall seek a sale, purchase, option, rental or lease of real property at the price and terms stated in the brokerage agreement or at a price acceptable to the client;

"4. Shall present all offers made to or by the client as soon as is practicable, unless the client chooses to waive the duty of the licensee to present all offers and signs a waiver of the duty on a form prescribed by the Division;

"5. Shall disclose to the client material facts of which the licensee has knowledge concerning the transaction;

"6. Shall advise the client to obtain advice from an expert relating to matters which are beyond the expertise of the licensee; and

"7. Shall account for all money and property the licensee receives in which the client may have an interest as soon as is practicable."

Index

About the Author

Garrett Sutton, Esq., is the bestselling author of *Start Your Own Corporation, Run Your Own Corporation, The ABC's of Getting Out of Debt, Writing Winning Business Plans, Buying and Selling a Business* and *The Loopholes of Real Estate* in Robert Kiyosaki's Rich Dad's Advisors series. Garrett has over thirty years' experience in assisting individuals and businesses to determine their appropriate corporate structure, limit their liability, protect their assets and advance their financial, personal and credit success goals.

Garrett and his law firm, Sutton Law Center, have offices in Reno, Nevada and Jackson Hole, Wyoming. The firm represents many corporations, limited liability companies, limited partnerships and individuals in their real estate and business-related law matters, including incorporations, contracts, and ongoing business-related legal advice. The firm continues to accept new clients.

Garrett is also the owner of Corporate Direct, which since 1988 has provided affordable asset protection and corporate formation services. He is the author of *How to Use Limited Liability Companies and Limited Partnerships*, which further educates readers on the proper use of entities. Please see CorporateDirect.com for more information.

Garrett attended Colorado College and the University of California at Berkeley, where he received a B.S. in Business Administration in 1975. He graduated with a J.D. in 1978 from Hastings College of Law, the University of California's law school in San Francisco. He practiced law in San Francisco and Washington, D.C. before moving to Reno and the proximity of Lake Tahoe.

Garrett is a member of the State Bar of Nevada, the State Bar of California, and the American Bar Association. He has written numerous professional articles and has served on the Publication Committee of the State Bar of Nevada. He has appeared in the *Wall Street Journal, The New York Times* and other publications.

Garrett enjoys speaking with entrepreneurs and real estate investors on the advantages of forming business entities. He is a frequent lecturer for small business groups as well as the Rich Dad's Advisors series.

Garrett serves on the boards of the American Baseball Foundation, located in Birmingham, Alabama, and the Sierra Kids Foundation and Nevada Museum of Art, both based in Reno.

For more information on Garrett Sutton and Sutton Law Center, please visit his websites at www.corporatedirect.com and www.sutlaw.com.

How Can I Protect My Personal, Business and Real Estate Assets?

For information on forming corporations, limited liability companies and limited partnerships to protect your personal, business and real estate holdings in all 50 states visit the Corporate Direct website at

www.CorporateDirect.com

or

call toll-free: 1-800-600-1760

Mention this book and receive a discount on your basic formation fee.

www.Sutlaw.com

Other Books by
Garrett Sutton, Esq.

Start Your Own Corporation
Why the Rich Own their Own Companies and Everyone Else Works for Them

Writing Winning Business Plans
How to Prepare a Business Plan that Investors Will Want to Read – and Invest In

Buying and Selling a Business
How You Can Win in the Business Quadrant

The ABCs of Getting Out of Debt
Turn Bad Debt into Good Debt and Bad Credit into Good Credit

Run Your Own Corporation
How to Legally Operate and Properly Maintain Your Company into the Future

The Loopholes of Real Estate
Secrets of Successful Real Estate Investing

• • • • • • • • • • • • •

How to Use Limited Liability Companies & Limited Partnerships
Getting the Most Out of Your Legal Structure
(a SuccessDNA book)

Bulletproof Your Corporation, Limited Liability Company and Limited Partnership
How to Raise and Maintain the Corporate Veil of Protection
(a Corporate Direct book)

Start a Business Toolbox
A Complete Resource for New Entrepreneurs
(a Corporate Direct book)